I0616217

AUTHOR OF THE CRITICALLY ACCLAIMED YA INTERNATIONAL NOVELS
"THE PRIEST AND THE PREACHES" AND
"THE DEMONS OF ABADON"

HORIZON HOMELESS

AUTHOR OF THE CRITICALLY ACCLAIMED YA INTERNATIONAL NOVELS
"THE PRIEST AND THE PREACHES" AND
"THE DEMONS OF ABADON"

HORIZON HOMELESS

LARRY PETERSON

Kravitz & Sons
INNOVATORS IN PUBLISHING, MARKETING AND ADVERTISING

Kravitz and Sons LLC
1301 Farmville Blvd, Suite 104
Greenville, NC 27834

© 2025 Larry Peterson

All rights reserved. No part of this book may be reproduced, stored in a retrieval system, or transmitted by any means without the written permission of the author.

Published by Kravitz and Sons LLC.

ISBN:(sc)   979-8-89639-222-4
ISBN: (e)   979-8-89639-223-1

Because of the dynamic nature of the Internet, any web addresses or links contained in this book may have changed since publication and may no longer be valid. The views expressed in this work are solely those of the author and do not necessarily reflect the views of the publisher, and the publisher hereby disclaims any responsibility for them.

TABLE OF CONTENTS

PROLOGUE

We are all aware of the seemingly permanent condition in our society that is called *homelessness*. This is an ongoing national tragedy.

Why this condition exists in the United States of America is baffling to many. But it can happen to folks easier than you might think.

It is very important to remember that there are millions of people across this great land of ours who are pre-homeless. These are the folks who are hanging on, the ones who still have a roof over their heads, who are still taking care of their kids, and who are still productive citizens. But suddenly and unexpectedly, after trying day after day to hold on for dear life to the roof over their heads and the beds that they sleep in, they begin losing their "grip." These families have started their journey into the bog called *homelessness,* and they do not even know it.

Having been a member of the St. Vincent de Paul Society (svdpusa. org) for more than twenty years I have had the honor of working directly with many homeless and pre-homeless people. I use the word *honor* because we are all God's children and they have privileged us by asking for our help. It is humbling to be given the opportunity to assist them. Therefore, the homeless tragedy begs the question; how do people become homeless?

Have you ever seen a homeless person and thought, *Why don't they just get a damn job?* Did you stop and think that maybe they had a job.

That maybe, through no fault of their own, they lost it. Is it possible they tried as hard as they could and could not find another. Maybe there was an illness or addiction or maybe mental illness. Who knows. Then, just like that, he or she was hanging on for dear life.

The following narrative is about a pre-homeless, fictional family living in the beginning of the 21st century. They are a composite of so many families that are spread all across our country, unnoticed, doing their thing, locked into survival mode. Say hello to Bob and Tracey Slider and their son, Jake. Can they "hold on" or will they "lose their grip"? What choices will they make? What will determine their success or failure?

"Come to me, all you who are weary and burdened, and I will give you rest" Matt: 11:28

*

*

*

CHAPTER 1

Memorial Day Weekend

Bob Slider, feeling contented, backed his blue pick-up out of the driveway, shifted into first, and let out the clutch. The truck accelerated smoothly as he reflexively shifted through the other gears. He smiled as thoughts leap-frogged inside his head.

The first leap took him to Jake's upcoming game that evening. The next leap was over to the three-day Memorial Day weekend beginning that afternoon. Another jump, and he, Tracey, and Jake would be fishing Sunday at Coronado Point. Then, it would be onward to the Memorial Day barbecue at home with many friends coming by. Yes, siree, life was good even though- well, there was no sense worrying about things that were rumored. No sense at all.

Bob is a 37-year-old, blue-collar guy who works hard, loves his family, and enjoys taking care of his house and yard. He and Tracey, childhood sweethearts, have been married for 14 years. They both love football and baseball and Tracey is even the team mother for 12-year-old Jake's Little League baseball team. The two of them sometimes share a "cold one" together on weekends and play fantasy football together. They live in a modest, three-bedroom, one-and-a-half-bath house in Pinellas Pines, FL, a town located in the Tampa Bay area bordering St. Petersburg. They might be considered your stereotypical, middle-class American family. Bob is an assistant manager at Bildot Building Supply which, at one time not long ago, had been one of the largest suppliers of commercial tools, construction equipment and materials in the area. Time and a downward economic spiral had changed all that. Now Bildot was hanging on, waiting for the next booming economic explosion to propel it back to prominence. That wait was proving to be much longer than expected.

Bob had worked for Bildot for 16 years and made the same morning drive to work thousands of times. For some reason, on this particular morning, a weird feeling grabbed hold of him as he turned and proceeded into the parking lot. He even felt a chill run down his spine. He shook it off, parked the truck, and headed inside. He clocked in and headed to his locker. His friend and co-worker, Zack Covello, was standing there. "Hey Zack, what's up buddy? How ya doing?"

"Hey, Bob, I'm hearing some rumors man. Like there's gonna be another layoff."

"No Zack, I haven't heard that."

C'mon, you would know. You're a boss around here. Clue me in. You hear anything?"

"Hey Zack, I said I didn't hear anything. I swear, man, nothing. I haven't heard anything about a layoff."

Zack, tying his Bildot work apron around his waist, looked at Bob and said, "Well, that ain't what I been hearing. I sure hope you're right. There ain't no other jobs anywhere. We'd all be screwed big time."

Bob shook his head, "Zack, I swear, if I hear anything, I'll let you know. Okay?"

"Yeah, okay. I better get busy. I still have that load of roofing to move."

Bob smiled at Zack, and as he watched him walk away, he felt very uncomfortable. He had heard a few rumors but he was a supervisor and he was sure he would have been let in on anything like that. No, he was sure that it was just a case of hearing unfounded rumors that seemed to take on a life of their own when a business slowdown occurred.

The construction industry and building material suppliers were always the first to feel the squeeze when the economy began to hiccup. Bildot, within a nine-month period, had laid off 26 workers leaving a skeleton crew of 12. Bob never considered that Bildot might lay off any more employees. That would basically close the company down. It was *impossible*. Plus, "Big Jim" would never allow it to happen. Zack was way off base or---maybe---Bob suddenly mumbled, "nah, no way."

It was the beginning of the much anticipated three-day holiday weekend. Every year, Memorial Day kicked off the summer season. School would be let out in two weeks, the Fourth of July was a little more than a month away, and Labor Day was two months after that. The "lazy, hazy days of another steamy hot Florida summer" were here. Bob shook his head, smiled to himself, and headed to his office.

It was 4 p.m. when James Bildot came out of his office and assembled his workers. They all gathered around, including Sally Weber, the bookkeeper and Mary Flanagan, purchasing agent and dispatcher. James Bildot stood in front of his Bildot "family" and you could hear a pin drop. The man had tears in his eyes.

"Big Jim", as he was affectionately called, had been a fine employer and treated his staff and customers with dignity and respect. Many times, when one of the guys had a financial problem or needed some time off to tend to family business, Big Jim would quietly slip the guy an extra fifty bucks. Sometimes, it was more. There were also times when Sally *knew* she was supposed to make a "mistake" and not dock a man's pay if the reason he missed work was a good one.

Jim looked at the 13 people looking at him. The only person not looking back at him was Sally who, standing next to Big Jim was holding the envelopes with the paychecks inside. Her eyes were cast downward. Jim shook his head and began to speak. "This is a very dark day for me. My dad started this company over 55 years ago with nothing but his sweat and determination. When he died 18 years ago I took it over. Lord knows, I have tried my best to be a good steward of the company and to treat everyone fairly and with respect. I love Bildot Building Supply and I have come to regard all of you as much more than employees----"

He had to stifle an unexpected sob. The guys were looking at him and half of them had teared up also. Big Jim took in a deep breath and continued, "Okay, here it is. Today I have to announce that as of 5 p.m. , Bildot Building Supply is closing its doors for good. We have, as the saying goes, 'gone belly-up' and I---I--" Big Jim Bildot could not continue and broke down in tears.

The crew standing there were numb. This they never expected. A temporary layoff, maybe. "Belly-up"? "Out of business"? Just like that, Bob Slider and his co-workers became statistics. They were unemployed. Bildot Building Supply was just another company that had failed. It, too, had become a statistic. The rumors had proven to be worse than ever imagined.

Standing in the parking lot after they had all received their final paychecks, all the guys appeared as if they were in a trance. It was Friday. They were going home. Just like every Friday. But this was no ordinary Friday, you see. They were never coming back. That reality was slowly but surely beginning to sink in. They were NEVER coming back.

Bob had earned $16.00 an hour and, for years, averaged 48 hours a week earning more than three grand a month. Take home was almost $2600.00 a month. As orders for supplies diminished, layoffs began to occur. Then the number of hours at work diminished also. The previous two months, Bob and the rest of the skeleton crew still working were getting about 30 hours a week, and for some of the guys it was less. Bob was now bringing home less than $400.00 a week. When the clock struck 5 p.m on this day, the now "former" Bildot workers had no idea where their next paycheck would come from. It would be on to the unemployment office.

As Bob and his former co-workers drove away from Bildot it was as if everything for Bob was moving in slow motion. He gave cursory waves to the other guys and choked back an unexpected tear. This place had been like a second home and just like that it was gone. It was almost as if someone close had suddenly died. Fear of the days ahead suddenly grabbed Bob Slider in a chokehold. He could not breathe. He pulled to the side of the road and got out of his truck. He stood straight up and tried to breathe in. As traffic passed by, he turned away and vomited.

Bob composed himself, took a deep breath and rinsed his mouth out with some early morning coffee that was still in his thermos. A "fender-bender" on US 19 delayed him even more, and he did not arrive home until a bit past six o'clock. Jake, dressed in his baseball uniform, was nervously pacing back and forth in the driveway. Bob had not even shut the engine off, and Jake was standing by the window, all hyper. "Dad, where you been? I'm supposed to be at the field by six. We gotta leave right now."

"Hey Jake, slow down, just slow down. Why didn't your mom take you?"

"Her car won't start."

"Oh great, just what I need. Okay, Jake, wait here. I have to talk to your mother. I'll be back in a minute."

"But Dad, coach said---

"Stop it, Jake. Just stop. Now, do as I told you and wait here while I talk to your mother for a minute. And don't worry, I'll talk to coach."

The boy was a bit unnerved. His dad was always upbeat, and when he saw his son he would usually grab him and pick him up and spin him around or at least mess up his hair with the palm of his big, calloused hand. Jake's lips tightened. He folded his arms and leaned against the truck. This was not the happy-go-lucky dad he was used to. He felt his stomach do a flip-flop.

Bob shook his head and walked into the house, glad Jake was staying outside. Tracey was sitting at the kitchen table and did not notice that her husband's usually pleasant demeanor was missing. She just started speaking. "Oh my God, Bob. Where have you been? My car won't start, and you're not going to believe this, but it is so crazy and---

"Whoa, Tracey, slow down, slow down. I can always fix the stupid car."

"I don't care about the car. I know you can fix the car. You always fix the car. Plus, Tommy is next door to help if you can't fix the car. You fix everything. I know, I know."

"Bob went over to her and pulled a chair close. He grabbed her hand. "Okay—what is it? What are you so upset about? What's going on?"

"What's going on. I'll tell you what's going on. They cancelled my unemployment because of that thunderstorm two weeks ago."

He looked at his wife and, squinting his eyes in confusion, simply said, "Huh."

Sarcastically she said, "You heard me Bob. Unemployment---cancelled--thunderstorm.""Look Tracey, I don't need you doing that sarcasm thing, okay. Just explain to me what you are talking about. What does a thunderstorm have to do with your unemployment being cancelled?"

Tracey took a deep breath and said, "I'm sorry sweetie. I'm just upset and a bit nervous, okay."

"Well, that's obvious. So tell me what is going on."

"Remember when our power went out in that thunderstorm a week or so ago?"

"Yeah, it was out for a while."

"It sure was. Long enough for me NOT to be able to sign in and re-certify. So their computer kicked me out of their system, and I don't even know if I can get it reinstated. and---oh my God, Bob, what a disaster. I needed that money for grocery shopping. I swear, I wish they would start giving you 40 hours again. This is getting a bit scary."

Bob was stunned and seemed to go into a bit of a daze. Only six months earlier, the two of them had been bringing over $4300.00 a month into the house. Then Tracey's company downsized and a new computer system replaced her and eight other people who had been reclassified as "non-essential".

Tracey's take home pay went from almost $1500.00 a month down to $126.00 a week in unemployment benefits. In less than six months the family's monthly income had been reduced by over $2300.00. Now, like a branch from a tree, another $504.00 had been lopped off and $4300 had plummeted to $1500.00. Just like that they were in a financial free fall and Tracey still did not know about Bildot.

Bob's head was spinning with thoughts akin to them being in a demolition derby. Smash! The rent was already one month behind. Bang! They had missed one truck payment. Boom! They were at the end of an extension on their delinquent power bill and the car insurance was due. May was ending and June was only three days away. All of these thoughts collided in a moment. All he could say was, "Huh."

"You heard me, Bob. They cancelled my unemployment."

Suddenly Jake hurried into the house. "Dad, Dad, we have to leave. I'm so late. I won't even be able to start if I don't get there."

Bob turned and snapped at his son, "Jake, I told you to wait outside, didn't I? Now do what you're told and wait outside like I told you."

Jake's baseball glove was on his hand and he smashed it against his thigh. He said nothing, turned and stormed out of the house.

Tracey hollered out, "You better watch it, mister. You behave like that, you won't be going anywhere."

Bob said, "Tracey, he's just upset. He doesn't understand what's going on, that's all."

"Fine, Bob, fine. But I will not tolerate him being disrespectful. Now look, we needed that money for food. Your check was supposed to cover the electric bill and a partial rent payment. Plus, Jake needs his inhaler and that's $68.00. Mr. Margolese has been real good about the rent but we have to pay him something by the beginning of the week. There's no way around it."

"Aw, c'mon Tracey. We're in this house for 12 years. I have maintained it for him, paid for repairs out of my own pocket, even repaired some of his other houses. It's like our own house."

"Oh Bob, oh Bob. Sometimes you sound so naïve. That sounds so nice. But---the fact of the matter is, this is NOT our house."

"Whatever Trace, he's a good guy. I'll talk to him."

"Look, you had better get Jake over to his game. Then come back and we'll talk about this. You have yet to miss a single inning of any of his games so you can miss a few tonight. You'll both live through it."

"Very funny Tracey, but you're right. We do need to talk."

"Yes, I know we do. You have had this strange look on your face and I know you have something to tell me."

Bob rolled his eyes upward, tightened his lips and breathed deeply through his nose. She could always see right through him. "Look Tracey," he said. "I might as well tell you right now and get it over with."

"Tell me what. It's bad isn't it?"

"Bildot closed down today. They closed their doors and went out of business. I don't have a job."

She stared at him, disbelief covering her face. Eyes wide open, tears began to pour down her cheeks. "Oh my God, oh my God."

"He went over to her, hugged her, and said, "Not to worry, Trace. We'll be fine."

Tracey stammered, "Fine, fine, how will we be fine? Today, I lost my unemployment, and you lost your job. Oh my God, Bob, what are we going to do?"

Bob looked at her and said, "Don't worry, Tracey, we'll be okay."

*

*

*

*

CHAPTER 2

Baseball, Pizza and Finance

Bob headed out to his truck and saw his son leaning against the front grill with his arms folded and a pouty look on his face. "Jake," he said, "wipe that look off your face right now or I'll do it for you. I got no time for this baby stuff. Smile and get in the truck or get inside and go to bed. You make the call."

Jake quickly got in the truck and they were on their way. Neither of them said a word for about five minutes. As they turned onto 49th Street Bob said, "You know Jake, you are old enough to understand when mom and I need to discuss a problem. I expect a little more maturity from you. You're not a baby anymore. I'm disappointed you acted this way."

Bob loved his son deeply and as soon as Jake could walk he became an ever present attachment to his dad's side. Bob did everything with him and by the time Jake was six years old he knew how to check the oil and fluids in the car. By eight years old he could do a tune-up on the lawn mower and weed-whacker and by ten he was able to change spark plugs in the car and truck. Bob would also take him to work at Bildot on Saturdays and Jake already had a working knowledge of construction supplies and equipment.

The boy did not like feeling as if he had disappointed his dad. Bob looked over and Jake was quietly sobbing. Bob felt lousy so he reached over and grabbed his boy around the back of his neck. "Let's forget it about it, okay. It was just a lousy afternoon. So, you starting tonight?"

Jake took in a deep breath and wiped his eyes with the sleeve of his shirt. "No Dad, Tommy Burns is starting. I pitched the other night, remember?"

"Oh man, see, I told you it was a lousy day. Yeah, like I forgot you pitched a two hitter. I don't think so. I was just checking to see if you remembered."

"Yeah Dad, nice try. Nice try. "

They both laughed and ten minutes later they were pulling into the parking lot of McKinney Field. Jake turned to grab his baseball gear out of the back and noticed that right behind them was his coach. "Dad, coach is behind us. He's late too."

"See that Jake, things work out. They always work out."

Bob parked his truck and stepped out. "Yo, Jeremy, how you doing?"

Jake's coach replied, "Hey Bob, we win tonight we're in. Playoffs here we come."

"I know, I know. That's awesome. You've done a great job with the kids this year

Jeremy, a great job."

"Thanks Bob, appreciate that." He turned to Jake and said, "How's my all-star pitcher/short-stop tonight? Ready to kick some butt?"

"Yeah coach, I'm ready."

Bob said, "Hey, Jeremy, can you do me a favor?"

"Sure Bob, if I can."

"Look, I have to go home for a bit but I expect to be back before the game is over. If I'm not, could you make sure Jake gets home?"

"Oh sure, no problem."

"Okay Jake, gotta run. Coach will bring you home if I'm not back in time, okay."

Jake said, "Hey Dad, I need that $35.00 for the all-star uniform. It was supposed to be in tonight."

Bob's stomach did a flip-flop. A bit taken back because Coach Jeremy was standing there he quickly said, "Oh nuts, Jake, with all the hurrying and all I forgot the check. I'll bring it when I come back."

Jake, like most kids his age, assumed that his father had a magic money maker inside of his pocket and said, "But you said you might not be back. Can't you just give it to me now?"

Bob glared at Jake, "No, I cannot. You have to wait until I return. It's not a problem, right Jeremy?"

"Of course not Bob, no problem. Hey Jake, get out on the field with the other guys and start stretching. I'll be there in a minute."

Jake shrugged and Bob said, "You have a good game Jake. You're playing baseball tonight and it doesn't get much better than that. See you later."

Jake was a bit stunned. His dad was always at his games. All of a sudden he was leaving and might not make it back. Jake just said, "Uh, yeah, okay Dad. See you later."

As Jake jogged out onto the field Jeremy said to Bob, "Hey Bob, I have the cash on me. I'll hand it in and you can give it back to me when I see you at the next practice. What do you say?"

It was the logical and simple solution and Bob knew he had to accept the offer. "Uh, oh sure, Jeremy. Thanks, sounds good. Appreciate it. Okay, hopefully I'll see you later."

He walked away hating the fact that he had agreed to take anything from Jeremy Zeller. It was a *pride* thing.

When Bob returned home the first thing Tracey asked him was, "Did you talk to coach?"

"Bob shook his head and said, "For crying out loud Tracey, he got there after we got there. Stop worrying. Everything is fine. I'll tell you this though, I felt like a jerk. Jake is like, 'Hey dad, I need that $35.00 for the all-star uniform' and I forgot all about it and Jeremy is standing there and---" "So what is the big deal? You forgot it. Who cares? Bring it later. You just don't like Jeremy, that's what this is about. If it was his boy he would have pulled a fifty dollar bill out of his pocket and told the kid to keep the change. You can't compete with that Bob. The guy has a lot of money. That's all there is to it. But he's a good guy."

"Yeah, you're right. He is a good guy. He did offer to put up the money and said I could give it to him later or at the next practice."

She laughed and said, "Oh my God, you're kidding. So, what's the problem? He did you a favor."

"Tracey, I don't know what it is but I just don't like the guy. There—I admitted it. I don't like him. He has this way about him and---oh, this is dumb. Anyway, Jake is fine and all is good over at McKinney Field."

"Okay, that's great. Jake seems to worry about every little thing lately. He wears me out sometimes."

"I guess it comes with his age."

"Yeah, I guess. Look Bob, we have to talk about money."

"I know, Tracey, I know. I know all about it. I live here too, remember."

"Well, you don't have to get nasty about it."

"Tracey, for God's sake, I was laid off today. I get home and find out that your car broke down and then you tell me you were cut off unemployment. Jake is pouting because he might be late for a game that doesn't even start until an hour after he gets there. So cut me some slack, all right?"

"It's just that we have a serious money problem Bob, and I'm scared."

"Bob took stock of his thoughts and said, "I know, I know. Hey listen, why don't we go down to Carmine's and get a pizza. We can talk there. Then we'll head over to Jake's game. If they win they make the playoffs. That should be fun to watch and it will do us some good to get out of here anyway. What do you say?"

She agreed and they got in the truck and drove over to Carmine's Pizzeria. He said toher, "So tell me, what happened with the car?"

"It didn't start, that's what happened."

He shook his head and sighed, "Tracey, come on, you know what I mean. Did it turn over, did it make any noise, did you check to see if the lights work?"

"It turns over but it won't start, okay. I know it is not the battery. If it was a dead battery it would just click-click or do nothing. You taught me, remember?"

Bob turned his head toward her for a moment and said, "Stop it, okay. You're talking to me like I'm an idiot or something. Just stop it."

She took a deep breath and said, "Oh my God, you're right. I'm sorry. I'm just---"

"I know, I know, me too. Let's just forget it. I'll check the car in the morning. Can't worry about that now."

Carmine's Pizzeria was doing its usual, brisk Friday night business and Bob and Tracy were only able to get a table for two that was situated in the middle of the dining area. "Bob, I don't like sitting here. There is no privacy. I wanted a booth."

"Tracey, the place is packed. We're lucky this table was open. It'll be all right. We'll talk low."

Bob ordered a large pepperoni pizza, a beer, and an unsweetened iced-tea for Tracey. After taking their first sips of the drinks, Tracey leaned forward and asked in a low voice, "Okay, tell me. How much do we have?"

An astonished look covered Bob's face. He leaned toward his wife and said, "Are you kidding me? You always know down to the last penny how much money we have. Why would you ask me that? Didn't you check the on-line balance this morning? We have direct deposit, right?"

She shook her head and said, "I don't believe you. Our computer is fried, remember? The storm, remember? You were paid today, and how much that was I do not know. There was no unemployment check, so I don't have a clue how much we have right now. All I know is whatever we do have it is not enough."

"Damn, I forgot about the computer. But look, I don't exactly understand what happened with your unemployment benefit."

"It is very simple. Every week I have to sign in and list where I looked for work that week and then I get re-certified and a check is issued. I was supposed to sign in yesterday. "

"Oh crap," he moaned. "No sign in, no check, right?"

"Exactly. So their computer automatically kicks me out of the system. You don't reason with a computer. It just follows instructions 24/7 and that is that. It's not like you can talk to a live person. Well, I finally got through to a real person this afternoon and they told me I could use their in-house computer to re-apply. I was all ready to run over there and guess what?"

"I know, I know. The car didn't start."

"It sure didn't. Now I have to wait until Monday to re-apply."

"You mean Tuesday, don't you."

"Oh my God, I forgot, the holiday is Monday. Well, I guess we can go together and apply."

"Wait a minute Tracey, don't think for a minute that I will need to get unemployment. I WILL be getting work. You just watch. No unemployment for me."

The server brought out the piping hot pizza and placed it on the elevated pizza stand. She removed a slice and placed it on Tracey's plate. Then she did the same for Bob. "Enjoy," she said and she walked away.

"Okay now, tell me how much money you were paid today. I think there was about $400.00 left in the checking account."

Bob reached into his pocket and pulled out his crumpled pay stub. "It says they deposited $876.34. Plus there is an extra $500.00 Big Jim gave me as sort of a severance pay. I think everyone got a little something. So I guess we have about $1775.00. Plus, we also have about $900.00 in savings. So, I guess when all is said and done we have about $2600.00. We're okay."

Tracey blurted out loudly," We're okay! Oh my God, are you kidding me!"

The noisy restaurant suddenly went quiet as all heads turned in the direction of the ear-splitting voice. Tracey, embarrassed, looked around and hurriedly leaned her head forward covering her face with the open palm of her hand. Bob looked around and nervously smiled at all the people he did not know. Within a few seconds, everyone in the place was back to their own personal world. Tracey said, "Oh my God, I am so humiliated. We have to get out of here."

"Tracey, it's okay. It's not a big deal. Nobody is even looking over here. It's okay."

"Well," she whispered. "This is a disaster, an absolute disaster."

"Why? We're okay right now, right?"

"Bob, Tuesday is June 1ˢᵗ. We still owe Mr. Margolese $700.00 for May's rent. Add in June's rent and that is $1650.00 we owe just for rent. The electric is $276.00 and I had gotten a ten day extension which is up Tuesday. If we don't pay that they will turn the power off. The car insurance is due and that is $156.00 and don't forget the May truck payment of $278.00. Since it is June that makes $556.00 due for the truck."

Tracey paused and was busy jotting numbers down on a paper napkin. Suddenly tears were rolling down her cheeks. Bob looked over at her and turned the palms of his hands up saying, "What?"

She wiped her eyes with her right fore-finger, smearing her mascara into dark smudges across her cheeks. She tried to speak but couldn't. Suddenly she stood up, grabbed her purse and hurried out of the restaurant. Bob, self-conscious and trying his best to maintain his manly aura, slowly stood up, placed a twenty dollar bill on the table and followed his wife outside. She was already sitting in the truck and he could see her just shaking her head. He got in and waited a minute before saying anything. Then he reached over and grabbed her hand. "Okay, what are you seeing in all of this that I am not seeing?"

"Bob, I love you and all but sometimes I just don't know where your head is. Do you realize that if we pay all of our bills we won't have a penny to our name. Not a penny. We could lose everything, our cars, our house, everything."

Bob began to get angry. He snapped at his wife, "Stop it Tracey, just stop it. I am not crippled. I will get work. We'll be okay. Greg Margolese is a good guy. Maybe I can do some work for him on some of his houses. He'll understand our situation. I'll talk to the bank about the truck payments. I'm sure they will work with me. Hell, I was never late with a payment until this month and there are only four or five payments left anyway. Don't worry, we'll be fine."

Bob's confidence was calming his worried wife. He knew they had not discussed the money. He also was fully aware that they still needed to buy food and repair Tracey's car. Factor in gas for the vehicles and Jake's medicine and the water bill, it was not looking very good.

Jake was growing and they went through six gallons of milk a week. That was $72.00 a month all by itself. He knew she would be bringing all of that up in a matter of minutes. However, on this particular Friday something else was going on. Hiding inside the big, burly, tough-looking man was a cowering and suddenly very insecure little boy. So far Bob had succeeded in hiding him well.

Just then there was a tap on the truck window. Bob turned and saw the server from Carmine's standing there. She was holding a pizza box and two take-out containers with drinks. Bob rolled down the window and the girl said, "Look, I hope you don't mind. But I did not want to see a whole pizza go to waste. So I boxed it for you and here are two ice-teas to go along with it. Hope you guys have a great weekend."

Bob and Tracey were moved by the kind gesture the girl had made. As she walked away Bob yelled out, "Hey, thanks. Appreciate it."

The girl, without turning back, lifted her arm and simply waved. Bob opened the box and both of them grabbed a slice and began to eat. "Man, Tracey, she didn't have to do that. That was really nice of her."

"Yes, it was. There are some good people out there. She could tell we were dealing with some stuff and she wanted to make it easier for us. She's one of those people who cares about other people. That was a nice moment." She took another bite of the pizza and said, "You want to talk about the other bills now?"

"Not really. What's the point anyway? We both know what they are. Plus, we need a mental break. Let's go to Jake's game and we can talk about all of this tomorrow when we're not so tired and worn out. Nothing will change from now until then."

"Yeah, I guess you're right and going to the game will be fun."

"You have the check-book in your purse?"

"Yes, why do you ask."

"I told Jeremy that I would bring him the $35.00."

Tracey sighed and said, "Oh brother, another $35.00 out the window."

Deciding to go to Jake's game proved to be a welcome diversion from the reality they were facing. It was the last game of the regular season and Jake's team, the Braves, was tied with the Tigers, for first place. The winner of the game would move on to the county playoffs.

There were two outs in the bottom of the final inning and the Tigers were ahead by one run. Jake was at bat and had two strikes on him. Tyler Anderson was on first base. All the players on the team had their faces pressed against the chain-link fence in front of the dugout. They were all screaming for Jake to get a hit. Tracey and Bob were standing near the grandstands. Tracey had her hands folded as if she was praying and her fingers were covering her lips. Bob's lips were tightly pursed and he was shaking his fist in cadence with his own mumblings of, "C'mon, c'mon, c'mon".

The pitch came toward home-plate straight and true. Jake Slider, head down, turned his hips and swung the bat into the strike zone and a beautiful swing it was. The sharp sound of ball and bat colliding as the two objects met in a violent yet beautiful confrontation reverberated into the night air. Momentary silence gripped the several hundred folks watching as the ball took flight.

When the ball sailed over the fence in left field the entire place went crazy. Bob began to cry as he watched his boy round the bases. So did Tracey. Jake had hit a "walk-off home-run" to win the game. It was one of those moments that neither a boy nor his parents would ever forget.

After all the yelling and hugging and congrats were over with, Coach Jeremy gathered all of the players and their parents together and announced that he had called Carmine's Pizzeria and they were setting up the back room for the team to have a celebratory pizza party. Bob and Tracey immediately looked at each other wondering how much this would cost. They had just spent $20.00 at Carmine's and given $35.00 for all-star fees. This would be another twenty bucks at least, turning the evening into an unexpected $75.00 hemorrhage. Tracey said to Bob in a whisper, "Do we have to go?" Her husband turned to her and just rolled his eyes. Twenty minutes later they were back at Carmine's.

The pizza party proved to be lots of fun with Jake the center of attention. The highlight for Bob and Tracey turned out to be when they found out that Jeremy Zeller had picked up the tab for the entire party. Jake asked if he could sleep at his best friend Tyler's house and he left with Tyler's mom. Bob and Tracey drove home still basking in the glow of Jake's home-run. As they pulled into the driveway Tracey said, "You know Bob, God was good to us tonight. We needed a break from everything going on so, while driving to the field, I asked God to help us out with a few good moments. I think He was listening."

"Sure Trace, whatever you say. Why don't you check your car. Maybe He fixed it while we were gone and it will start right up."

She looked over at him and said, "What is wrong with you? What, you don't believe in God anymore? Are you kidding me? Tell you what; I am going to see if my car starts right now. If it does you are coming to church with me Sunday. Agreed?"

"Sure, whatever you say."

Tracey got into her car quietly praying, "C'mon Lord, he needs this. C'mon, please help me start this car."

She turned the key and the engine began to turn over. But that was all that it did. It would not start. Quickly, the battery began to die. She got out of the car and walked straight into the house. He followed. The glow from the previous few hours was rapidly fading.

*

*

*

CHAPTER 3

Everyone Wants Money

It was 7:30 Saturday morning when Bob walked out of the house and over to his wife's car. The Florida sun was streaming in from the east and he squinted as its rays hit him in the face. It was already hot and a trickle of sweat rolled from his forehead. He ran his fingers across his brow and thought of how he had done nothing but was already sweating. He said to no-one, "Okay, let's do it."

He took a sip of coffee from his navy-blue "world's best dad" mug and opened the car door. He knew what was going to happen when he tried to start it. But, like the person pushing the already pushed elevator button, he had to try himself.

Tracey's car was a 1998 Chevrolet Lumina four-door sedan. Bob had taken good care of the car and it rarely gave them any trouble. Bob set his coffee mug on the dashboard and said, "Okay sweetheart, turn over for papa."

He turned the key and 'sweetheart' responded with a 'waawaawaawaaa'. "Terrific," Bob said. "That's just great. Come on, be a bad battery. That is SO easy. Why do you have to be contrary on the Memorial Day weekend. C'mon, start, will ya. Cut me some slack."

"Who you talking to, Bob."

Startled, Bob turned to see his next door neighbor, Tommy Pavano, standing outside the car. "Oh, it's you Tommy. Man, don't sneak up on a guy like that. That's wrong man."

"Kind of uptight, aren't you? What's going on?"

"Tracey's car is being temperamental. She won't start."

Tommy laughed and said, "And that's who you were talking to, the car?"

"C'mon, Tommy, give me a break. Tell me what's wrong with this thing."

Tommy Pavano was a top-notch auto mechanic. His dad had owned a garage in Tampa for years and Tommy had been working on cars since he was a kid. He and Bob were best of friends and he had helped Bob out many a time when Bob's vehicles were 'misbehaving'.

Tommy had a repair shop over in Largo and folks came to him from all over to have their cars repaired. He was not only a fine mechanic but he was an honest businessman who always did his best to give his customers quality service and prices. Once you took your car to Tommy Pavano, you came back again. "Okay, Bobby baby, start this puppy up. Let me hear what you got."

Bob shrugged and turned the key. "Waawaawaawaa." Tommy said, "Okay, enough. Pop the hood."

Bob pulled the hood release lever and Tommy lifted the hood. After a few minutes he yelled to Bob, "Okay, try it again."

Bob turned the key and "waawaawaawaa" and then 'click, click, click'.

Tommy shut the hood and walked over to his neighbor. "Hate to tell you but you have a bad fuel pump. There is no pressure. I checked. The worst part is the fuel pump is in the gas tank. It is sort of a big deal to replace it. Plus, I saw some gas leaking into the manifold. That has to be fixed too. We can't do it in the drive-way. I have to get it over to the shop. We're closed till Tuesday but you can use your truck for the next few days, right? "Yeah Tommy, of course. But I don't know when we can get this fixed."

"Hey Bob, you know I'm gonna take good care of you, right?"

"C'mon, Tommy, I know that. What I mean is, Bildot closed its doors yesterday. They went out of business for good. I'm out of work. The car will have to wait."

"What! No way man. You gotta be kidding me. Bildot closed. You were laid off. Holy crap, that's unbelievable. Bildot has been around forever."

"Yeah, tell me about it. I still can't believe it."

Just then a bright red, F-350 diesel pick-up with rear tandem wheels, rumbled to a stop in front of Bob's house. Bob said to Tommy, "Hey, that's my landlord. I need to talk to him. You and I can talk later, okay? "Yeah, sure. Hey, tell me quick, how did the game go last night?"

"Oh my God, Tommy. It was the bottom of the sixth with two out. The score is 3 to 2, a man on base and Jake is up. He has two strikes on him and he hits it out. My kid homered and they won the game 4 to 3. It was crazy. The place went nuts."

"Holy crap Bob, that must have been so cool and to think---"

Tommy paused and they both turned as Greg said, "Good morning, guys."

"Hey Greg, you're up bright and early. Did you ever meet my neighbor, Tommy?

"Sure Bob, we've spoken a few times. Hi Tommy, how have you been?"

"Good Greg, good. Look, I'll let you guys talk. See you later, Bob. Nice seeing you Greg.

And Bob, congrats on Jake's big hit. Wish I had been there."

Bob smiled and Greg said, "Jake had a good game I take it?"

"Hit a walk-off in the last inning to win it and send the team to the playoffs. It was so awesome. We'll never forget it. So tell me, Greg, what's going on? I'm surprised to see you so early."

"Yeah, well, I have to take care of a broken water heater over on 72nd Terrace and I wanted to talk to you anyway so---I thought I would just stop by."

"Sure, glad I was here."

"You know Bob, you still owe me $700.00 for May and June 1st is Tuesday. You think you will have the money?"

Bob suddenly felt intimidated and embarrassed. He had known Greg for a long time. The man was a savvy businessman and owned 18 houses and two motels. Bob had helped him out many times getting him discounts on materials at Bildot and personally doing minor repairs on some of his rental homes for him. He liked to think that they were friends first. But this Saturday morning there was a different feel in the air between them. Greg Margolese was exhibiting a 'business is business' attitude and Bob was feeling quite uncomfortable. Bob nervously said to him, "Uh---I was going to call you Greg. Truth is, I have a problem and---look, hold on a minute and I'll be right back."

Bob hurried into the house and wrote out a check for $700.00. He went back outside and, handing the check to Greg, said, "I would have asked you in but Tracey is sleeping and I thought it better if we talked out here. Anyway, here is the rest of May's rent. Sorry it took so long."

"Sure Bob, that's fine. Thanks. So, you mentioned you had a problem? What's going on?" Does this problem have to do with June's rent payment?"

Greg was cutting right to the chase and avoiding any verbal detours. Bob looked at him and felt himself getting a bit annoyed. He knew that Greg was asking the right question but he was also thinking that it was not June – not YET. Plus, he always was ready, willing and able to help the guy out any time he asked so why was he suddenly applying pressure when the rent was not even due for three more days.

It was not Greg applying the pressure though, it was Bob doing it to himself. Not having a job and realizing that your income flow had been shut off can make a man think and do all sorts of things to save "face". At that moment, Bob Slider was not equal to Greg Margolese in stature and he was squirming inside. He said, "Look Greg, the problem is Bildot. They closed down yesterday."

"What! Bildot closed. I can't believe it. My dad used to take me there when I was a kid. Wow, that is some news. That's a shame. This damn economy is starting to strangle the country."

"Yeah, it sure is."

"So what are you going to do for work?"

"Well, for starters I was thinking that maybe we can help each other out."

"Oh yeah, and how is that?"

"Well, I was thinking that maybe I can do some extra maintenance work and repair work for you and we can credit my work towards the rent. I know I can get some work but it might take a little time. And I do have the truck so I can do some hauling and clean-ups too. In the meantime I could start working towards July's rent now. What do you think?"

"I guess that means you will have June's rent, right?"

"I hope so but I might need a little time, okay."

Greg took a breath and raised his eyes. Then he looked at Bob and said, "I don't mean to seem indifferent or anything. But we all have problems. Right now I have four vacant houses and five other tenants late with their rent. I pay mortgages and insurance and taxes on all of my properties. Right now, I need cash. This economy is hurting everyone, me included. As a businessman I have to maintain a solid credit rating or my bank dealings could be seriously affected. So, I'm out of sorts a bit myself. You can understand that, right?"

"Of course I understand, Greg. Hey man, you've been good to me but I have been good to you too. So let's help each other a bit, especially now when things are sort of in the tank."

"Look Bob, let me think about it and we'll talk again Tuesday when I come back."

Bob was not about to ask him why he was coming back on Tuesday. He knew why, he was going to see about June's rent payment. "Sure Greg, see you Tuesday."

As Greg drove away in his large, growling pick-up Bob watched and a chill went down

his spine. Forking over the other $950.00 on Tuesday would leave them in a terrible spot. This is exactly what Tracey had been talking about the previous evening. The house did not belong to them and Bob never felt the reality of that fact as much as he did at that moment.

He slowly walked back into the house and by now Tracey was up and sitting at the kitchen table having coffee. She looked at Bob and said, "So tell me, how did it go with Greg?"

"All right I guess. I gave him a check for the $700.00. He's coming back Tuesday and we'll talk some more."

"Will he work with us on June's rent?"

"I'm sure he will. I'm sure he will."

"You know Bob, we never really discussed all the money we owe when we were at Carmine's last night. Like the phone bill, the cell phone bill or the three credit card payments that are due. We never added those bills into the total due. And what about my car? Did you find out what is wrong with it?"

"Yeah, Tommy looked at it. Fuel pump is bad and the fuel-injectors are leaking. It's a big job and he needs the car at his shop. I told him we have to wait."

"I need the car, Bob."

"Well Tracey, you will have to just use my truck until the car is fixed. At least we have one vehicle that runs."

"And how are we both supposed to use one vehicle?"

"Damn it Tracey, I don't know. I don't know. We are just going to have to. End of story."

Bob poured some coffee into his mug and walked out to the back yard. Standing on the back patio looking across at the partially dead grapefruit tree he mumbled to himself, "Damn it, can't believe I never tried to buy a house."

The previous evening they had tallied up a personal "fortune" of $2650.00. It was time to start trading some of that fortune for some groceries. Bob handed Tracey the keys to his truck and decided to mow the lawn. He knew he would feel a bit better about things if he worked up a good sweat. He pulled off his T-shirt, started the mower and went at it. Tracey headed to the supermarket. Pulling out of the driveway she blessed herself and prayed for the wisdom to shop wisely.

A practical and frugal woman by nature, Tracey always checked ads and looked for coupons before going food shopping. On this particular Saturday she spent an inordinate amount of time prowling the aisles for the best deals she could find. There were items that she knew she had to purchase no matter what. 'Store brands' were always less expensive than 'name brands'. The exceptions to that rule were when certain name brands were being offered as "BOGOs" (buy one get one free) or having a coupon that might give a good deduction on a name brand.

The first section of the store she went to was the produce section. She was surprised that she found herself getting a bit angry at the price of some of the produce. The bananas were .69 a pound and a head of lettuce was $1.89. She had wanted to buy tomatoes and actually had spent ten minutes sorting out two pounds, bagging them and placing them in her cart.

Fifty feet away from the produce section she stopped and looked at the tomatoes. They were the size of tennis balls and there were five of them. She picked the bag up returned them to the tomato display. She was NOT going to spend $4.38 on two pounds of crummy tomatoes. Five pounds of yellow potatoes were $3.89 and when she added in the lettuce and bananas the three items came to almost $10.00. She felt herself quiver and returned the bananas also. She shook her head thinking how five pounds of potatoes and a head of lettuce were going to cost her $5.78. It was crazy.

Tracey headed to the check-out and the total came to $112.64. She had managed to buy toothpaste and toilet tissue, laundry detergent, two gallons of milk, shampoo, and four frozen pizzas because they were a 'buy one get one'. There was ground beef for meatloaf and Hamburger Helper and chicken thighs that Bob would grill with his special marinate. She even managed to get two new filters for the air-purifier in Jake's room which were critical to keeping his asthma in check.

She left the store pleased with the money she had saved and the creative meal planning that would carry the family through the next week. She had just finished loading the groceries into the back of the pick-up and had closed the tail-gate when she blurted out, "Oh my God, I forgot Jake's inhaler." She headed back to the pharmacy located in the rear of the store and, just like that, another $68.00 disappeared.

When she arrived back home Bob was just finishing up the back yard. Covered in sweat and dirt with loose blades of grass and weeds stuck all over his legs, arms and chest, he walked out to the driveway. "Hey Trace, you're back and I just finished. I call that good timing. Let me help you."

"Oh Bob, look at you. You're covered in dirt and grass."

"Well why don't you come over here and give me a big hug."

She said, "You stay away from me, Bob Slider. You're filthy."

"Oh, come on. You know I'm sexy when I'm all sweaty and dirty. You love it."

She started to laugh and ran towards the house. Arms outstretched he laughingly walked after her pretending to be a monster. Working up a sweat had revived his good nature. He carried the groceries inside and placed them on the kitchen counter. He looked at Tracey and she looked at him. "Oh no you don't, Bob Slider. You stay away from me. Go take a shower. You're a sweaty mess."

He started to laugh and began to walk toward her. She ran out into the backyard and quickly lifted up the garden hose. As he slowly moved toward her she turned it on and blasted him. He laughed and as the cooling, refreshing water sprayed all over him, he kept on coming at her. Wanting him to catch her, she feigned an attempt to get away. He quickly caught her and tried to wrangle the hose nozzle from her hands but she held on. Laughter filled the air as the two of them, supposedly fighting for control of the hose, soaked each other.

They kept at it for a few moments and the whole time Tracey kept screaming, "Stop! Stop!" while Bob just laughed and laughed. Then, with the hose still spraying between them he grabbed her and kissed her and she threw her arms around him and kissed him back. Their tempered passions ignited and the heat between them exploded. Tracey pushed him away and said, "Go grab a quick shower and I'll meet you in our room."

It was a needed, spontaneous and silly moment that completely rejuvenated their dwindled spirits. They spent two hours together, alone, enjoying being married and in love. Afterwards, Bob helped Tracey put the groceries and other household items away. She made two ham and cheese sandwiches with fresh lettuce and mayo on rye bread for their lunch. As they sat together and ate, Bob said, "So babe, how did you make out at the store?"

"I swear Bob, the prices are nuts. But I think I did all right. I spent $112.00 and then remembered that I had to get Jake's inhaler. So, I spent a total of $180.64. Do you know that it cost $5.78 for a head of lettuce and some potatoes. Is that crazy or what? I put the tomatoes back. No way I'm paying over four dollars for some crummy tomatoes."

"Tracey, whatever you do with the grocery business is fine with me. I would buy all junk food and we would have lots of cake and dip and salsa and chips and be eating TV dinners or frozen pizza every night. You just do what you have to do. So, tell me, how do we stand money-wise?"

Tracey had a pad and pencil in front of her. She put her sandwich down and lifted the pad. "Well, I spent $180. You gave me $700.00, we spent $55.00 last night and you also got $30.00 worth of gas which, by the way, just about has the needle at half---"

He cut her off. "Tracey, I know where the gas needle is, okay."

"Of course, sorry, I didn't mean anything. I was just---"

"Tracey, forget it. Tell me the rest."

"Gosh Bob, you know what else. The electric bill is $278.00, the truck payment is $276.00, the cable and phone is $119.00 and, here look at this, the water bill is $64.00 and car insurance is $158.00 and oh yeah, the credit cards and---"

"Tracey, stop, okay. I get the picture. We're screwed. We still have to pay rent too."

"Yeah, I know. This is not pretty. When I add all of this up it comes to $2630.00. That leaves us with $20.00 to our name." The realization smacked her right between her eyes and she said, "Oh my God, we only have $20.00 in the whole world. What are we ever going to do? This is a disaster."

Bob became the voice of reason. "Stop Tracey, it will be okay. We can make arrangements on the phone and cable bill and Tuesday morning you will get your unemployment straightened out. I'll work something out with Greg. We hit a bump in the road, that's all."

"Well, I'm sure glad you are so calm about all of this. I guess our bedroom visit worked wonders for you."

"Absolutely, I needed that reconnection with you. It was great. Sometimes I forget how much I love you. Didn't you feel the same as I did?"

She was now putty in his hands. "Oh Bob, I sure did. I love you too and it was wonderful. We really need to give ourselves more time alone together."

"Yeah, I think you're right. We just get caught up in the daily routine and sort of forget about what we have together."

She smiled and said, "Where is this sensitive side coming from? I like it. Well, all I can say is, thank God we have each other at a time like this. You know, maybe you will even come to church with me tomorrow. "

He tightened his lips a bit and said, "Well see, Tracey. We'll see."

They hugged and kissed each other again and then Bob sat down and flicked on the TV. Tracey took her pad and pencil and sat down at the kitchen table. It was time to get back to "normal". She did some quick calculations and decided not to pay the car insurance, the cable and phone and the water bill. Making the truck payment and paying the delinquent power bill would have to take precedence. She figured that by doing this she had held back over $300.00 to keep in their pockets.

Tracey had forgotten one minor detail. If the truck payment was late and went delinquent into the following month the lien-holder would not accept one payment. They would demand that the account be brought current within five days of the first of the month—or else. Tuesday was the first and Monday was the holiday. There was no way to beat the deadline.

*

*

*

CHAPTER 4

Just a Quiet weekend

The holiday weekend quickly turned into one of quiet and restraint. To avoid buying extra gas for the truck and paying the tolls, the fishing trip to Coronado Point was put on hold. Jake was at Tyler's house anyway so that took the pressure off Bob and Tracey to 'entertain' their son.

Bob and Tracey were both born Catholics but did not go to church very much. Jake had never even been baptized. Tracey would occasionally bring Jake to Mass at Sacred Heart Catholic Church. This Sunday she made a point of being at Mass and sat through the entire service alone, having no idea what was going on. When she left she realized that she was glad she had gone and felt good about having been there even though she had no understanding of what she had witnessed.

The rest of Sunday vanished just like that and Monday followed suit. It was Tuesday and the real world once again beckoned. Bob, as usual, got up at 5:30 and began getting ready to go to work. It actually took him a few moments to accept the fact that he had no place to go. Somewhat lost inside of himself he walked outside and stood by his truck. He took a breath and looked up the black morning sky. The stars were shining so brightly that he could not believe he had never noticed them before.

He stared at the infinite beauty for a few moments and then decided to drive over to the Park Slope Café to get some breakfast. Bob loved Park Slope's "All-American Skillets" because they were loaded with so much bacon and sausage and cheese they had actually earned themselves a reputation around town. He dropped two quarters into the newspaper machine, pulled out a newspaper and headed inside.

He was surprised to see so many patrons there at such an early hour. He avoided looking around because he did not want to bump into anyone he might know. He was in no mood for idle chit-chat, truth being he did not want to have to tell anyone he had been laid off. The server came by, placed a menu on his table and asked, "Good morning sir, you having coffee?"

"Yeah, thank you."

The cup was upside down on the table and she turned it over and filled it. "I'll be back for your order in a minute."

He smiled at her and opened the menu. Quickly he was adding numbers in his head. *Dang, the skillet is $6.99 and coffee is $1.59 add in tax and that's over nine bucks. Two bucks for a tip and I just spent $11.00.* The server returned and asked, "So, what can I get you this morning?"

"I'm just going to have coffee, okay?"

He sipped his coffee, read the paper and was on his way home by 6:30. In the light of the new day he noticed all the cars and trucks going back and forth. He wished his truck was heading to a job like the rest of them. It was only his first day out of work and already he was feeling quite useless. He told himself to get home and start figuring out where to look for work. He said out loud, "I know I can find something out there."

The first call came in at 8 a.m. Bob, usually not home on a weekday, quickly answered. "Hello?"

"Is this Mr. Slider?"

"Yes, who is this?"

"Yes, good morning Mr. Slider. This is Jeanine from Avico Financial. Mr. Slider, I am calling his morning because as of yesterday you are two months behind in your credit card payment. This is about to be turned over to a collection agency and we want to see if we can avoid this happening."

Bob was surprised at what he had just heard and did not answer the caller. He took a breath, composed his thoughts and said, "Uh, I was sure that was paid. I have to check with my wife. She's not here right now but I can call you back in about an hour or so."

"If it is all right with you Mr. Slider, we'll call you back later today, okay?"

"Yeah, I guess. We do have to go out for a while. So make it after three, okay. We should be back by then."

"Fine Mr. Slider, after three it is."

Tracey had heard Bob talking on the phone and came out of the bedroom after he hung up. "She yawned, ran her hand through her tousled hair, and asked, "Who was that?"

"Avico Financial, calling about our credit card payment."

"I swear, Bob, they call three times a week and it's always a different person. They are relentless. I made an arrangement with them last week and we are supposed to send $25.00 by today. They should not be calling us this morning. It is SO stupid. I wish they would just have one person working the same accounts. I swear it is---"

Bob stopped her, "Tracey, whoa---slow down. You just got up. Grab some coffee. Don't worry about that dumb call. Go ahead, have some coffee."

She headed to the kitchen and filled a cup. They sat together at the kitchen table and she said, "We have to get to the unemployment office as soon as we can. Sometimes it takes a while when you go there so the earlier we go the better."

"You go Trace—I don't need unemployment. This is only my first day out of work. I'm

going to find something."

"Bob, you are going. It cannot hurt to put in your paperwork. If you get a job, great. If you don't, you have a cushion to fall back on. It takes about three weeks to get a check anyway, sometimes longer."

"He let out a big sigh and said, "Okay Tracey, okay. You're right. Truth is—and don't tell anyone, I am embarrassed to have to walk in there. I feel like a loser just thinking about it."

"Well, you are NOT a loser. Losing your job does not make you a loser. You are just one of millions, including your wife, in this predicament. None of us like it."

"Whatever Tracey, whatever. All I know is that when I walk in there I am walking in with my thoughts and feelings about it. Nothing can change that. And you know just what I'm talking about, don't you?"

She looked at him and, empathizing, said, "Yes Bob, I do understand, I really do."

Tracey began going over the numbers on her pad when Greg Margolese pulled up. Bob was out in the garage and Tracey had just come to the realization that they could not pay the entire rent. There was only going to be $789.00 left. She jumped up and ran to the garage, "Bob, Bob, come here, Hurry up."

He hurried in and she said, "Look, Greg just pulled up. We do not have the rent money.

I messed up with my numbers. We only have $789.36 left. We have to keep some money. Give him $500.00. That still leaves us with less than $300. And we have a whole month ahead of us. Go, go talk to him. He'll work with you."

Bob shook his head and headed outside. Greg was already near the front door. "Hey Greg, how's it going?"

"Hi Bob, I'm good, thanks. Look Bob, I know you're in a spot and I know I wasn't too cordial the other day. It was just that, well, I'm sorry for acting that way. Anyway, can you give me $500.00 today and maybe the rest in a week or so?"

Bob stood there absolutely dumbfounded. He did not even have to ask. Greg had offered to take less and it was the same amount that Tracey had mentioned. "Wow Greg, that would be a real big help. Thanks, thanks so much."

"Well, we have been together for a long time. I always know I can count on you if I need something. So, just give me the 'five' and we'll be good. If I hear of some work or if I have something I will let you know right away."

They shook hands and Greg left. Bob went inside and told Tracey. She smiled and said, "You know, you should go to church with me once in a while. Imagine if both of us were praying."

Bob, Tracey and Jake had become an official part of the Great American Paradox of their time; they were both rich and poor. They had everything money could buy yet they had no money. They had a nice house to live in, a refrigerator, a washer and dryer, a personal computer, two TVs, a DVD player, a Play Station, a stove and oven, central heat and air, a microwave , internet service, two vehicles, cell phones, took a vacation every year and had been to Disney World and Busch Gardens many times.

There was always plenty to eat, Jake always had the latest clothes and shoes and they even had a quality health care plan through Bildot. Suddenly, just like that, the family had zero income coming into the house and that put them about $19,000.00 under the national poverty level for a family of three. They had become a "poor, rich, American family".

It was 10:30 when Bob and Tracey left for the unemployment office. Jake had spent the weekend at Tyler's house and Tyler's mom had dropped them at school Tuesday morning. Tracey said, "I hope we get home before Jake does. He doesn't have a clue about anything that is going on. He doesn't know about your job and---gosh Bob, I'm just worried about telling him, that's all."

"He's a good kid Tracey. He'll understand. I'll tell him I will get another job and that it is no big deal. It's nothing to worry about, okay."

"I hope you are right."

They walked into the unemployment office and Bob was surprised that it was not more crowded. "This isn't too bad Tracey, I thought more folks would be here."

Tracey said in a low voice, "Most people apply on-line. Hardly anyone comes in here to sign up. If they did the lines would be around the block."

"So, what are we doing here?"

She looked at him and shook her head, "I swear Bob, what is wrong with you? Our computer does not work---remember? We are here to use their computer. Let's get a number and sit down. We have to wait for one of the computers to open up."

"Where are these computers we're waiting for?"

"Over there by that wall."

Bob turned and said, "There are only five of them. Is that it. There's a whole bunch of people waiting to use five computers?"

"I know, I know, but we have no choice. We have to do this. We'll probably be here a few hours. Let's just try to make the best of it, okay."

They took numbers from the dispenser and sat down. The number on the board flashed #23. They had numbers 41 and 42 respectively. "Dang Tracey, we'll be here all day. This stinks."

"No, no, no. It's not so bad. There are five computers so I figure there are three people ahead of each of us. Not so bad."

At 12:30 #41 flashed on the board. Tracey hurried over to the computer, sat down, gathered her thoughts and tried to sign in. She clicked 'enter' and nothing happened. She clicked again---nothing---and again---nothing. She started to look around and the on-line computer assistant came over. "Is everything all right ma'am?"

"No, I cannot access my page. Look for yourself."

The lady looked at the screen and said , "Oh my, it is a 'code-9'. You did not re-certify and you were dropped from the system. You have to re-apply."

Tracy could not believe what she had just been told and started to jammer, "But, but---all my information was in there. I mean, it is not my fault. The storm last week ruined our computer. I tried to log in and couldn't and the car broke down and I couldn't get here and then it was the holiday and...oh my God, I needed that check. My husband was laid off last week. There has to be a way to re-boot this or something. Please—help me with this. Please."

Bob, sitting next to his wife, was shocked at how upset she was. The pressure of their circumstances was bubbling over Tracey's 'high water mark'. Bob grabbed her hand and put his other hand on her shoulder. "Hey Trace," he said. "Come on, it will be okay. Take a breath, okay."

She looked at her husband and wiped her now wet eyes. "Okay, okay. I'm Sorry. I'm okay."

The assistant shook her head and said, "I'm sorry ma'am. My hands are tied---"

Tracey, once more composed, cut her off, "Look, this is crazy, it takes a few weeks to get a check when you apply. I was supposed to get a check today and the computer just kicks me out of its precious system because it can't think and no living breathing person has to take responsibility because the "computer did it" and—I swear, can't you override it? I mean, this is NOT my fault."

"Ma'am, I am so sorry. But you are not the first person this has happened to. They set the system up this way so folks could not over-apply and it hurt people like yourself. The only people that can override this are the IT specialists up in Tallahassee and they know about this and are working to correct it."

"But, but, what am I supposed to do today?"

"My advice is to fill out the forms and get yourself back into the system. Maybe the system will recognize you and hasten the process. I don't know. I do know that you MUST fill out the new forms. And do not forget that you have to show that you applied for at least five jobs a week. That is VERY important. If you don't you will get kicked out again. Now, here is the toll free number for someone in your situation. Take your access number from your new application and call these folks when you get home. It may take a while to get through. They will ask for this new access number. Maybe they can speed things up for you. Good luck."

"Tracey just looked up at the woman and said, "Thanks for your help. I appreciate it."

Three and a half hours after arriving at the unemployment office they were on the way home. There was very little talk going on. Both of them had been emotionally drained from the experience. As they turned onto Madison Ave. Tracey said, "Hey hon, you had better pull into the bank so I can drop off that truck payment. It is too far past due to mail it. This way we can get credit for the payment immediately."

A half mile down the road was the rear entrance to the bank. Bob parked his truck and

Tracey went in. He sat listening to his country-western station on the radio and tapped his fingers on the steering wheel as he sang along with Johnny Cash's, "Ring of Fire". Caught up in the moment he did not notice Tracey heading back to the truck. He snapped to when she jerked the door open and hurriedly climbed in. Tears were coming down her face. "Oh my God, Tracey. What the hell is wrong? What happened?"

Speaking through her sobs Tracey sounded like she was talking with a mouth full of water. "They –bllb---want---bllb---they want two payments. They won't---bllb---take one---I swear, these people, they won't take one because today begins a new month. They want two payments or the truck. And, guess what Bob? It is NOT their fault. And do you know WHY it is NOT their fault. I shall tell you WHY it is NOT their fault. Because the computer will not accept the payment. The computer is in charge. These SOBs have deferred to the computer. Give me a break!"

"Well, I'll see about this. We only have five payments left anyway. We have been paying this thing like clockwork for three years. I'm going in there. Give me the payment book."

Bob headed into the bank and a lady dressed in a gray suit was standing inside the doorway. She asked him if she could help him and he explained that he wanted to talk to someone about his truck payment. She showed him to a seat at a desk opposite the teller windows and told him she would be with him in a moment. Bob sat and after about five minutes began to get annoyed because the lady was busy talking to a colleague and they were laughing and obviously not talking about business. He started to feel as if he were being disrespected. He was right.

He stood up and began to pace and he noticed her look over at him. She looked away and continued talking to her friend who also happened to look at Bob and realized what was going

on. She motioned to Miss Gray Suit and Miss Gray Suit turned and slowly walked over. She never said a word to Bob about making him wait. She just said, "Yes, can I help you with something?"

Bob Slider felt an anger rising up in him and through tightened lips explained why he was there and what he wanted. Miss Gray Suit condescendingly smiled at him and informed him that there was nothing SHE could do. He asked to speak to the manager. When she informed him that she WAS the manager it was all he could do to constrain himself. He walked over to a teller station and paid the two payments. As he left he glared over at Miss Gray Suit who was talking on the phone and he thought how being married to someone like that would be like hell on earth.

Back at the truck Tracey asked, "So, what happened?"

"I'll tell you what happened. I had to give them two payments. That's what happened. That witch in there. Why do we even come to this bank? They do not give a damn about us."

Tracey just said, "Bob, what about the electric bill. We have to pay the electric bill. We have to pay it today Bob, today. They will turn us of if we don't. Now what are we supposed to do?"

He just replied, "Yeah, yeah, yeah I know, I know. The electric and the phones and the cable and the insurance, I know. Oh man, Tracey, let's just go home and try to figure something out. Maybe we can have a huge yard sale or something. One thing is for sure, I have to find some work real quick."

Tracey was drained and did not say anything.

*

*

*

*

CHAPTER 5

Lights Out

Tommy and Judi Pavano were standing outside their house chatting when Bob and Tracey arrived home. Tracey saw her friend and said, "Oh, good, Judi is home. I guess I'll have to tell her what's going on. I feel a little embarrassed."

"Embarrassed," Bob said. "Get outta here. Since when are you embarrassed by confiding in Judi. She's your best friend and you two share everything. You go talk to her and I'll get these trash cans put away. Embarrassed, that's a good one."

Judi had been staying with her sick mom over the Memorial Day weekend. Tommy had told her all about their neighbor's predicament and Judi hurried over to Bob and Tracey's driveway. The truck slowed and stopped and Judi grabbed the handle and pulled open the truck door. Tracey got out of the truck, wrapped her arms around Judi and began to cry. "Oh Judi, I'm so glad you're home. This is such a mess. I can't believe everything that has happened since Friday. I don't know what to do."

"Oh, Tracey, Tracey. I'm sorry. Tommy did say that things were more or less under control right now. I guess it is not that simple, is it?"

"Oh, I'm sorry Judi. It's just that—damn it Judi. They just made us pay two truck payments. Now we can't pay the electric bill. That was due by nine o'clock this morning. I had gotten a ten day extension and now it is over. What am I supposed to do now?"

"I'll tell you what you are going to do. Call them right now. Tell them what happened."

"Judi, I just got off the cell phone with them. I called them as soon as we left the bank. They told me to do my best to get the payment in today but that they could not promise anything since we already had an extension. Give me a break---I have not been late with a payment in 12 years and they tell me that 'their hands are tied'. 'Their hands are tied'! Can you believe it? What does that mean? Are they sitting at the computer all tied up and can't move the mouse? Doesn't 12 years count for anything? Unemployment told me the same thing. Their computer kicked me out of their system and 'their hands are tied' too. The whole world is 'tied up" and we cannot do a thing about it. It's unbelievable. I don't know what to expect next."

Tommy had already gone home and Bob was busy bringing in the trash cans. Judi said,

"I have a pot of meat sauce on the stove. I need to check it real quick and then I'll come over. Put some coffee on and we can talk and figure something out."

"Thanks Judi. You're the best."

As Judi hurried home Jake came walking up the driveway. He had been at Tyler's since

Friday night and Tyler's mom had taken them to school that morning. As far as Jake was concerned everything was fine at home. He did not even know that his father had been laid off and that Bildot had gone out of business. Seeing Judi Pavano leaving his house was as normal as the sun coming up in the morning. "Hi, Mrs. Pavano."

"Oh, hi Jake. Have a good day today?"

"Yup, sure did."

Jake headed into the house and gave his mom a cursory, "Hey mom, I'm home".

Without stopping he dropped his backpack next to the sofa and walked to his room. He never noticed his mom's swollen eyes or thought about his dad's truck being in the driveway on a work day. Why should he, he was 12.

Tracey was in the kitchen wiping her eyes when Judi returned. At the same time Jake came into the kitchen from his room. This time he noticed his mom's puffy cheeks and said, "Hey Mom, what's wrong? Why you crying? What happened? You okay?"

"I'm fine Jake. Lousy day, that's all. You know how I get sometimes."

Jake's antennae suddenly went up. "Is dad okay? Why is his truck here?"

"Jake, dad is fine. There is just some stuff going on and I'll fill you in later. It's nothing for you to worry about, okay. Why don't you grab something to eat. "

Jake shrugged, went to the refrigerator and pulled open the door. As is the way with kids he peered into the fridge and began to stare. Judi had begun talking to Tracey when, matter of factly, Jake said, "Hey Mom, the bulb just burned out in the fridge. It's hard to see anything."

Tracey shrugged and a few moments went by. Then they all seemed to sense how eerily still and quiet everything was. It took about a half minute for them to realize that the ceiling fan had stopped spinning. Then they noticed that the fridge had stopped humming, and that the A/C had stopped cooling. Jake had already plopped down on the sofa and was pressing the buttons on the remote to no avail. His voice shattered the strange silence. "Hey Mom, the TV won't come on. I think we need some new batteries in the remote."

In the meantime, Bob came in from the garage and Jake immediately yelled over to him, "Hey Dad, something's wrong with the remote. We got any new batteries?"

"I put new batteries in the remote two days ago. Nothing is wrong with those batteries."

"But nothing is working."

"What do you mean, nothing's working? I was just…" He stopped talking and looked around. The lights were off and the ceiling fan was not spinning. Indeed, it was very, very quiet. He looked over at Tracey and she said, "That's right Bob, lights out. Just like that."

Jake was confused and said, "What do you mean Mom, light's out? Why are the lights out?"

"Jake, it is okay. It's just a temporary power outage. No big deal."

Jake shrugged, got up from the sofa and headed into his room. The house was warming up quickly as the Florida heat rapidly gobbled up the last of its cool air. Tracey said, "My God, it must be ten degrees hotter in here already. Bob, we have to do something."

"When did this happen, Tracey? I was in the garage. I didn't see anyone."

Judi said, "They just come Bob. That's all. They don't ask permission or anything like that. They just want to finish their dirty work and leave. People can get very nasty when someone is shutting off their electricity. I'm sure the man just came while you were in the garage. He probably came through the back yard. Your meter is on the back of the house, same as ours."

"Bob, what are we going to do? We gave the last of our money to the bank for the truck payment. What are we going to do?"

Bob stood there with a sort of helpless look on his face. This was new territory for him and he felt his manhood being stripped away. It was a sickening feeling and he did not understand it. He also did not know what to do. He always took care of "stuff" whenever the need arose. But this time he just lifted his hands and turned them palms up as if to say, *Help me*. Instead, he said, "I'm not sure Tracey. But don't worry, I'll figure something out."

Judi said, "Hey, listen to me. I have an idea. First thing I want to tell you is that I apologize. We would gladly front you the money but—"

"Judi, are you kidding. Stop it. Why would you apologize. That's ridiculous."

"Well, we are sorry. We had to give my mom two grand for some medical issues

and well, just wait until I tell you that story, but anyway—we're short. But look, I think I can show you a way out of this."

Bob went into the kitchen and turned his back to the two women. He just stared out the back window and listened as Judi began to offer her idea. "Look, call the St. Vincent de Paul Society over at my church. They probably can help you out. They help people all the time who get in a temporary bind."

Tracey snapped at her friend, "I don't think SO, Judi. My God, how embarrassing that would be. Telling perfect strangers our business and asking for money. I could never. No way. We don't even go to your church."

"But that doesn't matter. They try to help anyone who asks. Plus, you do go to Mass there sometimes, right?"

" Look Judi, I know you mean well but we don't ask for handouts. Right, Bob?"

Bob shook his head and they heard the door slam behind him as he went back into the garage. Jake came out of his room and said, "It is really getting hot in here, Mom. When do you think the electricity will get fixed?"

Judi went over to Tracey and whispered, "Look, you guys are in a spot. You need the lights and air working. You won't be able to hide this from Jake. He's not a baby anymore. Go ahead, give them a call. You have nothing to lose, right?"

Tracey sighed and said, "I don't even go to your church and I don't even know who these people are. It is ridiculous."

"No, it is not ridiculous. This is what these people do. It does not matter if you belong to Sacred Heart Catholic Church or even if you're Catholic for that matter. If someone asks for assistance they follow the concept that we are all God's children, end of story. I'm going to run home and get the number. You think about it for a few minutes while I'm gone."

Tracey said nothing and Judi left. Jake said, "Hey Mom, it's really hot in here."

"I know Jake, I know it's hot. We'll just have to sweat for a while. We won't die. What

did people do before they had air conditioning anyway? They didn't even think about the heat. It was

just the way it was. So, let's just make do for now, okay?"

Judi returned and handed Tracey a piece of paper with the number on it. "Go ahead, Trace, give them a call."

Tracey stared at the paper and hesitated. "I don't know Judi. I just don't know if I can do this."

"Should I ask Bob to do it?"

Tracey looked at her friend and quickly thought about the arm twisting she had to do to get him to go to the unemployment office with her. "Okay, okay," she said. "Point well taken."

Just then Bob came back in the house. He was covered in sweat and grabbed a dish towel that was hanging from the handle of the oven door. Tracey hollered at him, "Bob Slider, that is not for wiping your sweaty face. It is a dish towel. I swear, I hate it when you do that."

Bob, disgusted, threw the towel on the counter and took the roll of paper towels and unfurled a handful. Tracey sighed, "I give up."

As Bob wiped the sweat from his face and neck he asked, "So, what's going on?"

"Tracey answered, "I'm calling these people about our 'little' problem. Maybe they can help."

Bob, expressing indignation, said, "No you're not. You're not calling anybody about our problem. I can take care of our problem." Then he turned to Judi and said, "You know Judi, I love ya and you are a great friend and all but sometimes---look, no way. What are we, some kind of charity case or something. Just forget the whole idea."

Judi looked at Bob and thought about whether she should leave them alone or keep butting in. She decided to speak. She just felt she had to. "You know Bob, I love you too but sometimes you let that damn pride of yours really cloud some good, old fashioned, common sense. Right now, at this moment in time, you need a bit of help. So what! It happens to everyone once in a while. So why don't you just let your wife call. Trust me, it is not a big deal. Heck Bob, you don't even have to do it. You can go back in the garage and sweat some more."

The remark did manage to squeeze a bit of a smile from Bob's tightly clenched lips. He lifted his left arm and waved it towards them and then headed back to the garage. It was his sign of surrender. He had also saved "face" by not having to make the call and not having to be present when Tracey did make the call. Pride, the great two-edged sword, combining positive and negative, a paradox unto itself.

Tracey shook her head and punched the numbers into her cell phone. She waited and then said to Judi, "I'm getting a recording."

Tracey held up both her hands and said, "Don't hang up. Just leave a message and they will get back to you."

Tracey waited and then began to speak. "Yes---my name is Tracey Slider . My neighborgave me your number and suggested that I call you. Anyway, our power is off and," suddenly she had to stifle an unexpected sob. She took a breath and continued, "Look, we need a little help. My number is 221-3790. Thank you."

As Tracey hung up, Judi smiled at her and said, "Good for you Tracey, good for you.

Just say a little prayer and things will work out. It is kind of late so I hope they can get back to you today. Look, I have to get home and back to that pot of sauce. I'll call you in a little bit to see how things are going."

Tracey and Judi hugged each other and, as Judi headed to the door, she waved to a concerned Jake who was sitting on the sofa. He waved back by simply lifting his hand as his arm rested across his leg. When Judi was gone Tracey said to her son, "Jake, I need to explain to you what is going on. First, I need to get some iced tea. Do you want a glass?"

"Sure mom."

She poured two glasses and could not help but notice how the iced tea was not as cold as it should be. The ice in the freezer was already starting to liquefy and she was suddenly glad she had made the call to St. Vincent's. She realized that it would not be long before things began to turn warm and she had just finished her food shopping the previous Saturday. She needed the food she had. There was no money to buy fresh food if it went bad.

She brought the iced tea into Jake and just as she was about to tell him what was going on the phone rang. She flipped it open and said, "Hello."

"Hi, is this Tracey?"

"Yes it is. Who's calling?"

"Oh, hi Tracey. This is Pete from the St. Vincent de Paul Society. We got your message. So tell me, how long has your power been off?"

Tracey was a bit taken back at how quickly the return call had come and said, "Wow, that was quick. I only called about five minutes ago."

Pete laughed and said, "Just good timing, Tracey. I was picking up messages and yours had just come in. If I had checked five minutes earlier it would not have been on the machine and we might not have gotten back to you today. I think God is just watching out for us, that's all." Pete let out a slight laugh and said, "Anyway, we have to come out to see you and can do it in the next half hour. How does that sound?"

"Tracey was stunned. "Uh, you have to come here? We don't come to you?"

"Yes, that's the way we do it. It's called a home visit and, trust me Tracey, it is not a big deal." He chuckled and continued, "Hey, don't worry, we're not the government."

Tracey felt herself smiling as Pete kept talking. "Look, we generally do not do a visit this quickly. In fact, most times it might take a day or so depending on people's schedules. Everything just seemed to fall into place with you. Maybe we can actually get something done today. I'm not sure. It is pretty late but it sure is worth a shot. What do you say? Should we come over?"

Pete's pleasant voice and down-to-earth manner had put her at ease. She simply said,

"Sure, that's fine." Then she gave him the address and he simply asked her to have her power bill available. As she hung up she felt no sense of intimidation or nervousness.

Bob came back a few minutes later. "Well Tracey, what's going on? Did you actually call those people?"

"Yes I did Bob. Yes, I did. They will be here in a half hour."

Bob slapped his hands together and sarcastically said, "Isn't this nice. Here come the church people to help out poor, pathetic, unemployed, Bob Slider."

Bob stormed out of the house allowing his pride to rule his outward emotions while inside he was actually glad that Tracey had made the call. Jake teared up never having seen his dad act like this. The word 'unemployed' was dancing inside Bob's head.

Tracey smiled reassuringly and went over to her son, sat next to him and said , "Aw Jake, don't worry." She rubbed his head saying, "Look Jake, Dad's okay. He has a right to be upset. Bildot went out of business Friday and he is temporarily out of work. But don't worry, everything will be fine."

Jake's life had been well ordered and predictable. Mom and Dad were always there and he was well cared for. His dad went to work every day, fixed broken 'stuff' around the house, knew how to barbecue the best ribs anywhere and could throw a baseball as well as any guy in the neighborhood. Suddenly, for the first time in his young life, Jake was facing the reality of life's "ups and downs". His dad was acting different and it was because he did not have a job anymore. The boy was suddenly scared about the future and it was a concern he did not understand. "Bildot closed? Gee Mom, you mean for good? Like they are really out of business? What about money? We need money, right?"

"Yes Jake, we do. That is not an issue. Dad will find work. And yes, Bildot closed for good. Sometimes in life things happen and you have to be strong and deal with whatever it is. But look, every family runs into things like this. That's all. Dad will be fine. Don't worry, we'll all be fine. Now, I don't want you worrying about anything, understand?"

As she hugged him he said in a low voice, "Okay mom, I'm not worried."

*

*

*

CHAPTER 6

The Home Visit and Onward

Their newly discovered sense of helplessness had Bob and Tracey emotionally drained and exhausted. They had $40.00 to their name and the electricity had been turned off. The inside of the house was hovering at about 90 degrees, the refrigerator was rapidly losing its coldness while the hot water heater was slowly losing its hotness. The stove could not be used and the washer and dryer had been temporarily relegated to useless objects just taking up space. Losing power because of a storm was one thing. Having it taken away from you on purpose by the power company was something totally different. A storm could not cause people to feel demeaned and degraded. People could.

It was about 3:45 when a white mini-van stopped in front of the house. A man and woman slowly stepped from the vehicle. Tracey, avoiding going to the front door until the last minute, watched them approach the house from inside the living room window. As they reached the front door she walked over and opened it. The man asked, "Hi, you Tracey?"

"Yup, that's me," Tracey answered.

"Nice to meet you. I'm Pete, this is my wife, Dee. You know, Tracey, it is amazing how this all fell into place. I'm glad you called us."

Tracey was still a bit uneasy and fumbled for a few words. "Um—do you want to talk out here or come in the house? It has gotten pretty hot in there."

"Oh, that's okay. We'll come in, that is if you don't mind. We don't care about how hot it is. Hey, don't feel funny about this. The same thing has happened to us. We understand how you feel."

Tracey was taken back by Pete's honesty and Dee's reassuring smile. Dee said, "Sure, we understand. In fact you would be amazed at how many people in town have had their lights shut off. It's unbelievable."

Tracey felt herself relax and a sense of calm came over her. These were folks just like her and Bob. They had no superior attitude, were down to earth and she sensed they were even the type of people she could be friends with. "Let me get my husband. He's out back."

Tracey stuck her head out the back door and looked left and right. She did not see Bob. She turned to Pete and Dee and said, "I'll be right back. He's out here somewhere."

She stepped outside and called out, "Bob, Bob, where are you. You need to come in here a minute."

There was no response and Tracey started to get annoyed. She looked in the garage and saw Bob sanding a piece of 1x6 pine which did not need sanding. She said in a low voice, "Bob Slider, you get in this house. These are nice people and you are acting like a child."

Bob scowled and dropped the wood and sand-paper and followed her inside. She was right, he was acting like a child but it was simply his embarrassment being displayed.

Bob stand-offishly came into the house and Tracey introduced him to Pete and Dee. Pete readily went over to him and shook his hand and started talking about the neighborhood. He told him that his son, Mikey, was going to Pierpont High School and was a junior. Bob told Pete that Jake would probably go to Pinellas Pines High School in two years. Mikey played football and Jake played baseball. Now they had common ground to share. Just like that Bob was sitting down across from Pete and they were talking about local things and different people in the area and it was as if they had been friends for a while. Then Pete said, "Okay, let me see your electric bill."

Suddenly Bob tensed up but Pete could sense it. He leaned toward him and said, "Bob, this is not a big deal. Trust me. Plus, it is completely confidential. No one will ever know about us being here except you guys, okay."

Bob slowly nodded and called over to Tracey who was in the living room talking to Dee. "Hey hon, you have the electric bill handy?"

"Yes Bob, it's right on the table next to those other papers."

Bob reached over, found the bill, and handed it to Pete. Pete said, "I need your social."

Bob jotted it down on a piece of scrap paper and handed it to Pete. Pete pulled out his phone and dialed some numbers. Suddenly all was quiet as they watched Pete sit there with the phone next to his ear. Bob felt ridiculous but there was nothing else to do. Pete waited and pushed in some more numbers. He waited some more and more numbers were pushed. Then he held the electric bill flat on the table with his elbow as he punched more numbers into the phone. By now the silence was becoming intense as they all sat quietly watching and waiting. Suddenly Pete said, "Oh, for crying out loud. Whatever. These people."

Bob said, "Something wrong, Pete?"

"No, it's fine. I apologize. I was just entering your info into their computer and the computer decided to transfer me to a real live person. See, the computers are telling the people what to do. Sometimes it can be exasperating. Boy, I wish I could just call some business up and have a real live person answer. Oh well, as they say, it is what it is."

Bob quickly thought about the truck payments and how Miss Gray Suit had said her "hands were tied" because of the computer. "Yeah, I know what you mean. Just went through that earlier."

Pete looked at Bob and raised his eyes as he pointed to the phone. "Hello, oh hey, is this Joe?" He paused and laughed and said, "Yeah Joe, it's me again. How's it going?"

Pete and Joe, who was the real live customer service rep at the power company, spent a few moments engaging in some idle chit chat. Pete and Joe had become more or less telephone buddies because Pete had talked to him so many times over the past several years. Plus, Pete was quite engaging and had a knack for putting people at ease. Then he said, "Yes Joe, whatever it is, the whole past due amount." He waited another moment and said, "Okay Joe, you're a good man. Thanks. By the way Joe, Rays and Yankees this weekend. I say we sweep."

Pete listened a few moments longer, laughed and said, "Okay Joe, good talking to you. Thanks again. And, you are wrong. Rays will sweep."

He hung up the phone and laughingly said, "Yeah, right, he thinks the Yanks will sweep the Rays. Not happening. What do you think, Bob?"

Bob was taken back a bit. He was focused on his electric bill. "I think you're right. The Rays have some great pitching and---"

Dee yelled in from the living room, "Hey Pete, what about the power bill. We can talk baseball later."

Pete said, "Oh man, I'm sorry. Okay, you guys are good to go. They will be out within the hour to restore power. Now, what else is going on. What about the water bill? Do you have groceries?"

Bob and Tracey were both stunned. "Tracey said, "Are you kidding? Just like that the power will be put back on? I can't believe it."

"They know our word is like gold. When we say we are guaranteeing to make payment we make payment. No problem. So, is your water bill current?"

"Well, actually no, it isn't," Tracey said. "You can't pay that too, can you?"

Bob said, "Actually no, we can't. Not today anyway. You know, the only monies we have come from donations from our parishioners. We don't get any outside funding so we have to play it close to the vest. But look, let me see your water bill. I know I can at least get a hold put on it."

Tracey brought the water bill out and handed it to Pete. He made a phone call to the

Pinellas Pine's Utility Department and talked to a woman named Nancy. Just like he had with Joe,

Pete spent a few minutes chatting and laughing with Nancy and then hung up and told Bob and Tracey that they were given an additional two weeks to pay their water bill. If they did not have the money in two weeks Pete told them that St. Vincent De Paul would cover it. That approach made Bob feel much better about things and he said to Pete, "Don't worry, I'll be able to cover that in two weeks, no problem. Thanks for backing us up. I really appreciate it."

The Vincentians left and Bob and Tracey both sat together at the kitchen table. Jake,

who had been asked to hang out in his room while Pete and Dee were visiting, came out and joined his mom and dad. He was drenched in sweat. "What's going on? The electric getting fixed?"

Bob was relieved to be able to say, "Yeah Jake, should be fixed within an hour."

"That's great dad, it sure is hot in here. Think I'll go shoot a few hoops."

Jake got his basketball and went outside. Bob had set up a regulation back-board and hoop in the driveway. Jake started shooting baskets. Tracey looked out at him and said, "That's amazing Bob. You can see the tension has just fallen off of him. I didn't realize how upset he was about everything."

"Really, I didn't think that. You sure?"

Tracey shook her head and said, "I'm his mother. I know my son. Yeah, he's upset."

There was a slight 'pop' and all of a sudden the ceiling fan was spinning and the refrigerator was humming. The A/C kicked in and Tracey said, "Thank God for Judi. I never would have thought***". She stopped mid-sentence and stood directly in front of her husband. Looking him in the eye she said, "We all need to start going to church every week, together, as a family. I want you to think about that for me, okay?"

Bob wanted to move on and said, "Okay Tracey, I'll think about it. Now listen, I was

thinking. Maybe we should have a yard sale this weekend. We have a lot of stuff. Maybe we could make a few bucks. What do you think?"

"I think that's a great idea. Let's do it. But I am very serious about this church thing. Plus, we need to get Jake going to church. It is important for him."

Bob just ignored the church talk and said, "Great Trace---I'll start making up signs and sorting through all of that stuff we have in the garage."

Suddenly a bit upbeat, Tracey replied, "Hey, this sounds like it might be fun. I'll start going through the closets. Maybe Jake has some stuff he would like to get rid of, too. We can talk about church later."

"Stuff" they had, lots of it. By Thursday the living room and garage was piled high with items they had pulled from the closets, under the beds, from the kitchen cabinets and from the garage. Bob had built shelves in the garage that were two feet wide and eight feet long. There were four of them, two on each side of the garage and there was a humongous amount of "stuff" that had been stored on them over the years.

Bob loved Christmas and had accumulated a vast array of decorations. He loved decorating his house and people would actually make a special trip over to see it. Lights covered the house from the ridge of the roof, down the sides, around the windows and across the lawn.

Illuminated figures were everywhere; Santa and his reindeer, snowmen, animals, a full Nativity set, and a ferris-wheel with teddy-bears in each seat appearing to be waving as they traveled round and round. Bob had a floor to ceiling Christmas tree that he placed in front of the picture window in the living room and Tracey and Jake would decorate virtually every square inch of its branches. Bob did not believe he would have it in him to give up one Christmas item.

Bob also had two circular saws, a reciprocating saw, a router and router table and accessories, a table-saw, two jig saws, a portable band-saw and numerous lawn tools. He had a small compressor and a power-washer kit, a refrigerator in the garage that was used mainly for holding drinks and ice, two sets of golf clubs, a weight bench and a treadmill. Most of these things he never used. In fact, the treadmill had other boxes stored on top of it and the weight bench had been dismantled.

Tracey had managed to fill half the living room with items that included picture frames, clothing, a crock pot, an old Smith-Corona Electric Typewriter rendered obsolete by computers an old Hoover Upright vacuum cleaner, an electric mixer, an electric skillet, a radio, two TVs and various other sundry items.

Jake managed to pull out things he had squirreled away in his room. An old skateboard, several video games, an aluminum baseball bat he used when he was eight years old and had outgrown, a NY Jets football helmet, and some old beer cans he had purchased from a local flea market with his allowance money. They were now ready to "wheel & deal".

Bob made up seven signs and at 6 a.m Friday morning he headed out to the seven locations where he had planned to place them. He had thought it out carefully, with signs at four main intersections directing traffic to the other three signs which would direct traffic right to his house.

Bob came home and he and Tracey set up the makeshift tables in the driveway and began to place items out. Tracey was feverishly at it when she noticed that Bob was sort of dilly-dallying in the garage. "Hey, hon, what are you doing? You have hardly put anything out here. Come on, put some stuff out here. People could be coming along soon."

"There is no rush, Tracey. Remember, it is Friday. This was your idea for today. I don't think many people come to yard sales on Friday. "Well, tell that to the people in the two cars that just pulled up. Come on, get some stuff out here. If we're doing this, let's do it right. Trust me, Friday is a good day. All the retirees are out looking."

Bob slowly came out holding an old rake and a beat-up driveway broom. He set them next to one of the tables. Tracey looked at him and said, "I don't believe you. You don't want to get rid of any of your stuff, do you? You're a packrat at heart. I don't believe it."

"I am not a packrat Tracey. I'm just not sure what to get rid of, that's all."

"Bob Slider, we need to raise some money, right? Most of this stuff you never use anyway." She laughed and went over and hugged him. Smiling, she said, "Suck it up, husband. Get ruthless and give up some of your stuff. You can do it. You don't need it anyway."

He knew she was right and he also could not believe how much he did not want to part

with his "stuff" even though he rarely used much of it. He picked up the older of the circular saws and placed it out on the table. Immediately a man walked up and said, "Hey, that thing work okay?"

Bob answered, "Yup, sure does."

"How much?"

"Ten bucks."

"Show me that it works and you got a deal."

Bob plugged it in and the man pulled the trigger and the saw screamed out as the blade spun. The guy handed Bob a ten dollar bill and just like that his saw was gone. It was not as traumatic as he thought it would be. He still had the "good" one. Onward and forward and by Saturday afternoon they had sold over $400.00 worth of "stuff" that they never used.

Then came the man rumbling up on a beautiful Harley. He was huge and he was a stereotypical biker. He was wearing black chaps, a black leather vest over an olive green tank top; his hair was pulled back into a long pony-tail and he wore sunglasses that made him look like he was a character right out of a movie. Leather gloves without fingers were on his hands.

The bike's engine went silent and the man pushed down the kick-stand, leaned the bike on it and got off. He stretched and walked over to Bob. Removing his sun glasses he suddenly lost his menacing appearance. He said to Bob, "Hi, my name is Jerry and my neighbor told me about your sale. He bought a circular saw from you on Friday, remember?"

Of course Bob remembered. It was the first sale of the weekend. "Yeah, sure. I remember. How can I help you?"

"Well, he told me about the car you had parked here. He said it was in nice shape and I'm looking around for a secondhand car for my son. You know, kids and all, he's going to be 17 and he has saved some money. I'm trying to find something that's not too expensive but runs okay. Anyway, I came over here to ask if that car might be for sale?"

Bob, never expecting the question, was startled. "Geez, Jerry, that was not the plan. It's the wife's car anyway. You would have to check with her. Plus, the fuel pump is shot. That's a pretty big repair job."

"How does it run otherwise?"

"Actually, I have taken pretty good care of this car. It is in nice shape. Plus, my neighbor, Tommy, is a mechanic and he has a kept tabs on it. So, it is in good shape except for the fuel pump."

"Do you want to sell it?"

Bob said, "I don't know. I have to talk to Tracey, that's my wife. Let me ask her about it."

"That's a 98' Lumina, right? I'll give you $1500.00 and I'll repair the fuel pump. See what your wife thinks."

Bob knew that it was a great offer for a used car with a blown fuel pump. He talked it over with Tracey and they agreed to sell the car. Between the sale of miscellaneous household items and the car they were suddenly $1900.00 richer than they were the previous Friday morning.

With a temporary financial reprieve in their pockets they paid the water bill, the car insurance, the cable bill, cell phone bill and even took $150.00 and had their computer repaired by their friend, Gary. They were good through June and into July. All Bob needed to do was find some work so they could stay "above water". They did not pay anything on the credit cards. They were so far behind they figured it did not matter.

*

*

*

*

CHAPTER 7

"Upward and Downward"

Tracey enjoyed managing money and probably would have been an excellent financial planner. She handled the family's meager funds in such a way as to get all their bills current except for the credit cards. That was a totally different issue and, being several months behind in payments, the collectors were calling them almost every day looking for money.

Tracey had tried to work out payment plans but, not having a steady income, she had not been able to keep her good faith arrangements with them. Tracey and Bob both got to the point that when their telephone rang it would trigger an involuntary stomach spasm in each of them. However, combined with unemployment kicking in during the third week of June and their yard sale, "bonanza" from a few weeks earlier. The Sliders were managing their financial lives okay. It was a balancing act for sure, but they were standing tall and moving forward.

At the end of June, Steve Jackson, one of Bob's former co-workers at Bildot, called Bob and asked him if he would be interested in doing a roofing job. Steve's neighbor needed his roof replaced and had offered the job to Steve who had experience doing roofing. Bob jumped at the chance and by the middle of July he had pocketed $1200.00 in cash for his labor.

It was a perfect scenario for both Bob and Steve. Both of them were collecting unemployment and did not want to report earning a lousy twelve hundred bucks. They both knew that all income was supposed to be reported to the Unemployment Office but the money earned was only for a few days work. You did not jeopardize unemployment benefits for that. After all, it was the only money they had been able to earn in over six weeks. They also could spot each other time away from the job to make sure they could fill out job applications so they could prove to unemployment that they were looking for work. Desperate times called for desperate measures and keeping food on the table and a roof over your head was always priority number one, no matter what.

Steve and Bob did such a good job on the roof another neighbor down the street hired the two men to do his roof also. By the middle of August Bob was able to put another $1400.00 in his pocket. In addition, Greg Margolese had come up with some painting and minor repair jobs at several of his rental homes and Bob did that work as a trade-off against some of September's rent. The Sliders were managing their financial lives, albeit a bit untraditionally and technically, illegally for not reporting the meager earned income.

Early in September, Greg called Bob on a Sunday evening and asked him if he could do some drywall repair at one of his vacancies. The plumber had torn out a wall to access a broken water pipe and the hole had to be closed up and finished. Bob said, "Don't worry about a thing Greg. I will take care of the that ASAP."

"Thanks Bob, I appreciate it. Can you do me one favor and pick up the material. I haven't had a chance. We just need two sheets of half-inch dry wall and some joint compound."

"No problem Greg. Will I see you out there tomorrow?"

"Yeah, I'll be coming over around noon."

Bob was up bright and early Monday morning. He had a job to go to and waking to a purpose in your day was such a nice thing compared to having an entire day ahead of you with nothing to do. He got in his truck and headed over to Home Depot.

Bob loved Home Depot. He loved Bildot more but at least when he walked into the home repair and remodeling warehouse there was a feeling of belonging there. He liked the atmosphere, the smell of lumber, the sound of the forklift loading pallets of cement onto the huge shelves and everything else about the store. Yes sir, to Bob Slider this was a man's place. He thought that maybe someday he would work there. He certainly had the experience.

He grabbed one of the orange carts that was near the fencing section entrance and pushed it inside. He was even enjoying the noise the cart made as it rumbled across the concrete floor. He pushed it to the drywall section and looked at the pile of 4X8 sheets. They were piled as high as his neck and he figured he had better get some help pulling a sheet from the top of the pile. But, as is the way with things, when you do not need help someone is always asking you if you do, and when you do need help, good luck finding someone. There was no one around.

He shook his head and reached up to grab a corner of the top sheet. He pulled it outward and the edge of the sheet slid toward him. He went to the other end and reached up to grab that side. Since the one corner had been pulled out the other corner naturally moved in. So, being a "I don't need any help" guy, Bob had a brilliant idea. He pulled the cart over, figuring he could step up on its edge and reach the corner that was evading his grip.

Bob, knowing in his gut that he was doing something 'dumb', stepped on the end of the cart to reach up. Naturally, the cart decided to do its own thing and rolled away from him. He more or less flew backwards and smashed into the pile of drywall. A light twinge ran across his lower back and the combination of surprise and "twinge" scared him. He took a breath, stood up and realized he was all right and called himself an 'idiot'. A voice from behind said, "Hey buddy, let me help you with that."

It was just another customer who saw Bob's dilemma and wanted to help. The guy was taller than Bob and he managed to reach the corner Bob couldn't. Bob grabbed the other corner of the drywall and, one at a time, they unloaded two sheets onto the cart. Bob thanked the guy and pushed the cart down the aisle to the pails of joint-compound.

As he lifted a five gallon pail onto the cart the almost 50 pounds of dead weight sent another sharp twinge across his lower back. Once again a touch of fear danced through him. The 'twinge' was something entirely new, something foreign, something that had never happened to him before. Once again it quickly disappeared. He headed to the check-out and, after paying, a worker at the exit helped him push the cart to his truck and helped him load it up.

Bob stopped at a McDonald's and went through the drive-thru getting a 'Bacon, Egg n Cheese' biscuit and a large coffee. Fifteen minutes later he pulled up to the house on Darby Road and backed into the driveway. He had already eaten the sandwich so he took a sip of the hot coffee and got out of the truck. He was glad the house was vacant. Vacant was so much nicer than 'occupied' because there was no furniture to worry about and no people to ask you a million questions.

He opened the garage door and went back to the truck to get the pail of joint compound. He dropped the tail-gate, removed the bunji cord that was holding the pail in place and reached across his chest with his right arm. He grabbed the handle on the pail and pulled. The pail of "mud" did not move. Its bottom edge had caught on the head of a bolt in the truck bed. Bob thought that he had been struck by lightning. Within a nanosecond, pain shot across his lower back, shot down both of his legs and exploded in his brain. He could not move.

For several moments the terrified man stood there. He did not know what to do nor did he have any clue as to what might have happened to him. He took some deep breaths and tried to stand up straight. The pain in his lower back was excruciating. He spent almost ten minutes trying to close the tailgate. He could not do it. He mumbled, "The hell with it. If it falls out, it falls out."

Slowly he began to inch his way to the front of his truck. Inch by inch he worked his way down the side of the truck to the driver side door. He opened the door and, after taking a few more deep breaths, slid sideways until his butt was against the seat. He pulled himself into the truck by holding onto the steering wheel.

The pain was so intense he was sweating profusely and tears filled his eyes. These tears were from both the pain in his body and from the fear of what might have caused it. As he sat for several minutes the pain subsided a bit. Bob knew he was in serious trouble. He managed to get the door closed and he headed home.

When Bob arrived home no-one was there. Jake was at school and Traccy had gone to the store with Judi. He managed to get himself into the house and sat down at the straight backed chair in the kitchen. It took him a few minutes to figure out how to sit with the least amount of pain.

Bob quickly learned that keeping his legs stretched out a bit and leaning his torso slightly forward gave him some relief. Then he would try to sit up straight for a few minutes. This movement backwards always increased the pain. But he kept hoping that if he did that, it would alleviate the pain. It did not. Determined, he did that off and on for the next hour and a half until Tracey came back home.

When Tracey came into the house she saw her husband sitting there in this strange position and looking at her with a pained expression on his face. She immediately said, "What's wrong? Why are you sitting like that?"

"I hurt my back Tracey, and the pain is really bad."

"Oh my God, Bob. What happened?"

"All I did was grab a pail of joint compound to get it off the truck. When I pulled it

something happened and it felt like something exploded in my back. I could hardly move. I don't know what I could have done. I just keep hoping it will go away."

When Tracey lost her job nine months earlier the "domino principle" had kicked in. The "dominoes" had been slowly but surely falling into one another ever since. One of the falling dominoes that was knocked over was when Bob's hours were cut and they dropped their health insurance so they could put another $372.00 per month back in their pockets. They did not want to do this but they needed the money to live on. Tracey immediately said, "I have to get you to the emergency room. Who knows what you might have done."

"Stop it Tracey, stop it right now. I am not going anywhere. This might just pass and I'll be fine. Don't forget, we have no insurance and we don't have any money to pay for any emergency room."

"They bill you. So that is not an issue right now. There is no reason you cannot go."

"I'm not going anywhere. End of story."

Tracey began to get angry. "Fine, Mr. Slider, or should I say Superman. Well, if you are Superman you were just hit by kryptonite and you are now useless. It seems like Superman needs someone to help him remove the kryptonite. Tell you what, Superman, if you can get up from that chair and walk across the room with no problem I won't say another word. If you can't, we go to the ER." He glared at her and began to stand up. The effort to do so was monumental and Bob was unable to fake anything. But he tried and took a step toward the living room grimacing as he did. Now sweat was exploding from his forehead and he stepped back and sat down. "Tracey, how about we do this. If I am not better by tomorrow morning I'll go then, okay. And—I am NOT Superman."

His cell phone began to sing its song as Tracey said, "Fine Bob, fine. You cannot take one step and you want to wait until tomorrow. You better answer your phone."

He looked at the screen and saw that it was Greg. "Hi, Greg."

"What happened, Bob. The garage door is wide open and no one is here. Where are you?"

"Look Greg, I hurt my back unloading the joint compound. I was lucky to get home. I still have the material on my truck."

"Bob, how bad is your back?"

"I don't know. Pretty bad. Tracey wants to take me to the hospital but I want to wait until tomorrow."

"I'm sorry, Bob. I wish that had not happened to you. Look, is it all right if I come by and get the stuff off your truck. I have to get that job finished. People are moving in this Thursday."

"Sure Greg, no problem. Come on by."

Twenty minutes later Greg backed his truck up to Bob's truck and transferred the drywall and joint compound. Then he went in to see his wounded handyman/tenant. Greg stood in the foyer acting a bit nervous. He asked Bob what had happened and Bob told him. Greg simply said, "Look guys, if there is anything I can do to help, don't hesitate to ask. I know you have been struggling lately and we've known each other a long time. Anyway, I'll check in with you in a few days, okay."

Tracey and Bob both smiled at their landlord and Bob said, "Yeah, thanks Greg. Talk to you in a few days."

When he left Tracey said, "Sometimes I can't stand that man. There is just something---I don't know what it is."

"Aw, Tracey, he's a good guy. He just comes from a different kind of world than we do, that's all. He's a good guy."

"He's probably worried that you will want to sue his homeowner's insurance or something. He's not fooling me any."

Bob looked at her. "Get outta here, Tracey. No he's not. He just told us that we should call him if we need anything, right?"

She shook her head and said, "Okay, okay, have it your way. You know him better than I do."

By 5 p.m. Bob gave in. The pain was too severe to wait until the following day. Tracey helped her husband into the truck and they headed to Gulf Shores Hospital over in St. Petersburg. Upon arriving they asked for Bob's proof of insurance and, of course, he did not have any. They made him sign papers saying that he was responsible for payment.

Three hours later a doctor came in to see him. An MRI was ordered and two hours after that Bob was told he had two herniated discs in his lower back, L4 and L5. They were pressing on his nerve endings causing the severe pain. The ER Doctor referred him to an orthopedic specialist and gave him some pain medication. He told him he should lie down in bed with a pillow tucked behind his knees and sent him on his way.

Tracey stopped at the 24 hour pharmacy on the way home for the prescription. The pain medication, which was oxycodone, did relieve the pain and Bob did manage to get some sleep although it was in the big recliner.

The next morning Tracey called the orthopedic doctor's office to set up an appointment. When she told them they had no insurance she was told that they would have to pay the initial $175.00 for the consultation fee. They did not have an 'extra' $175.00. Tracey told them she would have to call them back. The hope that had been resurrected inside them over the summer months was quickly put on hold.

Tracey shut the phone off and said, "They want $175.00 up front because we have no insurance. What are we supposed to do now?"

"I'll tell you what we are going to do. Nothing. That's right, nothing. I'll just get myself better. I'll take it easy and rest the back and

I'll bet you I can get by this. So don't worry that pretty head of yours about it. How's that sound?"

"Oh please, Bob, stop being ridiculous. For God's sake, you can hardly stand up. Wait a minute, wait a minute, I know what to do, I know what to do."

"Oh yeah, and what's that?"

"Call Greg. It was his house you were hurt at. He said if you need anything not to hesitate. Well, here it is. We NEED something right now. Call him and tell him what is going on and that you need $175.00."

Bob did not respond. She looked at him and said, "I know just what you're thinking. You feel stupid asking him for help, don't you? You already were behind with the rent and this would be too much to ask, right?"

"Bob raised his voice a bit, "Okay, yes, you're right. I feel dumb. I admit it. But a man has to keep some pride, doesn't he?"

"So this is a 'man' thing? Spare me, okay. This is not about a man's pride, Bob. This is about survival. You need medical attention. You will be cut off unemployment if you cannot be ready to work. This is not the time for this 'pride' nonsense. Plus, it is HIS house where you were hurt. You were going there to save him money. Give me a break. In fact, I'll call him myself."

Bob said nothing. He was glad that she was doing the dirty work and asking Greg. This way Greg would have no doubt as to the severity of Bob's condition and, of course, Bob would not have to be the one to ask. She called Greg and he told her, "No problem, Tracey. I understand. Glad to do it. I'll be over later with a check." The call lasted less than a minute.

She hung up and said, "He's coming over with a check. Now I can call and make that appointment."

"I guess he's not so bad after all, is he Trace?"

"Okay, okay. I have to admit, he did not hesitate at all. I guess you were right about him."

Tracey called and was staggered when the receptionist told her that they did not have an opening for three weeks. She stood there, staring at the phone for a moment. Then she went on the offensive, "You listen to me, the hospital gave us your number. This is an emergency. My husband can just about stand up. The pain is excruciating. Three weeks is unacceptable. This man needs help—NOW!"

"Ma'am, calm down please---"

"Don't you dare tell me to calm down.

I want to speak to the office manager.

"Hold on please."

Tracey listened as silence filled the next two minutes. Then the lady came back and said, "Mrs. Slider, can you bring your husband in tomorrow morning at nine o'clock?"

"Yes, absolutely, we will be there. Thank you."

Bob spent the night sitting at the dining room table in the upright chair with his head placed down on his folded arms. Even with the medication dulling the pain he could not lie down in the bed. It was 6:30 a.m when Jake, who was getting ready to go to school, went over to him and shook his shoulder. "Dad, dad, are you okay?"

Bob, who had only been able to doze off intermittently, lifted his head. "Huh, what, oh Jake, it's you. What's going on? Everything all right?"

"Yeah dad, I'm just getting ready to go to school. Mom will be out in a minute. You looked pretty uncomfortable sitting there. Just checking to see if you were okay."

"Bob slowly sat up, grimaced and said, "Thanks, Jake. Yeah I'm okay. I go to the doc this morning. Maybe he can fix me up."

Tracey came out from the bathroom and said, "So, good morning to both of you. Are you all right, hon? Sleeping like that cannot be very good for you."

"I'm okay, Trace, thanks."

"Well, I'm going to run Jake to school and then we'll head over to the doctor's. Can you get ready by yourself?"

"Bob groaned sarcastically, "Yesss, Dear. I can still stand up if I have to."

Doctor Victoria Nelson's office was located in a new medical complex over on busy

Haney Blvd. Tracey parked the truck and it took Bob almost 15 minutes to make the walk to the entrance. They took the elevator up to the third floor and when the doors opened they stepped right into the office. "Pretty fancy, Traccy. These people must charge a fortune."

"Oh Bob, right now, who cares. As long as they will see you and do something to help you is all that matters. You know, my love, you really need to get back to praying, you really do."

"Not now Tracey, okay. Not now."

Bob filled out the required paper work and only cringed when he had to write down that he was unemployed. He hated having to even admit it. Tracey brought the finished papers up to the receptionist and Bob was called into the examining room less than five minutes later. A nurse came in and took his vital signs and asked him a bunch of questions about his overall health, whether or not he had ever had any surgeries, what kind of vitamins and medications he was taking, and to explain exactly how he had hurt his back. Bob, not wanting to admit that he was working for someone, thought a moment and then answered, "I was a jerk. I tried to lift this pail of joint compound in my garage and, well, it did not move. Instead, my back screamed and here I am. What can I say. It happened so fast it is all a blur."

"She smiled and said, Thanks Mr. Slider. Dr. Nelson will be with you shortly."

Victoria Nelson came in about ten minutes later. A tall, attractive brunette she was wearing a white blouse, gray skirt and red heels and looked more like a TV newswoman or a business executive than a doctor. "Good morning, Mr. and Mrs. Slider. My name is Dr. Nelson. I'm glad to meet you. " She shook hands with each of them and continued, "Well, Mr. Slider, I was looking at your MRI and I see we have a disc problem."

"Yeah, I know. They told me that in the hospital. They referred me to you for treatment or therapy or something. All I know is the pain is very bad and I need to get better."

"Do you think you can get up on the examining table?"

As Bob gingerly moved his butt onto the examining table Dr. Nelson smiled at Tracey and said, "Hopefully, we can help this man of yours."

Dr. Nelson's caring manner helped relieve the tension in Bob and Tracey and they both relaxed. She smiled at Bob and stood to his side. She began to apply pressure with her fingers to his lower back. Suddenly he groaned, "Ohhh, that hurts SO bad."

She stopped and applied pressure in another direction and he said, "I think that relieved the pain a bit."

She stepped away from Bob and held up the MRI. Then she said, "Mrs. Slider, come over here and I will show you what is going on."

Tracey stood up and went over to her husband. Dr. Nelson held up the MRI in front of them and above their heads a bit. She pointed to the herniated discs in Bob's back. "There they are, two little demons that can wreak havoc in a person's life. We have to get them to go back where they belong."

"And how do we do that?" Bob asked.

"Well, first of all, I will not do surgery on a person's back unless it is a last resort. You may disagree and want another opinion. That is your prerogative and I have no problem with that."

She looked at them and waited a moment for a response. Tracey and Bob just looked at each other and shrugged. Bob said, "Sure, Doc, no problem. That's nice to know."

Dr. Nelson smiled and said, "Okay then, based on your test results I know that there are orthopedic doctors who would recommend surgery. That is fine with me. I do not pretend to know everything. But, at this time, I do not recommend surgery."

Bob and Tracey looked at each other a bit confused and then Tracey said, "He needs this fixed. What do you recommend?"

"Here is what I recommend. I would like to set you up for physical therapy treatments. PT can do wonders and I know a fabulous physical therapist. However, it does require a commitment on your part. Doing the exercises and following their orders and, most of all, being patient and persevering. It is not an immediate fix and it does take some time but, trust me, most times PT is extremely effective. It is also non-invasive and allows the body to work to heal itself, something of which I am a big proponent. Our bodies are amazing creations and will cooperate with our efforts to heal. So, what do you say?"

"Bob said quickly, "You're the doctor. I like how you did not want to cut me open right away. Let's do it. And trust me Doc, I'll do whatever I have to do to get back to square one."

"I know you will, Mr. Slider. Can't keep a good man down, right? Well, good for you.

I also see that the hospital ER gave you 21 oxycodone for pain management, correct?"

"Yeah, they did."

"Did that help the pain?"

"Yes, they did help. They helped a lot."

"Well, that's good. You got them Monday evening around 10 or 11 p.m, correct?

"Uh, yeah, I think so. Right, Tracey?"

As Tracey nodded in agreement Dr. Nelson looked intently at Bob and asked, "Well, this is Wednesday morning. They probably told you to take three a day for seven days. You should have 16 left. One for Monday night, three for Tuesday and one this morning. Do you have 16 left?"

"Um, I'm not sure. I may have taken an extra one or two. I can't remember."

"Okay then, I have to explain something to you. Oxycodone is a narcotic. It is part of the Opiod family and is quite habit forming. I do not like to give it out unless it is absolutely necessary. But it is highly effective for pain management. However, for right now, I would rather try an anti-inflammatory, 800 mg ibuprofen. They are non-narcotic but they definitely work on the pain because they bring down inflammation versus masking it. Do you understand?"

She paused and waited for a reaction from either Bob or Tracey. Tracey finally said, "If they work, great. Right, hon?"

He was a bit lost in thought. "Uh, oh yeah, sure, if they work. What if they don't work?'

Doctor Nelson said, "Call the office and I will write a script for oxycodone or something similar. But, for the time being, let's give the ibuprofen a chance and see if they do work. You will be a lot better off, believe me."

Bob and Tracey left the exam room and headed to the front office to get the PT referral and a prescription for 90 tablets of 800mg ibuprofen. Bob looked at the script and said to no one in particular, "I hope these work as good as the other ones."

*

CHAPTER 8

"Liking" Oxycodone

Bob was a bit quiet as they began the drive home. Tracey said, "So, what did you think of her?"

"Oh, she was good. She sure seemed to know what she was talking about. I hope these ibuprofen things work. I am in a lot of pain."

"Well, I'll stop at the pharmacy and we will get them right now. Hope they're not too expensive. Obviously Dr. Nelson is not one of those pill pushers you always hear about. She sure did not want to give you those oxycodones. She acted as if she was afraid of them."

Bob immediately said, "Afraid of them? Come on Tracey, she's a doctor. She's not afraid of them. And she did say that she would give more if I needed them."

"Hey Bob, how many have you taken since we got them? The doctor knew it should only be five and you said maybe one or two more. Did you take more than you were supposed to?"

"Maybe one or two, that's all."

Tracey had an unexpected empty feeling momentarily grab hold of her and then let go. She did not like it and she did not understand it. They drove up to the drive-thru window at the pharmacy and Tracey placed the script into the opened drawer. The pharmacist told her that it would only take about 15 minutes so they decided to pull around to the parking lot and wait. As they waited, Bob dozed off, his head leaning against the window. Twenty five minutes later they were pulling into their driveway. The price for the one month supply of generic ibuprofen had only been $12.00. Not bad.

The first thing that Bob did when he got home was to go to the medicine cabinet and get the oxycodone. Tracey watched as he reached for the small vial. "Bob," she said, "What about the new medicine we just picked up? Why don't you take that instead?"

Bob was quick to answer, "Shouldn't I finish these first? No sense letting them go to waste, right?"

Tracey just watched as he swallowed one of the oxycodone. Bob placed the vial on the dining room table and went back to the bathroom. Tracey picked the vial up and looked inside. There were nine pills left. Bob had already taken 12 when it should have been only six. She put the vial down and placed the large vial of ibuprofen next to it.

Bob slowly made his way to the dining room table and sat down. "Man oh man, Tracey, I was counting on that work. That would have been another $150.00 off the rent. This stinks."

"I know hon but...Oh my God, Bob, today is Wednesday. We have to recertify for unemployment by today and you still need two more job apps. You had better get on-line and fill out more. We cannot afford to get cut off from unemployment right now."

"You got that right. Okay, let me go and see what I can find. Do we still have yesterday's want ads?"

"Yes, they're still on the chair next to you. Here you go."

Tracey picked the newspaper up and handed it to him. Bob took it and walked back to the bedroom where the computer was located. In the meantime Tracey got some laundry going in the washing machine and cleaned up the kitchen which was still a mess from the previous evening.

She had just finished getting the dishes into the sink and the counter cleaned off when Judi called. She was home for lunch and wanted to see how Bob had made out at the doctor's. Tracey and Judi were chatting away when a bulb went off in Tracey's head. "Judi, hold on a minute. He's been awfully quiet in there. I better go check."

She got up and went to the bedroom. There was Bob, sitting at the computer station with his head down on the desk and fast asleep. "Oh God, Judi," Tracey said. "You won't believe this. He fell asleep at the computer. I'll call you back in a bit. I have to get him up."

She hung up the phone and said, "Bob, Bob, wake up. You have to do those apps. Come on, wake up."

He moaned a bit, opened his eyes and when he tried to sit up straight the back pain grabbed hold of him and he yelled out, "UGHHH! Damn—that hurt."

Tracey did not really know what to do. She said, "Bob, you fell asleep bent over at this desk. I had to wake you up. Those apps have to get done."

"Yeah, I know, I know. I had better get up and move around a bit first. Then I'll finish doing them."

Slowly he got up and walked directly to the dining room table. He was shocked not to see his oxycodone there but just the vial of ibuprofen. "Tracey—what happened to my medication? I need one of those pills. The pain is unbearable."

Tracey was suddenly sensing fear. It was less than two days since he had the pills and he was overly concerned with them already. Her antennae were up and they were receiving a scary message. Tracey quickly said, "You just had one of those and you fell asleep at the computer. You can't take another one now. Dr. Nelson gave you the new script. You haven't even taken one of them yet. She told you those oxycodone were dangerous. Forget them—try the new ones."

"Tracey, I'm a grown man. I do not need you telling me what medicines I should or should not take. Where are those pills?"

"Fine Bob, fine. Here."

She reached into her pocket and pulled them out. He sighed and popped one in his mouth. He swallowed the pill and looked at his wife. He calmly said to her, "I can't believe you had them in your pocket. Are you kidding me or what. You think I'm addicted or something? Damn Tracey—I just got these pills. There are only a few of them. I have tremendous pain in my lower back and I am entitled to some relief. Even Dr. Nelson said how effective they are. So please, cut me some slack. I'll take the other stuff later. Now, let me finish those job apps."

Tracey could not argue. He was right. She was making a big deal out of nothing. But—she had heard those horror stories about people getting hooked on prescription drugs. In fact, she and Bob had often discussed the rampant drug use that seemed to have permeated society especially now that Jake was getting older. But suddenly, here was her husband acting defensive and defending his use of them and he had never had them before. Her instincts began to make some noise and her anxiety levels amped up. She did not like this one little bit. She needed to vent so she took the phone outside and called Judi back. "Judi, tell me if you think I'm over-reacting."

"Over-reacting about what, Tracey?"

"Oh Judi, maybe I'm just being ridiculous but the hospital gave Bob some oxycodone for his pain and already he has taken double the amount he was supposed to. Those things are a narcotic and his having them is making me nervous. That's all. Do you think I am being over-protective or paranoid?"

Judi laughed a bit and said, "Maybe Tracey, maybe you are. They gave them to me when I had my gallbladder out and they helped with the pain but I was taken off them in two weeks. Tommy got them too,when he broke his foot. They did help his pain, no doubt about it, but then he went off them after a few weeks and started taking ibuprofen."

"That's what the doctor gave to Bob, ibuprofen."

"Well then, there is no problem. I wouldn't worry about it. The hospital only gave him a small amount anyway, right?"

"Right. And his doctor said she does not like giving them out, only as a last resort."

"Then I wouldn't worry about it. If she's not going to prescribe them what's he going to do? Don't worry Trace, it will be okay. Bob's a smart guy, he's not going to allow himself to get hooked on something like that."

"You're right Judi, absolutely right. I'm so glad you're my friend. Thanks---love you."

"Love you too. Okay, talk later."

Tracey went back into the house and walked back to see how Bob was doing. He was sitting at the computer station with his elbows on the desk and his head nestled into the upraised palms of his hands. His face was about twelve inches away from the screen and his eyes were half closed. It was like he was in a trance. "Bob, Bob, what are you doing? Did you finish yet?"

He turned his head slowly and with half opened eyes looked up at Tracey and said, "Oh yeah, I think so. Yeah, I finished."

"Oh," she said. "That's good. So, what did you find that you applied for?"

"Oh Tracey, I don't know. You expect me to remember that?" "You just filled them out, didn't you? How could you not---"

She stopped and hurried back into the kitchen and found his pill bottle. She opened it and counted the remaining pills. Then she charged back to the bedroom, held up the vial in front of Bob's face and loudly said, "There are only eight pills in here. You had 21 Monday night, This is Wednesday afternoon. That means you have taken 13 of these already. Two in the last half-hour. Are you crazy? What are you trying to do, kill yourself?"

Bob snapped to and opened his eyes wide. He yelled at her, "What the hell are you talking about? You're the crazy one. Am I hurt? Is my back a mess? Am I the one in all this pain? Answer---yes to all of the above. And all I want is a little relief from the pain and you're in my face about it. I don't believe you Tracey. Just leave me alone, all right?"

Bob's indignation and disbelief at his wife's apparent insensitivity took Tracey by surprise and she backtracked feeling terribly guilty. Her husband had gone to work for his family, had gotten hurt and was in serious pain. So he had taken a few extra oxycodone. So what. "Bob , oh, Bob, I'm so sorry. You're right. I just got worried about the pills. I love you and I just worry about you, you know that, right?"

"Fine ,Tracey, fine. Can we just forget about it. Give me a hug, okay."

They hugged each other and gave each other a cursory kiss. Then Bob got up and went

out to his lounge chair while Tracey sat down at the computer. Bob's access code and pin number for his unemployment file were written on a post-it-note that was stuck to the bottom of the computer monitor and she quickly finished his unfinished applications, entered the required numbers and completed the re-certification process.

When she went into the living room he was fast asleep in the lounge chair. She thought that he looked like a big galoot laying there and smiled because she was glad he was her man and she loved him. She also felt a twang of guilt about being so hard on him about the medication. After all, he did have two herniated discs. She went into the kitchen and began to prepare dinner.

Bob woke up at 5:30 p.m. He yawned and then pushed on the leg support of the lounge chair with his legs to make it go down. Pain surged through his back and down his right buttock into his leg. His reaction was a reflexive yell and Tracey came hurrying in to see what had happened. She saw him lying there with his face contorted in pain. "Oh my God, why did you yell like that? What happened?"

"Damn it, Tracey. All I did was try to push the leg support down. The pain in my butt and down my leg was unbelievable. This is so crazy. And this is all from trying to move a pail of joint compound. The whole thing is crazy."

"How is the pain right now?"

"It eased off. I have to get up and go to the bathroom."

"You need my help?"

"Let me see how it goes. I'll just be careful when I move."

Slowly he slid forward in the chair and then pushed down on the arm rests to help himself stand up. He stood up straight and headed to the bathroom. Tracey took a breath, shook her head and went back to the kitchen.

A few minutes later Bob quietly came into the kitchen, picked up the phone and walked out to the back yard. She watched as he pulled a card from his pocket and dialed the number that was on it. He waited, spoke a few words and turned the phone off. When he came in she asked him, "Who are you calling?"

"He snapped at her, "You monitoring my phone calls now? If you must know I was calling Doctor Nelson. Satisfied."

"I swear Bob, I asked you a simple question. What is wrong with you? I'm not your enemy. In case you didn't notice I have been on this ride with you. So don't be treating me like I'm some kind of outsider or something. I will not be treated like that, I just won't. I will not be treated like that."

Tracey stormed by him and went into the bedroom slamming the door behind her. She was wondering why he had called Doctor Nelson. For the time being, she could live without knowing the answer which came quickly enough, anyway.

Tracey had sat on the edge of the bed, bowed her head and spent a few minutes praying. She had no religious upbringing or training but Judi was Catholic and Tracey was a bit jealous thinking that maybe Judi was onto something although they had never talked about it very much. She had been to Mass a number of times not knowing what was going on but she knew that she always felt good when she left. She asked Jesus to help her do what was right and if He would help Bob's back get better. Fifteen minutes later she went back outside to the dining room.

Tracey got to the dining room table and Bob said, "Hey, I'm sorry, Okay. I'll be right back, I have to go to the bathroom. Stay right here."

She smiled and shook her head and he left the room. He had no sooner shut the bathroom door when the phone rang. Tracey picked it up, "Hello."

"Hello, Mrs. Slider. This is Doctor Nelson. Your husband called my office a short while ago and I wanted to speak to him. Is he there?"

"He just went into the bathroom. He should be out in a minute or so."

"Of course, what's going on?"

"Bob called asking if he can get oxycodone for pain relief. He said that the other

medicine does not help. I wanted to talk to him about it."

"Doctor, I don't think he has taken the ibuprofen yet. He has taken more oxycodone than prescribed. We even just had a little argument about them."

"Oh, I see. Are you sure he has never had these type of pills before?"

"Not that I know of. He never got hurt before or went to a doctor like he has done with you. Oh, here he is now doctor. I'll put him on. Bob, it is Doctor Nelson."

The toilet had not even finished flushing as Tracey handed the phone to her surprised husband who sort of stared at the receiver before lifting it up and beginning to speak. "Uh, hi Doctor Nelson. How you doing and thanks for calling me back so fast."

"Listen Bob, I heard your message. I need to talk to you. Can you come in tomorrow morning at nine?"

"Uh, yeah, I guess. Hey Tracey, can we come in at nine tomorrow to see the doctor?"

Tracey shrugged and Bob said, "Okay Doctor, see you then-- Umm, no, not really---Okay, I will. Yeah sure, she's right here. Tracey, she wants to talk to you for a minute."

Tracey took the receiver and hesitatingly said, "Hello--- doctor, yes?"

"Yes, Mrs. Slider. I just wanted to tell you that I told your husband that I want him to take those ibuprofen I prescribed. I would appreciate it if you watch him and see how he reacts to them. I also really feel it is necessary that I discuss this oxycodone request face to face. That is why I asked him to come in tomorrow morning. I just want you to know what is going on, that's all."

Tracey answered, "Of course Doctor Nelson. Thanks. We'll see you in the morning."

Tracey hung up the phone feeling uncomfortable about being asked to "watch" how her husband reacted to his medication. She already felt guilty for even mentioning the ibuprofen to the doctor. She felt like she had "squealed" and was not liking herself for doing that.

It was not an outrageous request. It even made sense for a doctor to seek assistance from a family member in monitoring a patient's reaction to medication. The haunting feeling came from the fact that this request was made because a narcotic was involved. Tracey had never been confronted with dealing with a "controlled substance" and the situation made her feel as if she had been placed between Bob and his doctor. The fact was, she had and she did not like it.

"Bob, she wants you to take the ibuprofen and she wanted me to remind you to do it."

He looked at his wife and said, "Oh really Tracey. She did, did she? So tell me, did you tell her that your husband is a big boy and can take his own pills or did you agree to watch me a like a

little freakin spy or something? You supposed to make a report about me too?"

Tracey was shocked. "What is wrong with you Bob? So what if I might remind you to take your pill. You are acting as if ---I don't know what it is. You are acting very weird about all of this and I do not like it. No, I do not like it at all. All I want to do is help you and you are acting like I'm trying to hurt you. I don't get it.

Suddenly Tracey started to cry. She could not speak and she stood there shaking her head with her hands over her mouth. Tears streamed down her cheeks and Bob instantly regretted his cutting remarks. He went over to her to apologize and she exploded, "Leave me alone. Just leave me alone. I do not want to talk to you right now. You are accusing me of spying on you. You hurt yourself Monday. This is only Wednesday night. Have you lost your mind in two days? What is your problem?"

He grabbed her and she tried to pull away. He would not let her. "Tracey, I'm sorry. I didn't mean anything. The pain has been so bad it has me crazy. That's all. I'm sorry."

He felt her body relax and she more or less went limp against him. Then she hugged him back and he looked down at her as she looked up at him. He wiped her eyes and they kissed each other. Just then Jake, who had been over at Tyler's house, came in. "Hey you guys, what's for dinner? I'm starved."

Jake's timing could not have been better. Tracey and Bob quickly composed themselves, smiled at each other and Tracey said to her boy, "We'll eat in about 30 minutes, Jake. Can you hold out for 15 minutes?"

"He laughed, "I'll try mom but it won't be easy. What are we having?"

"Your favorite Jake, "little meatloafs" with buttered noodles."

"Awesome!"

Instead of a standard sized meatloaf, Tracey had always prepared the meat in the shape of a half dozen or so small ovals and called them "little meatloafs". Jake just loved them and so did Bob for that matter. They all managed to sit and have a delicious supper together and were able to do some catching up with their son whom they had hardly seen since the previous Friday.

Everything was fine until about 7:30 p.m. when Bob, who was sitting in the lounge chair, tried to get up so he could go to the bathroom. As happened earlier in the day the pain seized hold of him and he groaned as it shot through his lower back, into his buttock and down his leg. He slowly stood up and, while hunched over, moved toward the wall. Bent over he extended his hands and placed his palms on the wall near the chair. Slowly he walked his hands up the wall allowing his body to straighten itself as he did. Once erect, he turned and stood with his back to the wall and heaved a sigh of relief as the pain dissipated. "Whew," he said. "That was not pretty."

Tracey and Jake, both looking at him and feeling somewhat useless, just stared. Tracey said, "Can you make it to the bathroom all right?"

He could not help but laugh a bit, saying, "I guess I had better babe, or we'll need a new mop."

Tracey and Jake started to laugh and so did Bob. Then he said, "Tracey, I'm taking another one of those pills from the hospital. I need one. Just want you to know."

Tracey simply said, "You don't have to tell me about taking the pills. You're a big boy. You know what you are doing. If they help, they help."

"Well, I tried the ibuprofen before and it didn't help."

"Oh, you did? I didn't know that."

"I tried one earlier, at supper, remember? It didn't do squat."

She knew he had not taken any pill at supper but did not want to get into another argument about pain pills. "Oh, that's right. I forgot."

The pills were definitely working. They had both just lied to each other.

The next morning they sat in Doctor Nelson's office waiting for her to come in.

Consumed by their own thoughts, they were not speaking. Tracey did not want to be '"tattling" on her own husband and was determined not to. Bob wanted more oxycodone and was determined somehow to get it.

Dr. Nelson came in and was all business. She immediately looked at Bob and said, "You brought the vial like I asked, didn't you?"

Bob reached into his pants pocket, pulled out the vial and handed it to her. She smiled at him and then opened the vial and looked in it. Looking back at Bob she said, "Okay, let me be clear about this pain medication business. First of all, I know the pain you must be in. I have seen the MRI so I know that it is quite severe."

She looked at Tracey and said, "The pain is pretty intense and he is not exaggerating any of it. The sciatic nerve has been compressed by the bulging disc and the pain level is, on a scale of one to ten, probably a nine. Do you understand?"

Tracey shook her head up and down but did not fully understand. She was just glad that Dr. Nelson had not asked her about his reaction to any of the medications. But both Tracey and Bob were not prepared for what came next.

Dr. Nelson, holding the oxycodone vial between her thumb and forefinger, said, "Bob, I have to be honest with you. I was surprised when you called me about getting more of these. Little red flags began waving inside my head. I mean, why would you be calling for more if you just got them for the first time on Monday evening? You should be inexperienced with these things. Do you know where I am going with this?"

Tracey looked at her and did not have a clue as to what she was talking about. Bob bit his lip and said nothing. "Bob, I am your doctor and my goal is to help you get better. So I want you to trust me , okay?"

Bob shrugged and nervously answered, "Sure Doc, of course. I want to trust you too."

She smiled a bit and stared hard at him. "Okay then, be honest with me and tell me the truth. This is not the first time you have taken oxycodone. Am I right?"

He looked at her, unblinking. Slowly, tears filled his eyes and a solitary tear ran down his cheek. He just kept staring at her. Tracey, blindsided by what she was hearing, teared up also. Bob lowered his head and ran his fingers across his brow. Momentary silence filled the small examining room. Bob lifted his head and said, "Yes, you're right. I have had some of them before."

Dr. Nelson asked, "Before what? What does that mean, before?"

Tracey anxiously started talking, "What is she talking about, Bob? What pills did you take 'before'? Are you one of those people I read about in the paper. Oh my God, is that why you lost your job?"

Bob could not believe what Tracey was saying and Dr. Nelson let the impromptu husband and wife drama develop. "Are you crazy, Tracey? Bildot closed down, remember. Everyone lost their job. And yes, I have taken a few of these pills before. Remember the time the plank fell on my shoulder and I could hardly lift my arm, remember?"

Tracey was stunned and did not know what to think. Suddenly her husband had revealed a side of himself that heretofore had been unknown. Bob went on, "Yeah, well Zack had some of these little blue pills and he told me they would help with the pain---and they did. So I took a few from him. And then when I sprained my ankle that time I took a few more. So what? I couldn't take off work and I didn't want to spend money on doctor visits and x-rays. You know, we DO have a co-pay. So, the answer is yes—I have taken some before. Big deal."

Dr. Nelson did pro-bono work over at the Pinellas Pines Rehab Center. The Center was a drug and alcohol treatment facility and folks who were addicts and wanted to get "straight" could spend 28 days there getting clean. Once a week, Dr. Nelson would treat patients at the center who had orthopedic problems. The lady was "street wise" to the illegal drug world and had seen right through Bob Slider the moment he mentioned going to the hospital ER and getting pain pills. "Thank you for being honest with me. Now, I need you to tell me how often you are taking pills."

Tracey said, "Oh my God, are you saying that my husband is a drug addict? Is that what is going on here. Oh my God---I----I—"

"I'm no addict, Tracey. Stop it. This is ridiculous."

He began to get angry and turned to Doctor Nelson and said, "So what, Doctor. I took a few pills from Zack, who cares. Tracey never even knew. Some addict I am. Give me a break. My wife and I trust each other and you're telling her that I'm a drug addict. You don't know anything about us. I swear, this has turned ridiculous."

Dr. Nelson raised her hands and said, "Hold on, hold on, both of you. We need to take a breath here. I apologize. I may have come on a bit too strong. I did not mean to imply you were a drug addict."

"Well," Bob said. You sure as hell did imply it. I did hurt my back, remember."

Dr. Nelson was taken back and said again, "I'm sorry, okay. It's just that I have seen so much disaster come into people's lives from these damn drugs. Look, Mrs. Slider, your husband has a genuine and legitimate reason for needing these kinds of pain pills. And Bob, as far as you go, the simple fact that you hid your use of only a few from Tracey proves you were protecting your use of these pills. In my world that is a "big red flag.".

All became quiet as Dr. Nelson began to write some notes on Bob's chart. Bob and Tracey had no idea what was going to happen next. The doctor lifted her head and said, "Okay, now tell me, how long have you been taking these pills and how often do you take them?"

Bob immediately said, "I told you, I have taken some in the past. I just got some from the hospital Monday. That's it, okay. Now, can you help me or what?"

"Yes, I am going to help you. But my way, not your way. So, the first thing I am doing is setting up an appointment with a physical therapist. Here are two numbers. One is for the PT the other is for social services. Since you are unable to work right now you might qualify for temporary Medicaid and, if you do, the PT will be covered. I am also giving you a prescription for 30 pills of 5/325 oxycodone. That is for two pills a day for fifteen days. That is all I can prescribe for you. If you still feel you need them I will have to refer you to a pain management doctor. Do you understand?"

"Yeah, I understand. A pain management doctor. Whatever. Don't worry, I won't need them."

She ignored his flip response and said, "Okay, that's a good start. I know you can do it. I truly believe that anti-inflammatories will manage your pain and the proper physical therapy treatments will get you better."

When they left Dr. Nelson's office it was after ten o'clock. Inseparable since high school, best friends always, lovers and companions, surfing the waves of life in sync with each other and never allowing the most disruptive argument or difficulty to get between them was how you would describe the relationship of Bob and Tracey Slider. They were a connected couple. But, in just a few short days, those "little pills" had put a breach between them. Their circuit breaker had been tripped. It would need to be reset.

*

CHAPTER 9

"Gripping" Tighter

Jake, the "shining star" in the lives of his parents, had not been overindulged. His parents were not afraid to say "no" to their boy. He had certain chores he was responsible for such as the daily trash removal, making sure that on Tuesday and Friday mornings the trash cans were out at the curb for pickup and then brought back in after school. Jake also cleaned the table off after dinner and was not to leave his dirty clothes lying around. Finally, his parents made a point of checking his homework every night.

Bob and Tracey were wise enough to make sure that their son was learning that people have responsibility in day-to-day living and that there are consequences to their actions or inactions. Jake's consequence for not doing what he was supposed to was an allowance reduction and a time out from video games.

Bob, a blue-collar, fix-it type of guy, had Jake by his side helping him with repairs and maintenance beginning when Jake was a toddler. When he was two years old he would be following his dad around wearing Healthtex overalls with a "Handy-Andy" hammer sticking out of his back pocket and a six-foot tape clipped to his side. By the time Jake was eight years old he knew how to use basic hand tools and by ten Bob was already teaching him about power tools. He could change the oil in the car, pull the spark plugs, maintain the lawn mower and, under his dad's watchful eye, had helped replace the broken belt in the electric dryer.

Of course there was baseball too. At four years old Bob had Jake out in the back yard teaching him how to throw, catch and hit a ball. Jake began playing Little League baseball when he was six. Jake Slider was well-parented, loved his parents deeply and his dad was his hero. But something was different. Smiles and laughter around the house had become scarce.

Bob and Tracey had decided to be honest with their boy about the family situation. They did their best to explain what had happened at Bildot, why they had sold mom's car and the two TVs, and why new clothes and shoes for the beginning of 7th grade were going to have to be put "on-hold".

Jake showed great maturity and actually thanked his parents for sharing their personal business with him. He really liked it that he had been treated like a "grown-up" by his mom and dad. What he did not understand were the changes in the moods, their new abruptness when they spoke to him, his dad's ongoing back pain with no fix in sight and his mom's chronically sad face.

The good-natured teasing and sudden lack of laughter that were missing cast a pall over the environment at home. Jake understood the layoff and lack of money but he did not understand his father's new behavior especially the way he was being ignored. He began to withdraw into himself. His grades began to slip and he was suddenly feeling insecure and unhappy. Tracey was noticing the changes in her son but, worn out herself, she did not know what to do. As far as Bob, he did not have a clue.

Life continued to spiral downward for the Sliders. Bob, unable to be "ready, willing and able" to work, lost his unemployment benefits. He applied with the Department of Family Services for emergency medical assistance and was waiting for approval. Since he had the documentation about his injury and Family Services had accepted his application, he was placed in the "pending" file. This showed the doctors and the physical therapy center that the medical care given would "probably" be covered under Temporary Medicaid. It got him started with PT treatments and medications.

September evaporated and October grabbed hold of the time-baton and charged forward. Things had changed for the Sliders in a more pronounced and noticeable way than they were aware of. Judi was the first to mention it when she stopped by Tracey's for coffee about a week before Halloween. Sitting at the table with both hands wrapped around her coffee mug she said, "Tracey, I have to say something to you. I feel a bit funny but you know I love you guys and I only have your best interests at heart."

"Of course, Judi, I know that. I don't know what I would do if you weren't around. You can tell me anything or say anything to me, you know that."

Judi said, "Well, I know. You say that but what if…,never mind, I have to say what I have to say. Look, you know, ever since Bob hurt his back he seems different. He is not that happy-go-lucky guy he used to be. And you seem so unhappy lately."

Tracey shook her head and said, "No Judi, we're okay. It's just been so tight with money and, and---" Just like that she started to cry. She managed to take a breath and continued talking, "Oh Judi, I don't know what's going to happen to us. We both have no jobs, he's always moaning in pain, we have no money---I can't believe this has happened to us. I get $131.00 a week in unemployment. His was cut off because he cannot work right now. That's it. That's all that is coming in. Well, we do get the food stamps, too. Anyway, the worst part is it's almost as if he doesn't care anymore. All he wants are those damn pills of his."

Judi was stunned. She had no idea things had become so desperate for her friends. All she could say was, "How is Jake? That's why I brought this up in the first place. He always had a big wave and smile for me and kidded around when we saw each other but lately—well, he sort of just waves his hand a bit and keeps on going. It has given me bad vibes. I guess those vibes were dead on."

"Oh my God, Judi, you're right. I have noticed some moodiness in Jake but I've kind of ignored it. He's such a good kid. He doesn't deserve this from us. What am I going to do, Judi? What am I going to do? I have to be strong for my son."

Judi just stared at Tracey. She did not have a clue what her friend should do. She said to her, "I have to go, Tracey. I'm here for you anytime, night or day. I don't care if it's 3 a.m."

"Thank you Judi. Thank God you are here."

They hugged each other and, as Judi began to walk to the front door, she stopped and said, "Come to Mass with me Sunday morning. Bring Jake along and then we'll go out to breakfast."

Tracey smiled because the thought itself presented a moment of relief. "Okay, that sounds nice. We just might do that."

Bob had started his physical therapy treatments ten days after seeing Dr. Nelson. He also had another doctor in his life. Dr. Nelson had been true to her word. As she expected, Bob called her for more oxycodone. She immediately referred him to Dr. Jeffrey McCaba, an anesthesiologist and pain-management specialist.

McCaba, a dour-faced, matter-of-fact, abrupt man, always seemed to be exasperated. Most of his patients did not care about his miserable personality. They only cared about getting their "pain meds". This mindset would quickly infect Bob Slider who was immediately given a prescription for 90 oxycodone a month. His temporary Medicaid card was all he needed to have the pills handed to him.

Bob was supposed to take three oxycodone per day. On October 12th he called Dr. McCaba's office and told Dr. McCaba's nurse, Jane, that his pain level was a #8 and asked if there was anything else he could get to "help" him. Bob was told to come to the office. He was given a prescription for 38 pills of .5 mg, Xanax (aka Aprazolam), and told to take two a day. This amount would carry Bob through until the 1ˢᵗ of the next month. He was advised that he had to make sure he took the number prescribed because they could not give anything more until then.

By October 28ᵗʰ, Bob was out of oxycodone and finished off his last two Xanax. He had four days to go before November 1ˢᵗ. He needed more pills and was beginning to panic. Judi, who did not even know about the Xanax, had noticed how her husband was sleeping more and more and that when he was awake his eyelids seemed to be half closed. He would begin pacing up and down, going into and out of the house, and just being abrupt with her. "What is wrong with you Bob? Can't you sit still for a minute? Either you're half asleep or prancing around like a wounded jack-rabbit. What's going on?"

"Nothing Tracey, nothing. I'm fine, okay. Just leave me be. My back hurts, that's all. You have no idea of the pain I'm in, no idea."

It was 8 p.m. on Halloween. Tracey was next door at Judi's and they had been greeting "trick or treaters" since six o'clock. Every Halloween Bob had dressed up as some kind of witch or monster and sat outside on stage for the neighborhood. His routine was simple yet very effective. If a child came close to him he would raise his arm ever so slowly and let out a low guttural groan. Some kids actually ran away screaming. His presence had almost become a tradition in the neighborhood. This was the first time in years that he had not put on his performance.

Jake and his friend, Tyler, decided to be a two-headed monster and they had more fun than the little ghosts, ghouls, zombies, witches, princesses, super-heroes and varied other creatures that ambled up to the front door. Since the trick-or-treaters had almost stopped coming, Judi and Tracey went inside to grab a cup of coffee and to chat a bit. Jake and Tyler headed over to Jake's to watch TV.

The two boys never noticed Bob passing them in the driveway as he headed to his truck. Boys are boys plus it was not a big deal. Tracey thought she heard Bob' struck start and was unnerved. She hurried to Judi's front door just in time to see the truck going down the street. "Anything wrong, Trace?"

"Bob just drove down the block. I wonder where he's going? I hope he's all right."

Bob was not all right but he soon would be. He had called his old friend from Bildot, Zack Covello. Zack was the guy who had introduced Bob to the little world of pain meds to begin with and he always seemed to have some available. There was a difference though. At Bildot, Bob was Zack's supervisor and it was in Zack's best interest to slip Bob a few pills here and there to help his boss with his aches and pains. It was a smart call on Zack's part because Bob did get to like having Zack around simply because he had those little blue pills.

Now, Zack was out of work just like his "former" boss and one of his under-the-table ways of making some extra income was selling pain pills. His fees for pill distribution were a lot higher than Medicaid's, which paid for the entire prescription. He charged $10.00 for one oxycodone and $5.00 for one Xanax. If Bob had to buy his entire prescription from Zack it would have cost him $1200.00

Bob met Zack at a convenient store on Missouri Ave. near Lake Street in Largo. He walked into the store and back to the refreshment bar where Zack was fixing himself a container of hazelnut coffee. "Hey Bob, how's my old buddy doing?"

Bob smiled and they shook hands. "How you been, Zack. What's going on?"

Zack took the $30.00 from Bob's hand and slipped him two oxys and two Xanax. "Oh man, you know. Still looking and collecting. I pick up some side work here and there but otherwise, man, I swear, things are dead out there. What about you?"

"My back is so messed up I can't do nothing. Can't even get unemployment because I can't work. It sucks. Anyway, I'm hoping the

PT starts to work. The doc was talking about surgery. We'll see. I don't want anyone cutting my back. Maybe it will just get better."

"Yeah man, I hear ya. Well, I gotta get going. Good seeing you Bob. Don't forget, you need me, give me a shout. You have the number."

"Will do, Zack. Thanks."

Zack drove off and Bob got into his truck, popped a Xanax and Oxycodone into his mouth and washed them down with the Bud Light he had brought from home. By now the beer was warm and he crunched his nose as he swallowed. He started the truck and shifted into reverse.

He looked into his rear-view mirror a second too late because he did not see the dark blue Toyota Corolla that had just pulled in back of him on its way to the gas pump. Bob promptly backed into the passenger-side door. The Toyota slid sideways about five feet and a lady jumped out of the car. She instantly began screaming at Bob, "Oh my God, what is wrong with you? Are you blind or something? You can't see another car in back of you? Oh my God, look what you did to my car! Oh, thank God, here come the cops right now. You're in trouble mister. I hope they lock you up."

The lady was totally overreacting to a minor traffic altercation which was actually her fault. Bob had the car in reverse and his back-up lights were on. The woman never paid attention and momentarily stopped directly in back of Bob's truck. Justice can be an illusion especially when no one has seen exactly what happened.

As is the way of things a police car had just parked in the parking lot. An officer, wanting to grab a container of coffee, stepped out to see the frantic woman running toward him. No one saw the officer roll his eyes and take a deep breath. "Officer, officer, some idiot just smashed into my car. He's probably drunk or something. My car is all smashed up. I want him arrested right now."

The big cop looked down at the woman and said, "Ma'am, please calm down. Let's go see what happened."

"He drove into me, that's what happened. I suppose you can't see either. I swear."

The cop knew immediately that the woman was unreasonable and aggressive. He turned his head toward his shoulder and spoke into his phone, "Officer 3452, requesting back-up at convenient store at Missouri and Lake, I have an 1182. 10-4."

He listened to the scratchy response and surveyed the scene. He quickly figured out what had happened and had the two drivers exchange their auto information. He cited the woman for failing to "yield the right of way" which was a judgment call on his part. Her behavior may have influenced his decision. Who was to say.

This really infuriated the woman who was not only brought to tears but it triggered a stream of expletives that tumbled from her mouth that could rival any stevedore's. Unfortunately for Bob, the back-up unit had arrived and the woman officer immediately noticed Bob sort of leaning against the side of his truck with his eyes half closed. The pills he had gotten from Zack were kicking in and were doing their job.. One hour later Bob Slider was being booked into the county jail. The charges were DUI and possession of an unprescribed controlled substance.

Tracey would not hear from her husband until 11:30. By then she was frantic and was sure he was hurt somewhere and needed her help. She never imagined for a moment that he would call her from jail. It took her a little time to actually process what he was telling her. When she did, she started screaming at him. "Oh my God, in jail. What did you do? Why are you in jail? Are you insane or something? What is going on?"

Fortunately, Judi and Tommy were both there. They too were concerned about Bob's whereabouts. Tommy took the phone from Tracey and began talking to Bob. Judi put her arm around

Tracey's shoulder and Jake went over and hugged his mom. Tracey was crying and this triggered Jake's crying and then Judi began crying.

The three of them were crying and no one had a clue as to what had happened.

Tommy grabbed a pencil that was on the kitchen table and began jotting down information on the side of the morning's newspaper. When he hung up he shook his head and held up his hands. "All right, everything is okay—"

"Okay? What do you mean, okay? My husband just called me from jail. Everything is NOT okay."

"Tracey, please. Let me explain."

"Fine, Tommy, you explain to me why my husband, a man who never did a wrong thing in his life, is calling me from the county jail. Go ahead. I'm listening."

"He had a slight traffic altercation and it was not even his fault. The cops gave the woman a ticket."

"So why is he in jail?"

"Oh boy," Tommy said. "Look, apparently Bob had taken an extra pain pill or two. He appeared to be a bit groggy so they arrested him for DUI and possession of an unprescribed controlled substance."

"But, but---the pills were prescribed. This makes no sense."

"Tommy tried to be the voice of reason. "Look, Tracey, I'm going to call a bail bondsman and find out exactly what is going on. They should have the arrest info on their computer.

So let's find out exactly what the situation is. Then we'll go get Bob."

In the meantime, Bob had been processed into the county jail and was wearing a standard issue orange jump suit with the words "County Jail" emblazoned across the back of it. He was also sober and in shock, engulfed in disbelief as to where he was. He had been searched, finger printed, and had his mug shot taken. He had to surrender his watch, wedding ring and everything that was in his pockets including the one remaining oxycodone.

Contrary to the prevailing belief, Bob was not strip searched but was patted down quite thoroughly from head to toe. He also gave his medical information and the name of his doctors. When he mentioned the name, Dr. Jeffrey McCaba, the processing sergeant paused and said, "Him again? You're the second guy in here tonight that gets his pills from this guy." The guard paused a second, looked up at Bob and said, "Hey man, know what, maybe he should be in here with you."

Bob had never been in trouble before and was able to document a prescription for the oxycodone. At 2:30 a.m he was "released on his own recognizance", more commonly known as ROR. His vehicle had been impounded and Tommy had to bring him home.

Tracey was an emotional basket case when Bob walked into the house. Jake was as wide awake as a 12-year old can be at 3 a.m. He was so relieved to have his father home and looking okay he fell asleep within ten minutes of Bob's arrival.

Tommy had gotten all the information from "Big Al Esterhaven's: the Friendly Bail-Bondsman" and Tracey had already been primed and was ready to hear her husband's story. Naturally, Bob started to ramble on and on and Tracey, so exhausted from the tsunami of emotions that had swept over her the past several hours, fell asleep the moment she sat down on the sofa. The last thing she said to her husband was, "The first thing in the morning we have to get our truck back, understand?"

Bob's blood work and urine sample proved that he was driving while under the influence of a controlled substance. The consequences of his actions kicked in immediately. The fine was $250.00. He was required to do 50 hours (the minimum by law) of community service. He had to complete a "Law and Substance Abuse" program that required his mandatory attendance once a week for 13 weeks and each class cost $20.00. He also received one year of probation and each visit to the probation officer would be another $30.00. Adding $260.00 for the class and the once a month probation fee which equaled $360.00 to the $250.00 for the fine came to $870.00. The coup de grace for Tracey was the fact that Bob's driver's license was revoked for at least six months. She instantly became the official household chauffeur.

They still were facing an impound fee for the truck. Those four little pills he had bought from Zack probably turned out to be among the most expensive pills he would ever buy in his entire life. And they did not have any idea where the money was coming from to pay for of it. They certainly did not have it stashed in a "rainy day" fund.

Since the truck was the family's only means of transportation it was released from impound for Tracey to use. The $200.00 fee was paid for by Tommy Pavano. Being caught up in the criminal justice system proved to be a miserable, unpredictable, expensive and downright scary place to be.

The arrest and its consequential aftermath joined forces with the two extremely painful, herniated lumbar discs to create a "double whammy". The protruding discs pushing into Bob's nerve endings in his lower back prevented him from standing up straight. The pain was hard to escape and it was chronically intense. Factoring in that he could not work and had no money pushed Bob Slider into a deeper and deeper pit of despair. He was pulling Jake and Tracey with him but Tracey had an unknown inner strength and resolve inside of herself that would enable her to pull back and begin confronting the forces working against them.

*

*

*

CHAPTER 10

Tracey's Challenge

Halloween was over and Thanksgiving loomed on the horizon. The stores already had Christmas decorations on the shelves, Christmas music was being played all over the airwaves and the newspapers and televisions were hammering away with the Christmas specials promoting Black Friday. The fast approaching holidays were pushing Tracey into a depressed state. Bob did not seem to care and Jake was just feeling an unexpected unhappiness claw away at his young psyche.

The Sliders were now fully fledged "grippers", financially battered and just barely hanging on to the life they had been living. As they tried to avoid being sucked under and lost in a deepening abyss of abject poverty, a sense of despair was setting in. Then along came a bit of good news and things happened quickly.

Judi Pavano was the front-end manager at the local Shop-Well Supermarket. Her store manager, Mr. White, wanted to hire a part-time cashier for the Christmas season and needed someone who could start work immediately. He asked Judi on Friday, November 1, if she might know someone qualified. Judi recommended Tracey for the job. First thing Saturday morning Tracey was at the store. She met Mr. White, filled out the application, got the job and grabbed onto that lifeline holding on for dear life.

She began working on Monday, November 4th. Her schedule gave her 20 hours a week and she would be paid $12.00 an hour. Her first biweekly paycheck came in on November 22 and the take home amount was $390.00. The $780.00 a month would only be $256.00 more than the she was receiving in unemployment benefits but it was a job and a beginning. When Tracey logged onto her bank account and saw the $390.00 posted she began to cry. Thanksgiving was only six days away. She raised her wet eyes upward and mumbled, "Thank you, Lord."

Tracey's days quickly became chaotic because it was difficult to establish an ordered routine. Jake had to be at school by 7:30. Bob had to go to physical therapy treatments twice a week and the appointments never were scheduled at the same time. Either it was 8a.m or 9:30a.m or 2p.m. depending on the schedule and it was always with the same excuse, "We are so booked we have to squeeze patients in the best we can." Plus, Bob's insurance was 'temporary Medicaid'. Many places would not even accept it. You had to take what you could get on Medicaid.

Judi was responsible for scheduling all the cashiers and baggers. Tracey quickly had proven reliable, competent and hardworking and Mr. White had no problem with Judi scheduling Tracey for the hours she requested. Mr. White's "generosity" also might have had something to do with the fact that Tracey always requested the unpopular, late evening hours. Having only one vehicle and being the only driver in the household required a lot of creative time management.

The consequences of Bob's conviction on the DUI did not just affect him. As is the way of things, consequences invariably produce slithering, sticky tentacles that reach out and grab onto others pulling them along for the miserable ride. Naturally, the first people dragged under were the immediate family members, Tracey and Jake. Others would get dragged into the whirlpool along the way like Tommy and Judi, who had already felt the powerful undercurrent over the Halloween weekend .

That was not all of Bob's traveling needs. He had to go to his probation officer every week for the first six weeks of his probation and the appointment time was usually 10a.m. every Tuesday. That conflicted with possible PT scheduling. These appointments were expected to be moved to every two weeks after six months. Probation would be for one year and there had better be no 'mess ups'.

Bob also had to be driven to the St. Vincent de Paul Thrift Store where he would be able to fulfill his 50 mandatory hours of community service. He would have to be there twice a week from one until 5 p.m. and then on Saturdays, from 8 a.m. until noon. What Bob Slider, disabled drug-user needed, was his own personal vehicle and driver. He was spending more time away from home than when he was working, or at least it sure seemed that way.

Let's not forget Jake who was dismissed from school at 2:30p.m. Tyler's grandmother would usually pick Tyler up and take him to her house on the other side of town so that more or less left it up to Tracey to get her son. Tracey was frazzled. She was finding it impossible to get Bob and Jake and herself to all the places they needed to be when they needed to be there. She wrote all of the requirements down for each of them and decided to take action.

Tracey, after some heavy duty pleading with the Physical Therapy center and the probation officer, managed to place some semblance of order into her frenetic life. Judi assisted her and she had her work hours set in place from 6p.m. to 11p.m. Thursday through Sunday.

She managed to get the probation officer to agree to Bob's seeing him on Thursdays at 10 a.m. and the PT center agreed to schedule appointments on Monday and Friday afternoons. The only activity unaccounted for was Jake's Winter Baseball League. Tyler was playing Youth Football and the field for the winter baseball league was on the south side of St. Petersburg. Jake was told he could not play this year. Judi could not cut herself that thin. She needed a few minutes to herself or she thought she might go crazy. After all, besides her new job, she still had a house to keep, laundry, cooking, shopping and all the other things that the men in her life did not seem to think about.

Jake did not take his being held out of winter-ball very well. Baseball meant so much to him. How could they let this happen? He did not understand. But it really was not the "baseball thing". After all, it was only winter-ball, sort of an instructional league where the kids kept in shape and prepared for the regular season. Missing the winter league program was just the catalyst that drove Jake's feelings to the surface and these feelings began to exhibit themselves in different ways. Jake's grades dropped, he seemed to have developed a moodiness and was becoming quiet and withdrawn. He even was caught playing hooky, not once, but twice.

Tracey did not know what to do. She tried her best to stay on top of Jake's activities but she was so physically and mentally exhausted it was almost impossible for her to do so in an effective way. As far as Bob went, well, as he always was quick to point out "You know, I'm in a lot of pain and nobody seems to care about me at all".

That ongoing comment was now making Tracey angry when she heard it. Her husband was always attending his own drug related pity party and everything that happened was someone else's fault. She discovered that she had the inner resolve to deal with the adversity, the confusion, the tension and the financial chaos that had entered her life.

She was managing to stay on top of the ever growing mountain of uncertainty as quickly as it grew. Working, communicating with Greg Margolese about the rent, dealing with the power company or the phone company, handling Jake and his problems at school, maintaining the home and everything else was not the true challenge facing Tracey Slider. Those things had a way of being dealt with.

What was seeping into her psyche and beginning to occupy more and more of her thought process was the fact that Bob had turned himself into a 'victim'. This was NOT easy for her to deal with. In fact, Tracey had slowly been developing an unwanted bitterness towards her husband. She truly loved the man but His behavior was like a slow moving knife, cutting deeper and deeper into that love. Bob Slider had no idea and could not see past himself or his need for "medication".

On Tuesday, November 26th, Tracey dropped Jake at school and headed to the supermarket. Three weeks earlier she was feeling despair. That despair had begun evaporating on her first day at work. This day a sense of pride accompanied her as she walked into the store.

She grabbed onto a shopping cart and immediately headed to the rear of the store where the meat department was located. As she stood before the freezer loaded with frozen turkeys she remembered how only a few weeks earlier she had doubted whether she would even have one for the holiday. She smiled and pulled a turkey from the pile. She deserved to be proud of herself. She had earned the money to give the family a Thanksgiving. She gently placed the turkey into the cart with two hands.

Tracey knew to the penny how much money was in her checking account. It was $143.56. She filled the shopping cart with about $60.00 worth of grocery items which included the 14 pound turkey, two cans of jellied cranberry sauce, two cans of sweet corn, a large can of sweet potatoes, string beans and dried onions for the casserole and, of course, a large bag of stuffing mix, all for Thanksgiving. There would be $83.00 and change left and $65.00 would go to the electric company as per her arrangement with them. There was enough gas in the truck to get them through the following week and she knew if she could manage to really limit her driving she might last until the next payday, which was a little more than a week away.

Tracey unloaded her items onto the checkout counter and watched as her friend, Helen, scanned the items. As she slid each item over the scanner they chatted about "turkey day". Helen finished the check-out quickly, paused and said, "Okay Trace, that comes to $60.28."

Tracey smiled and said, "I can't believe it, Helen. I wanted to spend only $60.00 and I went 28 cents over. Not bad, if I do say so."

"Wow, you are good, Tracey. I usually double what I plan to spend."

They both laughed as Tracey swiped her debit card. Then she keyed in her pin number and waited for the prompt to continue. A message popped up, *Insufficient Funds*. Tracey saw the unexpected message and instantly a sense of impending doom poured over her. She smiled at Helen and tried to remain calm. Again she swiped her card. Again she got the same message. *Insufficient Funds*. She looked at Helen, "I do not understand." She tried again. *Insufficient Funds*.

The customers lined up in back of her were watching as Tracey Slider tried to keep her composure. It is a fact that humiliation can embrace a person in a nanosecond and Tracey was firmly in its grasp. She could feel all of the eyes that were upon her and desperately wanted to be somewhere else. Fighting the panic rising within her she garnered a sense of composure. Taking in a slow, deliberate breath through her nose she exhaled and said, "Look Helen, I'm going to put this stuff back in the cart and you hold it here for me, okay? I'll be back in fifteen minutes."

Helen smiled and said, "Oh sure, Tracey. No problem. Take your time."

Tracey left the store without her Thanksgiving dinner. She walked to Bob's truck, got in and began to tremble. Taking in a few deep breaths she wiped her teary eyes and headed home. All she could think of was, *It has to be a mistake, It has to be a mistake. How could they do this?*

She pulled into the driveway so fast she actually screeched to a stop. She jumped out of the truck and hurried into the house, walked right past Bob who was sleeping on the sofa and sat down at the computer in the bedroom. She tapped her fingers on the desk as the computer seemed to be taking forever to boot-up. Then she said to it, "C'mon, c'mon, hurry up already. Hurry up."

It may or may not have been paying attention because in a few moments the screen was waiting for her commands. She clicked on her bank icon, the web site opened and she keyed in her username and password. It took several moments and then her checking account balance showed itself. There was negative $89.00. Tracey gasped and blurted out, "Oh my God. Are they crazy or what?"

There had been two transactions posted. On Friday afternoon a $100.00 cash withdrawal had been made. The same afternoon another $60.00 had been taken out. Then there were the two bank charges of $36.00 each, one for "insufficient funds: and one for an "over limit" fee. Unblinking, she stared and stared and stared at the screen. The she blurted out, "Oh my God!"

She jumped up from the chair and rushed into the living room yelling, "Bob, Bob, wake up! Wake up right now."

Bob remained still and quiet on the sofa. Tracey began to yell at him and pull on his shoulder. "Bob, wake up right now. Wake up, damn it. Where is our money? What did you do with our money?"

Her opiate dazed husband turned toward her and opened his eyes. "What are you screaming about? What's going on? Why you pulling on me like that? You're hurting my back."

"You want to know what's going on? I'll tell you what's going on. And—right now, I do not care about your back. I just had to leave our Thanksgiving dinner at the store because there is no money in our checking account. Do you hear me, Bob? NO MONEY! What did you do? Where is our money? You took our money, didn't you?"

Now Bob was somewhat alert and said, "Take money? What money? When."

"You took money from the ATM Friday and never told me. That was our food money. That was for Thanksgiving. I want that money right now so I can go back and get our groceries."

Bob sat up and, looking at his wife through half opened eyes, said, "What are you talking about, Tracey? I don't remember taking any money from any ATM."

"Damn it Bob Slider, you are the only one with an ATM card besides me and I know what I do with our money. So, you had to have taken it. Where is it? I need to go pay for our groceries."

Bob scratched his head, sighed and ran his hand through his hair. He looked at his wife and said, "Well, now that you mention it, I did need some medication. So, you're right, Trace.

I did take money. So what."

"So what! Are you nuts? All you can say is 'so what'? I need that money and I need it right now. And what medication are you talking about? You can't get any pills until December 1."

"Whatever Tracey, I needed some so I got some. End of story."

"You're buying from Zack Covello, aren't you. That drug dealing son of a bitch. If I ever see him around here I'm calling the cops."

" Well, I don't know what to tell you, Tracey. You know I need that medication. You should have checked the account before you tried to spend money we didn't have. Don't blame me for your screw-up."

Tracey Slider was stunned. She stared at the man who was her best friend, her partner, her confidant, her lover and her husband and did not know who she was looking at. Her thoughts smashed together like a collision of speeding vehicles hitting each other head on. The ensuing internal explosion inside her brain thrust her into a momentary petrified state. She had mentally shut down and just stood still, not moving, not breathing, not thinking, just staring.

Her body quickly sought fresh breath and when it instinctively took some in Tracey exploded and started screaming at her husband. "Oh my God, what is wrong with you? You're blaming ME for the money? Are you crazy or what. You took it and now you are blaming me. You know what Bob, you have turned into nothing but a full-blown drug addict. You don't care about anyone or anything but yourself. You don't care about me or Jake or anything anymore. The man I loved and the man I married has vanished. I do not even know who you are anymore. If you keep this up I swear—."

"You swear what, Tracey? Don't threaten me. Don't even try it.""

His billfold was on the coffee table and she saw it. She grabbed it and he tried to get it away from her. Quickly she rifled through it and found the ATM card and yanked it out. "Okay Bob, watch this." She hurried to the kitchen cabinet and took out the scissors and cut the card up before he even had a chance to get up from the sofa. "You won't ever do that to me again. Ever."

A voice from behind drew her attention. Tracey turned and it was Judi. Judi said, "I was knocking at the door and I heard the yelling and the door was partially opened and I thought something might be wrong. I'm sorry, I didn't mean to intrude. I'll come back later."

"Oh Judi, what a disaster. You stay right here. I need you. I---I---"

"Tracey, I have your groceries out in my car. That's why I stopped by. Are you all right?

How can I help?"

"You have my groceries? What are you talking about? How, why---?"

Tracey began to cry and Judi went over and hugged her. She wanted to get her friend away from Bob who had laid back down on the sofa and covered his eyes with his forearm. She was nervous being in the middle of their 'husband and wife' business and said, "Come on Trace, come outside and help me get the stuff and I'll tell you what happened."

They walked outside and Judi said, "Look Tracey, I was working the front-end when you came in this morning. I was behind the courtesy counter and you didn't see me. But I saw you leave without your groceries. Helen told me what happened and I covered it for you. I figured there was some kind of glitch with your debit card, that's all. You can pay me later, no problem."

Tracey held her hands over her mouth and said, "Oh my God, I cannot believe you were there and you did that. It's like a miracle. I did not know what I was going to do. Thank you so much. What would I do if I didn't have you for a friend?"

"That's' what friends are for, right? Now, tell me, what is going on? What's the matter with Bob?"

"Oh Judi, I don't know what happened to him. He took our money to buy drugs. He calls it 'medication'. I knew I had enough money for the groceries and then it said insufficient funds and I was so shocked and then I found out he took the money and he tells me I should have known better and—Oh my God, he blamed me."

"Whoa, Tracey. Slow down, please, slow down a second."

"Thank God Jake is in school and didn't see or hear any of this. It's not right, Judi. It's not right and I do not know what to do. The man I love is not in that man's body. He looks the same but he isn't the same. I do not know how to handle this."

Bob came to the front door and, acting as if nothing had happened, said, "So, what's going on girls? How you doing, Judi?"

Tracey and Judi looked at each other. Tracey said, "Yeah Bob, sure. What's going on? I'll tell you what should be going on. You should be down on your knees thanking our friend, Judi, for paying for our Thanksgiving groceries, that's what should be going on."

"You know what Tracey, I got no time for your crap." He went into the house and slammed the front door behind him.

Tracey and Judi both stared at the closed front door. Judi said, "You are absolutely right, Tracey. That man may look like Bob Slider but he sure isn't acting like Bob Slider. I think that your husband has been invaded by an alien and that alien is called narcotics. He will have a huge war to fight to overcome this demon. You, too, have a huge challenge facing you and will have some hard choices to make."

Tracey looked at Judi, smiled and said, "I had better go inside. I'll be all right. And Judi, thanks for the groceries. I'll pay you back on payday."

"Don't you worry about that now. When you have it you have it. No problem."

"Thanks for being there for me, Judi. You are my strength right now."

Judi said, "No Tracey, it isn't me. You have been to Mass with me the last two Sundays.

God has your back. That is your new strength. You have been reaching out to Him. Look, there is one Mass on Thanksgiving Day at 9:30 a.m. Come with me and bring Jake and see if Bob will come along too."

"Bob won't come. The way I feel right now, I don't care either."

"Well, ask him anyway. He might come along. You never know. He might be in a good mood that morning. And you might feel a bit differently too. It would be a nice way for you guys to start the holiday."

They hugged and Tracey said, "Okay Judi, I'll try. Thanks."

*

*

*

CHAPTER 11

Christmas Lights?---Not Today

Tracey had the turkey cleaned and stuffed and in the roasting pan by 8a.m. A string bean casserole was already in a baking dish waiting to go and the sweet potatoes were ready to go into the oven. Her plan was to have dinner around 3 or 3:30, right after the football game. All she had left to do was peel the potatoes and she could do that after church. She headed to Jake's room and knocked on the door. "Come on Jake, wake up. Time to get up."

There was no answer and she knocked again. "Jake, wake up, let's go, wake up."

Again there was no answer so she knocked hard on the door and opened it. Jake was sound asleep with the sheet pulled over his head. "Jake, come on. I want you to get up. It's Thanksgiving and we are going to church today. Let's go, get up"

Jake rolled over and stretched his arms up and over his head. He grunted and rolled back over pulling the sheet up and over his head again. His mother pulled it off. "Jake Slider, get up right now. Don't make me drag you out of that bed. Just get up and get ready. We are going to church today."

"Oh man," he moaned. "Do I have to? I'm so tired."

"Jake, I still have to get your father up. So please, just get up and get dressed. I don't

want to have to drag you out of bed."

She left Jake's room and went into her bedroom. Bob was still snoring. She shook his shoulder gently and said, "Bob, hey Bob. It's Thanksgiving. Jake and I are going to start the day by going to Mass over at Sacred Heart. How about getting up and going with us. It would mean a lot to me if you would."

Bob rolled onto his back and squinted up at his wife through half opened eyes. "Ugh, well, okay, why not."

He sat up and let out a big yawn as he rubbed his hand through his disheveled hair. He had no idea how he had shocked his wife. She never even expected him to wake up, no less get up and go to church with her. Over the years they had been to several church weddings and funerals but this would be the first time they would actually be going to a church together just to go for the sake of going. At that very moment Tracey Slider felt a sense of peace and calm that she had not experienced in a very long time. She took pause to consider if she might be dreaming.

Tracey prepared her two men a batch of pancakes and sausage patties and they all had a fine Thanksgiving breakfast. Bob appeared to be as normal as could be and he was even moving around without complaining of back pain. She knew he had already taken a pain pill but she did not care. So far this was a good day. Bob and Jake even cleaned up the kitchen so Tracey could get ready for church.

Judi and Tommy were at Mass and the Sliders sat with them. As the congregation prayed the "Our Father" everyone held hands. Tracey holding hands with her husband on her right and her son on her left stood motionless as tears flowed freely down her face. Silently she was giving "Thanks" to God for the very special moment.

After Mass was over the celebrant, Father Jim Daniels, was greeting folks outside wishing them a happy Thanksgiving. Judi stopped and said, "Good morning, Father Jim, Happy Thanksgiving."

"Good morning Judi, good morning Tommy. Happy Turkey Day to you too."

"Same to you Father. By the way Father, I would like to introduce you to my neighbors, Bob and Tracey Slider."

The priest smiled and shook hands with each of them. "So good to meet you folks. Tracey, I have seen you at Mass here before, right."

"Yes Father, I have come on occasion."

He looked at Bob and squinted a bit, "Pleasure to meet you, Bob. I don't think I have seen you before but I am really glad you came today." He turned to the side and said, "And who is this good looking young man?"

Tracey said, "I'm sorry Father. This is our son, Jake."

The priest reached out and shook Jake's hand, "Nice to meet you Jake. You know, we have a wonderful youth group here at Sacred Heart. Stop by for a visit sometime."

Jake did not say anything. Tracey said, "Father, we're not Catholic."

"That's okay. There are some kids in our youth group who are not Catholic. That's not an issue. In fact, many of the kids who go to our school are not Catholic. So, it is not a problem."

Tracey said, "Thank you Father. We will definitely talk to Jake about it. Sounds like a good idea."

Well, it was sure nice meeting you folks. If you ever have a need to ask any questions about this Catholic thing, you call me. I'd be glad to answer any questions you might have."

Tracey smiled and said, "Thank you Father. I might do that."

A voice yelled out, "Yo, hey Jake."

Jake turned and it was his friend from school, Richie Sanchez. "Hey Richie, what's going on?"

"What are you doing here? You don't go to this church, do you?"
"No, this is my first time coming here."

Father Jim seized the moment. "So Jake, you and Richie know each other?"

"Sure Father," Richie said. "We're in the same class and on the same baseball team."

"Wow, isn't that something. Goes to show what a small world it is. Hey Richie, maybe you can talk Jake into coming to a youth group meeting. The young folks do a lot of fun stuff here,

Jake. You should think about it. Like I said, don't worry about being Catholic. It doesn't matter."

Richie and Jake both felt a bit awkward being put on the spot by the priest. They both turned and walked away talking together as the adults said their goodbyes to Father Jim. By 11:00 a.m they were home and watching the Macy's Thanksgiving Day Parade. At noon the traditional football game with the Detroit Lions would come on. This year they were playing the Tampa Bay Buccaneers. Bob and his boy were amped up and ready to cheer their home team Bucs to victory.

Their Thanksgiving dinner consisted of more than just a bounty of delicious food. More importantly it included true, family camaraderie. Bob and Jake joked around and laughed together as they reminisced about silly things. Things from the past like when Jake's baseball shoe fell off as he was running the bases or how Bob had, without thinking, broken the front window when he went to smash a crawling bug and forgot he was holding a hammer in his hand. They even zeroed in on Tracey and teased her about the time she colored her hair and it came out bright pink instead of strawberry blond. Bob had told her that she should stand on the front lawn and people going by would think she was one of those 'pink flamingoes' you saw placed as lawn decorations on Florida lawns. The three of them laughed and ate and laughed some more.

After dinner the father and his son went outside and threw around the football.

Tracey, watching her two "guys" toss the ball around, thought that this was the best Thanksgiving that she had ever had. She lifted her eyes and whispered, "Thank you, Lord."

The holiday proved to be only a temporary reprieve from the tension filled days of the preceding months. Traditionally, Bob had decorated the house for Christmas on the Saturday after Thanksgiving. He would be up early and in the garage pulling out boxes of lights and all sorts of other

Christmas stuff. He would also be upbeat and jovial as the Christmas spirit embraced him.

The Slider house was always one of the best decorated in the entire neighborhood and people actually came from all parts of town to see the display. This year was a bit different. Bob's primary focus was now pain pills. The "need" for them trumped all else and he knew he would need more very soon.

It was noon and Bob was sitting in the lounge chair, feet up, heating pad plugged in and pressed onto his lower back and his eyes half shut. Tracey had been offered extra hours and had to be at work at one o'clock. She stood next to her husband and said, "Bob, it's Saturday. Are you going to start putting the lights up or what?"

"I don't know, Tracey. My back is killing me. Maybe tomorrow."

Tracey had come to a point where she did not believe for a minute that Bob's back condition was as serious as it was originally. Bob never said it was any better and any time he needed an excuse not to do something he blamed his back for it. He had been to physical therapy twice a week for over three months and Tracey was acutely aware of how often he would move around looking perfectly normal and seemingly pain free. She knew what she saw and Bob's actions and behavior had numbed her into an ongoing cynicism. "Bob," she said, "Jake has been waiting to help you put them up. You told him Thursday you would do them today. He even stayed home from Tyler's to help do them."

"Come on Tracey, give me a break. I can't help it if my back has me down. What am I supposed to do? I suppose I should go outside and start climbing up and down a ladder just to put up some stupid lights. Jake can still go to Tyler's. It's not a big deal."

"And how much pain medicine do you have left?"

"Not much, that's for sure. Not much."

"That's what I thought. Well, this is Saturday and the first is Tuesday. I hope you have enough until then."

"What's that supposed to mean. You think I'm overdosing again. You worried that your drug addict husband is going to steal your precious food money. Well, I don't rightly give a damn what you think. My back is messed up and I need pain meds to keep me going. You don't like it, too bad."

The simple fact was Bob's back was better but still in a tenuous situation where a wrong twist, turn or pull could set him back to square one. Tracey had tried to be understanding but ever since the drug bust and the money vanishing from the checking account her patience and tolerance had worn thin. "I swear Bob, you have no idea how much you have changed since you hurt your back. As soon as you start thinking that you don't have enough of your 'medicine' you start getting so miserable. I don't know how much more of it I can stand. I just don't know."

"And guess what, Tracey? I don't care."

The peace and tranquilty of Thanksgiving Day had quickly evaporated and things in the Slider house were back to the "new normal". Jake came out from his room and headed right to the refrigerator. He reached in and stuck his fingers into the bowl of leftover stuffing. Tracey, upset and near tears, yelled to him, "Leave that stuffing alone Jake. It is for dinner. It's almost all gone. I need all of it for tonight's dinner." "Okay mom, okay. You don't have to yell right away."

"Don't tell me what I should or should not do. If I want to yell at you I will, understand?"

Jake looked at her and sighed. "Okay, okay, okay. Sorry. Hey Dad, when are we going to start putting the lights up? It's getting late?"

Tracey said, "So Bob, what's it going to be? You could let Jake do the ladder work."

"Damn it Tracey. I told you not today. Maybe tomorrow if I'm feeling better."

"But Dad," Jake said, "we always do the lights on the Saturday after Thanksgiving."

"Well not this year. I can't be getting up and down the ladder with this damn back of mine. It's killing me."

"I can do the ladder stuff, Dad. I'm not a baby anymore."

Jake, not today. Maybe tomorrow, but not today. That's it. So drop it."

Jake shook his head and mumbled, "Your back is always hurting. Whatever."

"Bob sat up in the chair and said to his boy, "What did you say to me?"

"Jake got nervous and said, "Nothing, I didn't say nothing."

"Yeah, well, don't get smart with me Jake. I'm not in the mood for any of your 12 year old nonsense. Understand? I swear, you and your mother both have no idea what I have been going through, no idea."

Tracey looked at her husband and just shook her head. She was ready to blow-up at Bob but she bit her tongue, walked over to Jake and said, "Look, we'll do the lights tomorrow, okay. Now, how about a turkey sandwich. There is still enough for me to squeeze out a sandwich before dinner."

"I don't want no stupid sandwich."

Tracey looked at her boy and felt his pain. "Jake, I'm sorry for yelling at you. Look, let me fix you a turkey sandwich. Things will be okay."

Jake loosened up and said, "Okay mom, sure."

"Great, now give me a hug."

Mother and son hugged each other and the hug helped ease the tension. But the behavior of Bob toward his wife and son more or less set the tone that would embrace the family on its four week trek toward Christmas Day. Compared to years gone by it was different this year, very different. Unemployment, disability, lack of money, overdue bills, and Bob's addiction had joined forces to create a constant, unending anxiety that was slowly but surely tearing the family apart.

Tracey made Jake the sandwich and then said to him, "Listen, if you still want to go over to Tyler's, I'll run you over there. No sense hanging around here today."

"Okay mom, sounds good. Thanks."

Tracey drove her boy over to his friend's place and then went to work. She arrived back home about 5:30 and Judi came hurrying over. "Hi Trace, I wanted to talk to you for a few minutes without Bob hearing us. Can you come over for some coffee?"

"Well yes, I can. In fact, that would be great. Jake is at Tyler's and Bob is still sleeping on the couch so, yeah, coffee it is. It has been one lousy day so far and I don't feel like fixing dinner anyway. Maybe later."

Tracey sat down at Judi's kitchen table and the first thing Judi did was hand her $80.00. Tracey was puzzled and said, "What's this for?"

"Just put it in your pocket and do not let Bob know you have it. I had a little extra cash and I just want you to have it, that's all. ""I don't need this, Judi. Plus, I still owe you for the groceries."

"Well, I want you to hold onto that money too."

"Judi, I don't understand. I mean---"

Judi held up her hand and said, "I just want to do it. That's all. It's only $80.00, a little extra pin money. So please, as your friend, just do me a favor and take it."

Tracey shrugged, smiled and said, "Okay Judi, thank you."

"Okay now, let me explain something to you. You know my brother, Anthony?"

"Of course I do. He's the guy who is the computer expert. Has that consulting company over in Orlando. The last time you mentioned him you said he had been hurt on his vacation."

"You mean the guy that USED to have that company over in Orlando. Look Tracey, Anthony is a user. He has lost everything because of his addiction. We don't even know where he is. We have not heard from him in over two months. "

"Oh my God, Judi, I had no idea. That's awful."

"Yes, well Anthony was water skiing and, I really don't know what happened, but he crashed trying to jump from one of those water-ski ramps. He was in the hospital and he needed surgery for a ruptured spleen and his back was all messed up. Well, the next thing you know he's doing pain killers and—that was almost two years ago."

"Two years, that's unbelievable. I had no idea."

"It sure is and now you are having a similar situation with Bob. It's like an onslaught of pain pills has attacked injured or sick people and, instead of helping them get better, changes them into strangers even their families don't know."

"Judi, suddenly I am very scared. What can I do?"

"I'm not sure. I think I understand what you are going through with Bob. I have been going through that with my own brother but a husband is different than a brother. It's in your face every single day. I don't have that to deal with that. Don't know if I could. I have my husband to support me. You need support to help you with your own husband. That's rough Tracey, rough."

"Well, all I know is I have my son to look out for. He is only 12 and I have to be strong for him. And, trust me on this one, I WILL be strong for him. He didn't ask for this and he doesn't deserve it."

"Yup, I know you can be tough Tracey Slider, especially when the chips are down. I have been going to Nar-Anon meetings for the past few months to help me deal with Anthony. I think they can help you too. I would like you to come with me to a meeting."

"You know Judi, to be fair to Bob, I know he hurt his back and between losing his job and not being able to work at all has affected his manhood. He feels so useless. The fact that I'm the only one working drives him crazy. So, I think you are right. I do need help in dealing with all of this. Nar-Anon might be just the thing. I don't want to be too hard on Bob yet I have to look out for Jake too."

"And you have to look out for yourself. Don't forget you."

"Tell me about Nar-Anon."

You know about AL-Anon, right?"

Tracey nodded and said, "Sure, they're for the families and friends of alcoholics."

Judi continued, "Well, Nar-Anon is for families and friends of people hooked on drugs. My mom and I have been going to meetings for a few months. My mom lives on Social Security and Anthony was getting her to give him almost half of it. He kept telling her it was for medicine and she was not going to deny her 'poor baby' his medicine. Good thing her house payment is an automatic payment or he probably would have gotten all of it."

"Oh my God, he actually took the Social Security money from his own mother?"

"He sure did. Anyway, she wasn't eating and---"

"She wasn't eating? What do you mean? Why wasn't she eating?"

"Because he took her money and she couldn't buy food. I mean she had some soups and stuff like that but she never told me. I stopped by and I looked in her fridge and it was almost empty. I wanted to know why and then she told me. I couldn't believe it. It was so awful to me I started to cry."

"I cannot imagine, Judi. I cannot imagine."

"Well, it has stopped. I got control of her bank account and he can't touch it. I made sure of that. Mom gets mad at me like I'm doing something bad to her son. It is crazy, Tracey, crazy. She feels sorry for him and wants to help the 'poor thing' and gets angry at me for helping her."

"So, he takes her food and money and she gets mad at you. It sounds almost insane."

"It is. That's why I started the Nar-Anon meetings with my mom. Tommy has even come along with me to a few. It has helped me and my mom so much because we are learning that we cannot do a thing about Anthony's situation. He has to take charge. I will help him but, so help me God, I will not enable him. I think he knows it and that's why I have not heard from him. I know that you are in that same situation with Bob. He doesn't have a clue what real help is. So you and I can really be able to reinforce each other."

Tracey sighed and said, "You know Judi, I may not have any family but having you is the same thing. I'm so thankful to God that we are friends. You are just like having a sister."

*

*

*

CHAPTER 12

"Strange, Scary Feelings"

Tommy Pavano had driven over to Tampa to visit his brother, Ronnie. Judi said, "Hey Trace, why don't you and I go over to Park Slope for supper? Tommy won't be home until nine and Bob's sleeping. What do you say?"

Tracey thought for a moment and answered, "I say let's go. I can pick Bob up a cheeseburger and fries. Let me just run home and freshen up."

Tracey hurried home and, to her surprise, Bob was not there. Even though he was not allowed to drive, the first thing she did was check to see if the truck was in the driveway. It was. She checked and he was not in the garage. She could not imagine where he could have gone. She called his cell phone and a faint ring-tone popped out from the sofa. "I don't believe him," she mumbled. "He forgot his phone." She felt between the sofa cushions and pulled the phone out. She stared at it and mumbled again, "Whatever Bob, whatever."

She changed from her work uniform into slacks and a pullover sweater sort of procrastinating in hopes that Bob would show up. She still remembered the shock she received the last time he was gone. Getting a call from the county jail is something you tend to remember. It is a moment that is indelibly etched into your memory bank ready for retrieval at a moment's notice. She left him a note and headed back to Judi's.

Sitting in the Park Slope Diner, Judi shook her head and said, "Look at you Tracey, just look at you."

"Why? What's wrong?"

"I can see the worry written all across your face. You cannot stop worrying about Bob's whereabouts. He has you so worn down you're going to make yourself sick."

"I can't help it, Judi. Ever since he was arrested, every time he goes out I do worry."

"Just more fallout from the drug use. If Bob was not so dependent on those pills you would not be worrying about him at all right now and we could enjoy this time out. Those drug tentacles reach out in all different directions and here they are at Park Slope wrapping themselves around you."

Tracey looked at Judi and said, "I never thought of it like that. It is true, isn't it? I'm afraid he's going to get thrown in jail again and I cannot relax if he's out of the house. He's like having an unpredictable teenager to deal with."

Judi reached across the table and grabbed Tracey's hand. "Slow down Tracey. I'm sure Bob is fine. You just can't help worrying. You were traumatized with his arrest. Time will help to dull the pain."

"Damn it Judi, I never worried about my husband or mistrusted him before, ever. I do not like this."

They finished their supper and headed straight home. Judi turned off the car and said, "I'm going to the 9:30 Mass tomorrow morning Trace. You going?"

"Yes, I am. I'm hoping that Bob comes along. I have to pick Jake up at Tyler's but he and I will be there."

"Great, see you tomorrow. If you need anything give a shout."

"Thanks Judi, I'm fine."

When Tracey walked into the house Bob was sitting on the sofa watching TV. "Oh, there you are. Where did you go? I was worried about you?"

"Why are you worried about me? I'm a big boy, Tracey. For your information I walked down to the 7/11 on 94th Ave. I had to get out of here for a bit and I thought I would buy a lotto ticket. Maybe we'll win ten million and then you won't have to worry about the freaking bills anymore. You should have called me."

"Actually Bob, I did call you. Your phone was between the sofa cushions so I guess you couldn't answer."

Quickly Bob patted his pockets and then he saw the phone on the coffee table. "Oh damn---okay Tracey, you got me on that one. Tracey one, Bob zero."

She sighed and shook her head. It was almost as if he was getting into a habit of talking down to her. "You have to stop treating me this way, Bob. It is wearing me down. I am not going to be talked to like I'm some damn fool. I deserve respect from you."

"Yeah, well fine, and I deserve respect from you too. It's a two-way street sweetheart, a two way street."

She had no response and said, "Okay Bob, you're right. It is a two-way street. Here is a cheeseburger and fries I got for you. I figured you would be hungry."

He grabbed the bag from her hand and tore it opened. With one bite almost half the sandwich was gone. "My God, Bob, you must have been starving?"

"Yeah, I guess so."

Bob finished eating and dozed off again. He never mentioned to his wife that smoking a joint can amp up a person's appetite. Tracey, exhausted from working and from being on an emotional roller coaster for the entire day, was asleep by 8:30.

Sunday morning arrived and Tracey tried to wake Bob up so he could go to Mass with her and Jake. He would not budge. She gave up and called Tyler's house. His mom answered. "Hello."

"Hi Samantha, it's Tracey."

"Hi Tracey, how are you?"

"Fine, I'm fine. Could you tell Jake I'll be by in about 15 minutes to pick him up for church? I hope he didn't forget."

"Tyler and Jake are still sleeping. Do you want me to wake him up?"

Tracey paused for a moment and felt herself get a bit annoyed. There was a feeling inside of her that Samantha was questioning her decision to wake her own son up. She answered, "Yes Samantha, wake him up. He promised he would be up to go to church with me. So yes, please, wake him up. I'll be by in a little bit."

Tracey had hung up the phone before Samantha could finish saying, "Sure Tracey, if you say so."

Tracey pulled up to Tyler's house and Jake was not outside waiting as she had expected. She honked the horn a few times. He still did not come out. She started to get angry. She leaned on the horn hard and Samantha opened the door and yelled out that he would be right there.

Tracey waited and was about to go to the front door when Jake came hurrying out. He climbed into the truck and his mom looked at him and said, "My God , look at you. Didn't you even wash your face or comb your hair. And are they the same clothes you had on yesterday? Didn't you bring clean clothes for church with you?"

"Oh mom, I forgot. I just woke up a minute ago. Don't yell at me right away, okay."

"You know what Jake, it's fine. You can go like that. I don't care. But you and I are going to church together. I don't care what you have on or how you look."

"What's wrong, Mom? Dad wouldn't come to church, is that it? Well, don't take it out on me, okay. I asked Mrs. Anderson to wake me and she said she thought that she would give me a few more minutes. That's why I wasn't outside waiting for you."

Tracey smiled at her boy and said, "I'm sorry Jake. I'm sorry. You didn't deserve that from me."

After Mass, Tracey and Jake were walking to the truck when Father Jim came walking by. "Good morning Tracey, good morning Jake, happy Sunday. Good to see you both."

"Good morning Father," Tracey said. "Good to see you too."

Jake smiled and the priest said to him, "How are you this fine morning Jake?"

"Good Father. I'm good."

"Father Jim, never one to miss an opportunity, said, "So, I guess Mr. Slider couldn't make it today."

Tracey felt a bit foolish and was going to say something but the priest beat her to it. "No big deal Tracey. It's okay. In fact, sometimes I should think before I speak. Hey, at least you guys are here. Okay, I have to run. I have the next Mass."

He hurried off with his hand waving in the air. Tracey and Jake also waved but his back was to them. Jake said, "He seems nice, Mom. I think I like him."

"Yes Jake, I know what you mean. There is just something, I don't know, genuine about him."

"He kind of makes you feel like you have known him a long time or something."

"Come on Jake, let's you and I go get some breakfast at Park Slope."

"Absolutely Mom, I'm starved."

The diner was always very busy on Sunday morning as many of the church folks would come after services. Jake and Tracey were in luck and got a booth by a window. A server came over and said, "Well, hello again. You must love this place."

It was the server that Judi and Tracey had the previous evening. "Hi young man," she said. "My name is Karen. I waited on your mom and her friend last night."

Jake just sat and smiled looking up at the woman. She had a naturally friendly way about her and Jake was a bit intimidated by her outgoing behavior. "What can I get you both to drink?" She paused and looked at Jake. Then she slowly said as she rolled her eyes, " Oh boy, Tracey, this son of yours is going to be a heartbreaker for sure."

Tracey laughed and said, "Please Karen, don't say that. He's only 12 for goodness sakes."

Innocently, Jake said, "I'm almost 13, Mom."

Karen, a very attractive woman in her late twenties or early thirties, was actually flirting a bit with the boy because she noticed how Jake had been trying to keep his eyes off her but couldn't. His testosterone was starting to bloom and the young man was feeling uncomfortable. The lady sensed it and so did Tracey. "Karen, get me a coffee please. What about you, Jake? Orange juice?"

Karen answered for him. "Well, he's almost 13, maybe he wants coffee too?"

Tracey became a bit angry. The mother lion's claws were beginning to extend as her man-cub was being toyed with by an interloping female. "Karen, can you just bring a coffee and some orange juice."

Karen sensed Tracey's disapproval and backed off. "Okay, be right back to take your order."

Karen was all business after that. They both ordered the Park Slope favorite, "skillets". They ate quietly and headed home. Tracey had never considered her son's impending manhood and had been unnerved by the brief interaction between Karen and Jake. A moment had unexpectedly arrived in Tracey Slider's life where she would no longer think of her son as just a boy. She was not even aware it had happened.

Back home Tracey said, "Okay Jake, Dad's still in bed. What do you say we start the lights ourselves?"

"I don't know mom. He might get mad. He likes doing them."

"Jake, I don't care. It is almost Sunday afternoon and he has not even started them yet. You know where everything is, right?'

"Mom, why is dad acting so weird lately? Did he turn into a drug user?"

Tracey was stunned by the question and looked at her boy. "Oh my God, no, no Jake.

Look son, your dad lost his job, hurt his back, and then they gave him all of this medicine. When things like that happen to people they have a tendency to act different. That's all."

"Mom, I'm not a little kid anymore. We even learn all about drugs in school. I know dad has prescription drugs. I know he got in trouble because of them. I know what's going on and it drives me crazy that you act like I don't know anything. Dad has a problem and WE have to help him, not just you. He is my father."

Tracey Slider's protective shell was starting to show its cracks and imperfections. She was determined to be upbeat for Jake, strong enough to support the family and always have a ready smile available while working. Jake had, like an adult, addressed the situation about his dad directly to his mom and in so doing had shattered the remaining shell. Standing in the living room she started to cry.

Jake was stymied. He did not know what to do so he instinctively put his arms around his mother and hugged her. Feeling as if he was protecting his mom he said, "It'll be okay Mom. It'll be okay. Dad is strong. He'll figure this out. And you and me will help him, right?"

Tracey hugged her boy back and then gently pushed him back. "Jake, I'm sorry. I'm all right. And yes, you and I will help him.

Sometimes I forget that you are growing up. Come on, let's get those lights out and decorate this place. Christmas is coming."

Bob came out from the bedroom just as they were heading into the garage. "Hey, what are you two doing?"

"We're going to start the lights, Dad. Get dressed and come out and help us. You know where everything goes."

"Maybe later Jake. I didn't even have coffee yet. We can always do them next Saturday."

Tracey was not falling for any of that 'next week' stuff. "Bob, don't worry about it. Jake and I will get them out and begin putting them up. If you feel like helping fine, if not, that's fine too. Come on Jake."

'Hold on Tracey, you don't know how the wiring goes or the where the different sets go or the order they are in."

"Well then, you better come out and help us because those lights are going up today, one way or another."

Now Bob started getting angry. ,"Tracey, what's your problem. I just woke up for crying out loud. Didn't even have coffee and you're in my face. This is bull shit."

"No Bob, your excuses are 'bull shit'. I am not listening to them any longer. You just got up, big deal. It is noon already. Half the day is gone."

"Okay Tracey, have it your way. It obviously does not matter how much pain I am in. No, no, the precious Christmas lights have to go up right now."

Tracey held her ground and said, "You got it Bob. Today the lights go up no matter how much pain you are in. We can do it ourselves. Jake, let's go. Show me where everything is."

Bob was speechless and simply walked over to the counter and poured himself a cup of coffee. Jake, shocked at his mom's determination, just followed her out to the garage. The boxes with the outside decorations were all neatly stacked on the shelves and labeled.

131

Jake pulled the ladder over, climbed up and began handing them to his mom. Ten minutes later Bob came out. He was showered, dressed and looking good. "Okay, let's see what you have here."

Bob quickly separated the overhead fascia lights from the bush lights. There were lights that ran the length of the ridge of the house and down the sides along the eaves. There were small sets of lights that went around each window and other lights that were for the entranceway. Finally came all of the figurines; snowmen, elves, an illuminated toy train, Santa's sled and the eight reindeer pulling it which went on the roof, and lastly, the manger scene which they put out every year even though they never went to church.

Bob Slider went at it and it was like Thanksgiving Day all over. The pills he had gotten from Zack Covello at the 7/11 were doing their thing. Everything was fine and they were all enjoying the day. By 6 p.m., the day's darkness had snuck in from the east. Bob's anxiety levels were beginning to amp up. He owed Zack $60.00 for the pills and was supposed to pay him first thing Monday morning. He had no money.

The Slider Christmas display was illuminated at 6:15 p.m. Full darkness had descended and the lights looked beautiful. The three of them stood out in the street looking at their handiwork. Jake said, "Hey dad, they look great."

Tracey said, "He's right hon, nice job."

Judi walked over and stood with them. Other neighbors came out from their houses to see the lights and several cars slowed to a crawl as they came up the street, stopping just long enough so the people inside them could take a long look.

"Yeah," Bob said. "I guess it is a nice job especially seeing how bad my back has been.

Nice job for sure."

Tracey looked at him and thought that there was no way she would let him ruin what had been a wonderful afternoon. "Yes Bob, thanks. It was nice all three of us working together like that. Hey, how about some burgers?" Jake did not hesitate, "Great mom, I'm starving."

"Bob, why don't you light the grill and I'll get the burgers ready. What do you say?"

"Uh, yeah Tracey. Sure, why not."

Tracey asked Judi if she wanted to have burgers with them but she declined. Tommy was due back from his brother's soon and Judi wanted to wash her hair and take care of some personal needs before he returned, so she headed home.

Bob was getting a bit frantic. He needed $60.00. He also needed more pills. He did not know what to do. He noticed Tracey's purse on the chair in the dining room. He bided his time until she went to the bathroom and hurried over to the purse. He really did not expect to find anything but, to his wide-eyed delight, there was $80.00 in cash. He had hit the "mother-lode".

Bob's frontal lobe kicked into high gear and he could not resist. The "need" for more drugs took charge and just like that the money was in his pocket. He hurried back outside to the grill never realizing that Jake, who was coming back in from the garage, had seen his father take the money from his mom's pocketbook.

Tracey came out from the bathroom and walked into the kitchen with a bounce in her step and a song on her lips, *"Jingle bells, jingle bells, jingle all the way—".* She was still enjoying her Sunday and the now twinkling Christmas lights outside had ignited the Christmas spirit in her. They had put the tree up in the living room and after dinner were going to string the lights on it. The ornaments would be put on the tree Monday . It had been a good day all right, a good day for sure.

Dinner was pleasant enough except Jake kept glancing back and forth at his dad. Finally, Bob looked at his son blurted out, "What the hell is wrong with you? Why do you keep staring at me? "

"I wasn't staring at you, dad."

"Yeah Jake, sure you weren't. Do you need something? Do you want to ask me something? Come on, spit it out. Just don't keep staring like that."

Jake bit his lip and looked down at his food. Tracey said, "Is something wrong Jake?"

"No Mom, nothing is wrong, okay. Nothing is wrong. Can I be excused and go to my room?

Tracey was startled and confused. It had been a good day and she did not understand this strange altercation taking place between father and son. Bob was still glaring at the boy and Tracey said, "You didn't finish eating, Jake. Are you feeling all right?"

"Mom, I am fine. Please, let me just go to my room."

"Okay," she said. As he got up she stopped him and felt his forehead with the palm of her hand. "Well, your not eating a hamburger is strange. I hope you are not getting sick or something."

Jake went into his room, plopped onto his bed and began staring at the ceiling. His thoughts were cascading round and round, moving bumper cars without drivers just smashing into each other. He knew his father had taken the money from his mom's purse. But how could he "narc" on his own father? He also knew that his mom needed the money. He did not know what to do. It was a lousy spot for a 12-year old to be in. His eyes filled up with tears and he had to breathe in deeply through his nose to clear out the fluid that had started to run out of it. He wiped his nose with the back of his hand, took in another deep breath and fell asleep.

The next morning Tracey dropped Jake at school. It was another routine stop on another routine day. Cars would pull up in front of the school and the turn up a long curved driveway. Each car would stop momentarily as the student being dropped off would get out. Sometimes two or three cars emptied at the same time. The process was fairly efficient and the line usually moved right along.

It is strange how a seemingly mundane, simple moment can sometimes cause an emotional tsunami to explode and inundate those in its path. Jake got out of the car and began to walk towards the school. At the same time Tracey began to drive away. Suddenly Jake turned and ran back toward the car yelling , "Mom, hey Mom, wait up! Wait up!"

Tracey heard him and stopped. As he reached the passenger side door she rolled the window down. "What wrong sweetie?"

"I forgot, I needed five dollars for Mr. Petrossian's science class today. It was supposed to be in last week."

Tracey knew she had the money in her purse from Judi and said, "Oh sure hon, no problem."

Tracey looked inside her purse and there was no money there. She instantly had a sickening feeling engulf her whole being. She started yanking papers out of the purse and fumbling through them. The line of cars was quickly turning into a traffic jam. "Jake, I know I had money in here. I can't find it. I don't understand. Where is it?"

Drivers were now starting to honk their horns and some were trying to get around Tracey's truck. Jake had the same sick feeling his mom had but his feeling came because he knew the truth. He wished so badly that he had never asked her for the lousy five dollars but how was he to know what was going to happen. Tracey took a breath and said, "Jake, just tell Mr. Petrossian I'll bring the money after school. Okay? Tell him I forgot my money. It must have fallen out at home."

Jake stared at his mom. His mind was racing. He knew the truth. His dad had taken it. Should he tell. His mom should not have to go through this. *What should I do? What should I do? Should I tell her?* He just blurted it out, "Mom, I think dad took the money from your purse."

"The woman's eyes opened wide and she said, "Excuse me Jake. What did you say?"

"Mom, I saw dad take the money out. You were in the bathroom. He must have forgotten to tell you."

"Oh, he did, did he?" Tracey put the brakes on her reaction and shut up. She thought for a moment. She did not want to upset Jake who was obviously already upset. She looked her boy in the eye. "Thanks for telling me. At least I know where the money is. I thought I had lost it or something. Now, get into school and tell Mr. Petrosssian I'll bring him the money after school."

Horns were honking and traffic was backed up right down the street. Tracey said, "Oh my God Jake, I had better move this truck before they call the police on me."

Jake, feeling relieved by his mom's reaction to the missing money, said, "Okay Mom, see you later."

Tracey pulled away from the school and she was furious. Her plan had been to drop Jake off and then head over to the Cash-Advance Store on Robert's Blvd. Besides giving cash-advances it was also the place to pay utility bills. Tracey had promised the power company $50.00 by noon on Monday. She did have her emergency ten dollar bill she had put in with the registration. She found it and put it in her pocket. She headed straight home to confront her husband about the money.

As Tracey drove home her anger began morphing into a disdain for the recent actions of Bob and these feelings were causing her to actually dislike him. She did not understand these strange and scary feelings. She loved Bob, had always felt secure with him and trusted him totally.

Now, feelings of contempt for his behavior were turning into feelings that were making Bob into a person that Tracey did not even like. How can you love and not like someone at the same time? It was sort of like mixing mustard with vanilla ice cream. It just could not work.

She started thinking, *Well, maybe Jake is wrong. If he's not wrong Bob better have that money. Jake's just a kid. He can't be wrong. That is his father. Oh God, he tattled on his own father. He's going to hate himself for that. Maybe not. I won't tell Bob that Jake told me. Get a grip girl, he told you innocently enough. Oh my God, I can't trust my husband anymore. Judi's right, I do need help. I cannot stand this. Maybe I had better go to Nar-Anon. I know, maybe I should talk to that priest. Stop Tracey—go home and find out what is going on. You are driving yourself crazy. Just go home.*

When Tracey pulled up to the house Bob was outside talking to a guy in a gray SUV. Tracey did not know who it was and when she stepped from her truck Bob waved her over. "Hey Tracey, you remember Zack Covello from Bildot?"

Tracey only knew Zack in a cursory way from the Bildot days and really knew nothing about him. He had always given her "bad vibes" and then she found out that it was Zack that had introduced Bob to pain pills. That was it for Tracey. She could not stand Zack Covello and did not want him at their house. Tracey responded coldly, "Oh yes, hello Zack."

She turned from Zack quickly and said to Bob, "I have to talk to you. It is very important."

Bob and Zack both felt Traceys' cold indifference wrap itself around them. Bob looked at Zack and rolled his eyes upward, his embarrassment at his wife's behavior obvious. Zack sort of gave a hint of a smile and said, "Okay then, Bob. We'll talk soon. I have to go. See you, Tracey."

By the time Zack pulled away Tracey was already halfway up the driveway. Bob ran after her. "Hey, what the hell was that all about? You were rude as hell to my friend."

"What was he doing here? Making a drug drop?"

"A drug drop! Are you nuts? He was just in the neighborhood and stopped by to say hello. That's all. What's your problem?"

Tracey got right to the point. "What's my problem? Actually, I have two problems. First of all, I do not like that man. I do not know him, I do not trust him and I know he is not your friend. Secondly, my other problem is that I was supposed to pay the power company $50.00 this morning. I knew I had $80.00 in my purse and when Jake asked me for five dollars for science class the $80.00 was not there. You wouldn't know anything about that would you Bob?"

Bob Slider was a good man but he had chosen to become "best friends" with some extremely influential stuff. His 30 mg. Roxicodone and 1 mg. Xanax had become his masters. A little marijuana once in a while wasn't hard to take either. He was also a lousy liar.

Looking as if he was a child who had just been caught with his hand in the proverbial "cookie jar" he said, "Uh—what? $80.00? No, why should I? You mean you lost $80.00?"

"You're a filthy liar Bob. I know you took that money. It's written all over your face. Well, I need it to pay the electric bill or we will be shut off this afternoon. Give it back to me."

Bob began to get angry. "Okay Tracey, fine. I did take the money. So what? I needed it for some medicine."

"Oh God, please don't tell me it's gone. Oh, wait a minute, I get it. So that is why Zack was here. He really is your supplier. He sells you drugs. I have to pay the electric bill with that money. Please Bob, tell me it isn't all gone."

Bob felt foolish and a bit guilty about what he had done. He also felt better knowing that he had just scored with Zack. The 'better' feeling dominated the 'guilty' feeling. "You know what Tracey, I can't believe you would rather see me suffer with this back pain than have the lousy $80.00 that can give me some pain relief. "

"Give me that money. I have to pay the electric bill."

"I don't have it Tracey. It's gone. What can I tell you. I'll make a few calls and see what I can do."

Tracey Slider stood there, absolutely flabbergasted. Who was this man in Bob Slider's body. Where did he come from? "You're going to make a few calls and see what you can do? Have you lost your mind? Call who? Zack Covello maybe. You going to ask him to give you some of MY money back so I can pay the light bill."

Bob did not want to hear anymore. "Please Tracey, can you just stop with all your paranoia. I'm tired of it."

"Bob, the bill is supposed to be paid by noon or they will turn us off today. Do you understand what is happening here?"

"I'll call them up and tell them we need another day or two." "Sure, you do that. Good luck."

"You're so negative, Tracey. I said I would take care of it and I will."

"The bill is delinquent, Bob. They do not give extensions on delinquent bills. Thanks a lot."

Tracey was like a prizefighter who had been dazed from a sharp left hook to the side of the head. Her jumbled thoughts were moving slowly and she appeared lethargic as she went into the kitchen to sit down. She sat, placed her elbow on the table, closed her eyes, lifted her arm and began rubbing her forehead with her fingers. She had to pick Jake up at 2:30 and she had to be at work by 4 p.m. Bob was supposed to see his probation officer at 10:30 a.m. She sat and rubbed and rubbed her forehead. She did not know what to do.

*

*

*

CHAPTER 13

"Lights On—Lights Off"

Bob was in the bathroom shaving. Staring at himself in the mirror he was not sure who was looking at whom. He had fallen into a terrible place and did not know how to climb out. He thought that he wanted to but he also thought that he had no choice but to be where he was. He continued staring, just holding the razor still by his cheek as he and his image glared at each other. There was conflict raging between the two. Then he saw himself reach into the mirror and slice open that other guy's throat. He gasped as blood spewed out on the inside of the mirror.

"Old Bob" was feeling guilty about how he had been treating his wife. He loved her and he needed her and he had no idea what he would ever do without her. Yet, he did not give a damn about what he was doing to her. Slowly, he reached for the mirror. He realized he had not actually broken it. He took his hand to wipe some of the blood away and realized that it was only fog. "New Bob" looked and began to feel sorry for himself. *Damn, it ain't right that I'm not allowed to drive.*

Tracey was still sitting at the kitchen table and she was feeling lonely. She missed her husband, the guy that made her laugh, the guy that was always upbeat and acted goofy and would sneak up on her and tickle her in her sides and she would scream out, "Stop!" while loving every second of it. She was in a fight and she was in it alone. She needed her man back.

Tracey's forearms were leaning on the table and her hands were unconsciously fumbling around with some of the papers that were laying there. There were some bills and coupons and a notice from Jake's school and the church bulletin from Sunday. Tracey, her mind in neutral, pulled it towards her and flipped it open. Something in the upper left hand corner caught her eye.

Ironically, it was an announcement for an AA meeting. She lifted the bulletin and began to read. There were AA meetings every Thursday evening at 7p.m in the Sacred Heart Parish Hall. The announcement was followed by the Serenity prayer. *God, grant me the serenity to accept the things I cannot change, the courage to change the things that I can and the wisdom to know the difference.* Tracey read the prayer and was moved by its simplicity. She read it again and then she read it again.

She suddenly felt a bit more powerful. This was a message of hope that had been unexpectedly given to her. It was not an earth-shattering moment or anything like that. It was, however, like a sign posted on a road to nowhere that gave the traveler a sense that a rest stop was not too far away. She folded the bulletin into four smaller squares and placed it in her purse. She stood and said, "Hey Bob, we have to leave for your appointment. You ready?"

Bob came out from the bathroom and said, "Okay, I'm ready."

He did not say anything else and Tracey watched as her husband walked outside and got into the truck. She was about to step outside when something made her stop. She removed the church bulletin from her purse and opened it again. Directly under the announcement for the AA meetings was a small blurb about the St. Vincent de Paul Society. Tracey, without hesitating, pulled out her cell phone and called the number.

She left a message simply asking that someone return her call. She flipped the phone closed and looked at it. She could not believe that she had made such a call in such a spontaneous way. She was actually glad she had done it. A shiver ran down her spine.

Husband and wife barely spoke during the twenty minute trip to the probation office. Tracey parked the truck and said to Bob, "You won't be long. I'll just wait here, okay?"

"Yeah, sure, no problem."

Tracey watched as Bob slowly walked toward the entrance of the six story, concreteand glass municipal office building that took up more than half a city block. She continued watching, noticing how much smaller he was getting as he got further and further away from her. The once big, burly guy who always walked tall and erect, exhibiting an air of quiet self-confidence, seemed to have become older, slower and stooped at the shoulders. She had never actually paid attention to him just walking away from her. He looked pathetic and she shuddered.

Tracey reached into her purse and once again lifted out the church bulletin. She flipped it open and, for the second time in less than an hour, began to read the Serenity Prayer. The funny thing was she had not really thought about doing this. She just did it because her brain wanted a temporary, non-narcotic, gentle sedative. She read it four or five times and then thought it one final time with her eyes closed. Then she opened her eyes and said it out loud. She had it memorized. The best part was it began working as soon as she finished saying it.

Tracey took a deep breath and watched as Bob walked through the entrance doors. It was at this point in time that she began to develop a resolve and determination that she was not going to lose her husband to a nether world of drugs, drug pushers and self-pity. She got out of the truck and began the walk to the building entrance. She was angry.

She moved toward the building thinking how even with the bright, Florida sun washing over it, the place still looked curiously cold and bleak. It stood there, surrounded by parking lots filled with vehicles. Except for the forty-foot tall Queen Palm trees spaced about 50 feet a apart around the perimeter of the property, everything outside the building was exposed to the intense sun. Tracey realized she could not have waited in the car even if she kept the A/C running.

Once inside the lobby she had to pass through a metal detector and leave the contents of her purse and pockets in a tray that was inspected. It was the first time she had actually waited inside for Bob and the experience was a "wake-up call" because she realized what a mess the Slider family had become. She began to pray again this time just more or less talking to God. He was becoming a very close Friend and she was beginning to enjoy the relationship.

Tracey sat on a pre-fab plastic bench that was anchored to the travertine mosaic of manatees sleepily swimming near Weedon Island. She watched as all the different people came and went going this way and that absorbed in their own anxious lives. Besides the offices of the Probation Department this was also the county courthouse where trials were held, traffic fines were paid, real-estate records were kept along with marriage records, divorce decrees, child-welfare cases and custody information etc. It was a big place and many people came and went. Tracey Slider did not want to be there.

After about ten minutes Bob stepped from the elevator. He saw Tracey sitting along the wall and walked over and plopped down next to her. He did not say anything but instead let out a big sigh. Naturally, Tracey took the bait and asked, "Okay, what's wrong this time?"

Bob leaned his head back against the wall. His eyes were closed and his lips tightly held together. He took in a deep breath and a tear came from the corner of his right eye. Then one came from the other eye. Tracey was shocked. "What is going on? What happened?"

Bob could not speak. He just shook his head back and forth and then lowered his head into his hands. Tracey, now upset herself, grabbed his one hand and held it tightly. "Bob, please, what is going on. Why are you so upset?"

He lifted his head and said, "For crying out loud Tracey, I did not have the $30.00 fee. She says 'give me something, anything, even five dollars.' Well, I didn't have a freaking penny in my pocket. So I have until 5 p.m. to pay or she is violating me to jail. That's why I'm so upset."

Tracey was disgusted. "Oh for God's sake, what is wrong with you? Why didn't you say something to me before you went up there? I have ten dollars. They have to take whatever you have. Let's just go back up and give her the ten dollars. I can't believe you didn't mention it going in."

"Look Tracey, you made such a big deal about the $80.00 I didn't want to ask you if you even had $10.00. Okay?"

The elevator doors opened and Bob went to get on. Tracey grabbed his arm and pulled him backward. She was furious and said with at least ten people in earshot, "If you think for one damn minute you can pin this fiasco on me, think again. What, you were afraid to ask me? What, am I your big mean 'old lady' that treats you like a dog or something. All of a sudden you are afraid of me? Give me a break, Bob. I think you have put yourself on a self-destruct course and I am telling you that Jake and I are not going along for the ride."

The elevator had made a return trip and this time Tracey stepped into it and pushed the button for the third floor. She did not look at Bob as he slowly followed her in. Together they went and paid the $10.00 toward his parole visit. The rule was that even one dollar would be accepted if that was all you had and the balance would be tacked on the back end of the parole.

Tracey and Bob Slider left the building walking side by side and it was as if each of them was alone . There was no conversation and no interaction whatsoever. They might have been strangers. The quiet disconnect continued during the entire 20 minute drive home. Bob did not know what to say. He also knew that if he said anything, anything at all, it would be Tracey's cue to unload on him.

Tracey pulled into the driveway and pushed the shift up into neutral before the truck had fully stopped. It was like jamming on the brakes and the two of them flew forward as the vehicle stopped short. Bob yelled, "What the hell are you doing? You trying to kill us and wreck the truck too?"

Tracey turned and glared at him. "Is that it?"

He looked at her and knew the storm was about to open up and rain down hard on his head. "Whaddaya mean, is that it?"

"Don't play dumb with me Bob. Just don't. You know what I mean."

The truth was, he did not know for sure. His mind was racing. *Is this about the $80.00? Must be. No wait, she wasn't that pissed off on the way there. It must be the fee. That's another ten bucks. Oh man, she is just pissed off at everything. I guess I can't blame her. Wait a second, that's bull crap. It wasn't my fault I got arrested.* "Look Tracey, I'm sorry about the money and all but---"

She held up her hand and stopped him mid-sentence saying, "Whatever, I don't care."

She got out of the truck, slammed the door and walked quickly toward the house. Bob watched and noticed her wiping the tears from her eyes as she disappeared from view. "Oh great," he moaned out load. "This is going to be just great."

He went into the house and headed into the kitchen and sat down at the table. He heard Tracey in the bathroom and just waited. He was thinking he would just let her vent away and then she would have to go and pick up Jake and by then it would be over. A few moments passed by and Tracey came out from the bathroom. She looked at Bob and with a condescending look spread across her face said, "Okay, love of my life, now what?"

Bob nervously shrugged and Tracey glared at him. He held up his hands, "What? What is it? Just say it, will you."

"What is it? Let me show you, what it is."

She moved next to the wall and flicked the light switch up and down. Nothing happened. Bob was momentarily puzzled but it only took a few seconds for the reality to smack him between the eyes. "Oh shit---No power."

Tracey, raising her voice said, "No power is right. Way to go Bob Slider. Way to go. I think I will let you explain to your son, Jake, how his father took the money for the electric bill and spent it on some freaking pain pills instead. "

Bob was thinking fast and furiously. Quickly he said, "Can you call them and see if they will still take the $50.00?"

"And what should I say, oh, forgive us please but my husband needed to buy some drugs so we were not able keep our agreement?"

"Oh God, Tracey, just call and ask. If they agree I can get $50.00."

Tracey, furious and hurt, also felt a sense of hope coming from Bob's words. "Fine, I'll call them. I don't know where you are going to get the fifty bucks but I'll go along with you for now."

Tracey called and after 20 minutes of going through voice-mail directions and waiting on hold she got through to a real live person. The customer service rep listened and agreed to accept the $50.00. There was a catch. They also wanted an additional $25.00 for a reconnect fee which was basically a punishment for not living up to the agreement to pay before noon.

Tracey, angry and disgusted, hung up the phone. She looked at Bob and said, "We need $75.00, fifty for the payment and another twenty-five to reconnect. If we bring them that amount they will turn us back on."

Bob said, "Damn Tracey, that's almost like extortion. They want an extra $25.00 or they won't give us our electricity back. That seems criminal." "Maybe so, Bob, maybe so. But that is the way it is and we cannot do one damn thing about it except pay it. So, you said you can get fifty. What about the rest?"

"Give me a few minutes."

She watched as he went out to the garage. Almost immediately she heard banging and clanging and stuff being moved this way and that. She looked out the front window and saw him loading things into the back of the pick-up. Fifteen minutes later he came back into the house and said, "Well, I'm sure glad I didn't sell everything at the yard sale. I want you to drive me over to 'Big Jim's Pawn Shop'. I can hock all of those power tools and get at least a hundred bucks for them."

Tracey's first thought was that he had sold her car and held onto most of his tools.

She did feel relieved though, and perked up a bit. She was not about to smile though. These were his prized tools and he would need them again. "Well, okay, I guess we have no choice. I have never been to a pawn shop. You can get them back, right?"

"Sure Trace, they hold them as collateral, that's all. You have to pay interest on theamount they give you. It is a simple process."

She shrugged and off they went. This was the first time either of them had ever been so desperate that they were forced to pawn anything to get cash. Feelings of relief combined with shame joined together forming an uncomfortable new feeling that they had never experienced before. When they parked the truck in the pawnshop's driveway Tracey took a deep breath, reached over and squeezed her husband's hand. She said, "Don't worry, things will be all right."

He smiled slightly and, feeling the love, said, "Yeah, they will. Okay, you wait here and I'll take care of this."

Bob began carrying his power tools into the pawn shop. He had his worm drive circular saw, a sawz-all, his router, router bits and router table, and his compound miter-saw and table and it took him three trips to get everything inside. The clerk, who had been watching Bob, walked over to him and said, "Is that it?"

Bob nervously answered, "Well yeah, that's it. Should I have more?"

The guy was totally indifferent. It was a situation where if you were not so bloody desperate you might abruptly leave. Bob felt like a 'low-life' and all the guy had said was, "Is that it?"

"So, whaddaya want to do with this stuff?"

"I want to pawn it. Truth is, I need $75.00 to get the lights turned back on and I know all of this stuff is worth way more than $75.00"

The guy shrugged and said, "I'll give you fifty bucks."

Bob was stunned. "Fifty bucks? You gotta be kidding me. The circular saw is a worm drive commercial saw. It cost two hundred and fifty bucks alone. And that was wholesale. C'mon man, I need $75.00, not $50.00. Give me a break, will ya."

The guy did not care. "Look pal, we have tons of this stuff here. We certainly don't need any more circular saws. That's the best I can do. Fifty bucks, take it or leave it."

Bob filled out the paper work, showed his ID, had his thumb print taken and was handed $50.00. As he walked back to the truck and his waiting wife he felt sick to his stomach. He had been demeaned and he felt awful. Tracey could tell by his body language that Bob had been through a difficult few moments. He slowly got into the truck and she asked, "So, did everything go all right? Did you get the $75.00?"

An unexpected tear came from the corner of Bob Slider's eye. Looking straight ahead, he reached into his shirt pocket, pulled out the fifty and handed it to Tracey. "That's all I could get."

"All of that stuff and that is all they would give you. That is sad. Well, don't worry. You said we can get it all back and we will. Between the power company wanting an extra twenty-five and this place almost taking your stuff for free we are really having a day of it. Tell you what, take this and go get some more money."

She slid off her engagement ring. It was worth well over a thousand dollars. She handed it to Bob. "Don't say a word. Just go and get some more money."

He looked at the ring and stared at it. "Tracey, I can't---"

"Bob, just go. Please."

Ten minutes later Bob came back out with another $150.00. He handed it to Tracey. She counted it and said, "What? Only $150.00? Unbelievable. When you are down and out you sure can get stepped on. Okay, let me have the pawn tickets. I am going to make sure we get these things back."

Tracey had softened when she saw all of the tools that Bob was going to pawn. She knew how much he loved those tools and how hard that had to be for him to do. When her ring joined Bob's tools in the pawn shop they had each sacrificed personal things to help each other. Their actions created a huge crack in the shadowy barrier that had grown between them. They drove over to the Cash-Advance Store on Robert's Blvd and paid the electric bill. They still had $125.00 in their pockets.

Just as they were about to back out of the parking lot the phone rang again. Tracey answered and it was Pete from St. Vincent de Paul. Tracey apologized for calling and told Pete that they had managed to take care of the electric bill. Pete said, "Please Tracey, do not apologize. We are here for you if you need us. Simple as that. Tell me, are you okay with your water bill?"

Tracey was taken back. "Oh, Pete, yes I think so. Thanks for asking."

"No problem. Now, one more thing while I have you on the phone. We have our Christmas Giveaway coming up. You want in on it?"

"I don't know. What is it exactly?"

"You come to our parish center the Sunday before Christmas and we distribute a complete Christmas dinner to you plus we give you some kind of gift for your son."

"Thanks Pete, but I think we are okay. I did get a part time job in the supermarket so that has helped a lot."

"Well, good for you Tracey. Okay, if you get in a jam give us a shout. If I don't see you before, best wishes to you, Bob and Jake for a merry Christmas."

"Well, merry Christmas to you too, Pete. And thanks for all of your help."

Tracey closed the phone and Bob said. "What was that all about?"

Tracey, forgetting what she had already said to Pete, said, "Oh, that was Pete, from St. Vincent de Paul. He just called to see how things were going. That was nice of him don't you think?"

Bob said, "Yeah, well if he called you why did you apologize for calling him?"

Tracey sighed deeply and said, "Fine Bob, I did call them earlier because I had a feeling we were going to need some extra help today. That's all."

"So, now you're lying to me about stuff?"

"Damn it Bob, we just got a bit of a break and some relief and you start with me. I just did not want you to be embarrassed so I didn't say anything. I was worried about you and right away you get in my face. Unbelievable."

They did not speak the rest of the way home.

*

*

*

CHAPTER 14

Beginning Nar-Anon

Christmas was rapidly approaching and the family storm clouds that had begun to gather twelve months earlier were now on a collision course.

The reprieve from the murkiness between them lasted only a few days. Bob, able to renew his prescriptions at the beginning of the month, had already used twice the amount of prescribed pills. He should have had enough until New Year's but the way he was popping them he knew he would not make it through the middle of the month. As far as Bob was concerned his stash of pain relief pills was almost gone and it was not his fault. After all, 'no one understood' the pain he was in and he needed them. It was December 12. There were twenty days left before he would be eligible for a refill. His addiction rapidly began to expose itself.

As his amount of pills dwindled, Bob's personality took a noticeable downward spiral. He would get irritable, fidgety, pace around and be abrupt and demanding. There was no pleasing him and if he began to speak about something there was no sense answering him. He did not listen and what he was talking about usually was about his 'miserable existence' and how he was just a poor slob who had a few bad breaks. He even started to blame God, which was more or less a way to mock

Tracey who was now going to Mass every Sunday. "A lot of good all your damn praying is doing for us. If God was really listening to you this pain of mine would go away and He would help me find a job."

Tracey was at her wits end. She needed a break from the constant negativity. As for Jake, he was inside a vacuum he did not really understand. His dad had changed so much and his mom seemed so unhappy. He was keeping more and more to himself and also spending more and more time over at Tyler's. Why not? Tyler had his own TV, a Play Station 4, his own laptop and he had been given an iPod Touch for his birthday. Jake did not even have a TV anymore and it sure was no fun hanging around with his miserable dad and dispirited mom.

It was December 15 and Bob was almost out of pills. Jake was at Tyler's and Tracey was sitting in the kitchen looking across the room at the twinkling lights on the Christmas tree. There were no gifts under it yet and she was dragging herself down into the dumps thinking that Santa Claus might have to cancel his annual visit to the Slider home. Then the phone rang and it was Judi. "Hey Trace, how about we go to one of those Nar-Anon meetings I told you about? There is one over at Calvary Baptist Church at seven o'clock."

"Oh geez Judi, I don't know. Jake isn't home yet and I have to feed him. I'm not feeling so good and---"

Judi cut her off. "Tracey, it's me, Judi, remember. You don't have to give me any stories. Let's take Jake with us. It will do us all some good. We can grab a burger after."

"Oh Judi, I don't know. Isn't Jake too young for that kind of stuff?"

"Actually, they have a group that meets there called Narateen. It's for kids. He'll fit right in and it will do him a world of good."

Tracey agreed and left to pick up Jake who, surprisingly, was glad to leave Tyler's. Tracey said to him, "I thought you would give me an argument about coming home. But I understand. Sometimes it is just nice to be home and away from everything."

"Mom, Tyler and his mom are always fighting with each other. He talks to her like she's dirt or something. I don't like it. She IS his mom. It's not right. I told him that but he said that she don't care. I just wanted to get out of there. I'm glad you came and got me."

Once again Jake's developing maturity had shown through. Tracey smiled and said, "You're right Jake. It isn't right. I'm glad you can see that. So, how about you come along with me and Judi. We're going to a Nar-Anon meeting tonight."

"Oh man, come on Mom, gimme a break. I don't want to go to any dumb meeting. What is Nar-Anon anyway? Can't I just stay home and lie in my room by myself? Do I have to go?"

Tracey sighed and said, "Jake, you know Dad has a problem. You even brought it up to me. You told me you wanted to help, didn't you?"

"Well yeah, but what is Nar-Anon?"

"It is a place for people who have loved ones who are having drug issues. Judi's brother, Anthony, is a user and she goes to these meetings."

"Really mom, Judi's brother? I thought that was the guy with all the money and stuff."

"You mean, 'used to have'---not anymore. Anyway, Judi said the meetings have helped her a lot and she has learned a lot about addiction. They have a group called Narateen for kids like you. Let's go together. We can be teammates working together to help your dad. What do you say? Afterwards we'll stop for a burger somewhere."

She looked pensively at her boy waiting for his response. He looked back and shook his head up and down. The "teammate" analogy had hit home.

Bob was dozing on the sofa when they left and Tracey was relieved because she would not have to worry about him trying to go anywhere. Ever since his arrest she had the nagging fear that he should not be left alone and she could not get past the anxiety she felt. Usually, when Bob nodded off that way, he would be asleep for several hours. Tracey knew it was from the pills but she didn't care. He was home and could not get into any trouble. It was 6:30 p.m. when Tracey and Jake got into Judi's car and headed to the meeting.

~~~~~~

As soon as Bob heard Judi's car leave he got up. He had planned on leaving right after they did and had faked being asleep. Bob had a new prescription in his pocket and he had not told Tracey about it.

The law did not allow controlled substances to be renewed over the phone. They had to be physically picked up by the patient who had to bring the actual script to the pharmacy. If the patient was homebound that had to be confirmed before the pharmacist would release the drug for delivery. Tracey , as usual, had driven Bob to Dr. McCaba's office on December 1 for his check-up. It was also the day he could get the hand written script renewal for his pain meds.

There was one little detail that Bob had failed to share with his wife after that visit. Dr. McCaba was going away for the Christmas Holiday and was leaving on December 12 not to return until the middle of January. When Bob saw the doctor on December 1, the "good doctor" also handed Bob a script dated January 1. He said to him, "I don't like doing this but I will not be back until the middle of January and I want to make sure you have your script. Whatever you do, do not try to submit it before January 1st. They will not honor it and it could get you in trouble. Understand?"

Bob looked at the script and a strange, almost euphoric feeling filled him. One part of his brain was telling him he had just won the lottery. The other part was cowering in terror. Bob said, "Oh, absolutely Doc. I would never mess around with something like this. But thanks for filling it ahead of time."

"Okay then Bob, my best wishes to you and your family for a Merry Christmas. I'll see you the beginning of February."

Bob was an addict and the prescription was only going to lay dormant until Bob's supply of pills began to diminish. But, addicts always believe they need more than they have. Dr. Jeffrey McCaba may just as well have given a banana to a monkey and told the monkey not to eat it for a few days.

The anxiety started to build by December 5. Every day Bob would look at the script and think about tampering with it. Then he would hide it. By December 15 his anxiety was raging. Bob succumbed and carefully and meticulously changed the date on the script to the current date. He had some pills left but he was sure he "needed" more.

Bob always renewed his prescription at the supermarket where Tracey worked. She was also the one who usually picked it up for him. Not this time. He was not taking any chances that Tracey could discover what he was doing. Zack Covello had clued him in about the Kauflin Pharmacy that was across the street from Largo General Hospital over on Missouri Ave. It was an old-fashioned neighborhood pharmacy that had been in the area for over 40 years and it was always easy getting a script for a narcotic filled there. Most of the Kauflin customers always paid a bit more for their prescriptions and were more than willing to do so in exchange for the "prompt" courtesy they were shown.

Bob, a captive of the now illegally redated prescription, climbed into his truck and headed out to get his renewal. Six months earlier he was a solid, hard-working citizen, taking care of his family and doing the "right thing" every day. Now, ten days before Christmas, he was on probation, driving with a suspended license and carrying a falsified prescription for a controlled substance. He even had one of Tracey's checks in his pocket that he was going to use to pay for it. He did not look to see if the money to cover the check was in the account. If he would have only glanced at the check register he would have discovered that it was not. He simply did not care.

It turned out that none of that mattered because Bob never made it to Kauflin's Pharmacy. Ironically, he was rear-ended by a drunk driver on Missouri Ave., two blocks before he got to Kauflin's. Bob Slider, not at fault for the accident, would be on his way to jail right after the police checked his license and it came up as suspended. He would not get to present the falsified prescription and then attempt to pay for it with an overdrawn check. He would be going to jail and he would have no idea how fortunate he had been.

~ ~ ~ ~ ~ ~ ~ ~ ~ ~ ~ ~ ~ ~ ~ ~ ~ ~ ~ ~

An apprehensive Tracey followed by her nervous, self-conscious son, walked with Judi to the side door of the church meeting hall. Jake had an expression on his face as if he was being dragged to an opera or a ballet.

They entered the meeting room and there were about a dozen people milling about. There was a lectern in the front of the room, folding chairs randomly spread about and several long tables against the wall. One table was holding pamphlets and a sign-in sheet on one end and on the other end was a coffee urn, cold drinks, doughnuts and cookies. Judi saw a lady near the table and waved over to her. The lady smiled and waved back. Judi said to Tracey, "Come on Trace, I want to introduce you to Grace. She is more or less in charge here."

Tracey and Jake timidly followed Judi across the room as a dozen or more folks watched. Grace smiled as they neared her and Judi said, "Hi Grace, I want you to meet Tracey and her son Jake. This is their first time for them doing anything like this and they are both a bit nervous."

Grace was a stout, middle-aged woman with short, blond hair that was seemingly stuck to her head in a mass of small, tight curls. She had a big, round face emblazoned with a gentle smile and her twinkly blue eyes were filled with kindness. She reached out for Tracey's hand saying, "Hi Tracey, I'm so glad you will be joining us." Then she looked at Jake and shook his hand saying, "And you too, Jake. Thank you for coming tonight."

They both said "hello" to Grace and Grace asked them to take a seat anywhere they liked. Within five minutes everyone had almost reflexively arranged their chairs in a sort of semi-circle facing the podium and had sat down. Tracey and Jake were at the end of the row.

Grace stepped to the lectern in front of the group and asked everyone to say the Serenity Prayer along with her. Some people, Tracey included, already knew the prayer. For the folks that did not know the prayer, Jake among them, it was printed on a large poster that was hung on the wall. Everyone said it along with Grace, some reciting and some reading. Saying the prayer took less than 10 seconds.

After the prayer Grace asked who was there for the first time. Tracey, Jake and six others raised their hands. Grace explained that this was a "Beginner's Meeting" where some general information about the disease of addiction would be provided. These meetings would also be an opportunity where they could open their hearts and share with others, who were in similar situations, what they were going through with a family member. It was not mandatory for anyone to speak. Simply sitting and listening was also quite acceptable.

Grace then handed out sheets of paper on which were printed "The Twelve Steps of Nar-Anon Family Groups". She asked everyone to read them over and, after several moments, said, "Okay, I would ask you all to read out loud the First Step on the sheet.

Slowly but surely someone began to read and all the others quickly followed saying, "We admitted we were powerless over the addict and that our lives had become unmanageable."

When everyone finished reading the First Step there was a silence that ensued. Grace looked out over the small group of people and effectively let what they had just read, sink into their minds. After a few moments had passed she said, "Would anyone here like to make a comment on the First Step?"

No one responded and Grace said, "Does everyone agree with the First Step. Are we or are we not powerless over the addict we love? Can we change them by ourselves?"

Despairing looks appeared on the faces looking up towards Grace and most of the heads began slowly moving back and forth. A woman stood up and said, "Hi, my name is Angela and my husband is a prescription junkie and he has almost destroyed our family because of his incessant need for pain pills. He calls them medication. What a crock that is. Maybe they used to be pain pills but now they are the drugs he is addicted to. So, yes, the First Step is correct. We are powerless over the addict. They do not care anymore. They just don't care."

Angela began to cry and could not continue. She sat down, lowered her head and reached into her purse for a tissue. Jake stared at this woman and actually felt her pain and actually wanted to go over and hug her. He also knew what she had said was true. It scared him. His mom, sitting next to him, was thinking that maybe the woman should stop crying and get a bit tougher with her husband.

Grace said, "Thank you Angela. Okay, since this is a Beginner's Meeting I should explain something to you all about prescription drugs. I'm not a doctor or anything like that. I'm just like you, dealing with a loved one who is an addict. But here is what I have learned. Just as you have no control over the addict in your life, addicts have lost control of their lives to the drug. Prescription drugs are usually opioids and cause a rush of dopamine into the system. Dopamine makes us feel good and, given enough of it, euphoric. The brain decides that it needs the opioid for survival, like eating or drinking water. It follows that the addict becomes a prisoner of this false need. It is very hard to overcome. Some are quite successful, others not so fortunate."

Tracey raised her hand. Grace said, "Please, stand and tell us who you are. Just your first name."

Tracey stood up and said, "Hi, I'm Tracey. I was wondering if you could sum up in just a few words how coming to these meetings will help someone like me deal with my husband's addiction. And how will it help my son?"

Grace smiled and looked around the room. Tracey had asked a question that was dancing in everyone's minds. Grace said, "I can only speak for myself. I have been coming to these meetings for over a year and here is what I know. I am powerless over the addict as we read in

Step 1. I have also learned to be able to say 'NO' which has been very hard because it always seemed that everything that went wrong was my fault or someone else's fault. I know now it is not. Saying NO is truly a challenge because the addict refuses to accept it and then usually acts as if they are a victim and nobody understands or cares. I'm sure you all know what I mean."

The meeting lasted 45 minutes. They learned that Nar-Anon was not a religious program but it was a spiritual one. There would be six Beginner Meetings and then the beginners would begin attending regular meetings. Jake would start the Narateen meetings on the same evening as the regular meetings but in a classroom inside the adjacent school.

They left the meeting both feeling a bit uplifted and also a bit scared. Bob Slider, husband and father, had been cast in a different light. He was an addict. He was a victim of his accident. He was a victim of unwanted pain. He also needed to accept responsibility for his actions. It was a two-edged sword. They definitely needed to attend more meetings.

There was a Burger-Barn on Haney Blvd. three blocks north of Dr. Nelson's office. Judi parked the car and they walked in. The emotional effects of the evening were acting like a subtle sedative and it was obvious that they were worn out. They ordered their food and sat down at a booth next to a window. Slowly they removed the burger wrappers and began to eat. Tracey, feeling the need to force some conversation, said, "Is your burger okay, Jake?"

"I guess."

"Well, mine could have been cooked a bit more."

Judi said, "Don't eat it Tracey. Bring it back."

"Oh no, I've had worse. It's fine. I'm just tired, that's all."

"Yeah, me too. It will be good to get home. So, tell me, what did you think about the meeting?"

Tracey looked over at Judi and shook her head. "Judi, the truth is when I was sitting there I kept telling myself this was no place for me. That these things were not happening in my life. That I should get up and just wait outside for you. But when that woman Sally got up and talked about her lights being turned off, reality hit me. We were just like each other so I guess I do belong there."

Jake said nothing. Tracey turned to him and put her arm around his shoulder, pulled him toward her and kissed him on the top of the head. She did not say anything to him and he simply absorbed the love that came from his mom. And then they were done and headed home.

It was almost 9 p.m. when Judi pulled into her driveway. They said their good-nights and they all gave each other hugs. Judi walked to her front door while Tracey and Jake walked toward their house a hundred feet away. Both mother and son walked up their driveway and into the house and it was not until Tracey had closed the bathroom door that a light bulb lit up inside her head. She yelled out, "Oh my God, the truck is gone, the truck is gone!"

She ran from the bathroom hollering out, "Bob, Bob, where are you? Don't tell me you took the truck. Are you crazy or something? Where are you? Oh my God, you took the truck, didn't you? You took the truck." She was talking to someone who was not even there.

Jake had come out of his room and was standing there feeling the dark cloud of crisis fill the entire house. "Dad took the truck somewhere. Is that what you're yelling about?"

"Yes Jake, it is. He is not here and neither is his truck. What should I do?"

"Call his cell mom. Call his cell."

Tracey snapped back to the real world and patted her boy on the arm. "I'm sorry Jake—it's just that---"

Jake cut her off, "Mom, just call dad, okay."

Tracey pulled the phone from her purse and speed dialed Bob. She waited and redialed when voice-mail kicked in. The same thing happened and this time she left a message. "Bob Slider, where are you. Where is your truck. Are you all right? Are you crazy or something. Call me as soon as you hear this Bob. You better call me, you're scaring me, Bob. Oh God, where are you?"

She turned off the phone and stood there, a blank look covering her face. There was nothing she could do, not a thing. She had no vehicle and even if she did she had no idea where to look. It was frustrating not being able to do anything but she had no damn choice whatsoever. She had to wait until he called or came home. Jake said, "You know Mom, they talked about this stuff at the meeting. We can't do anything about it. All we can do is take care of what is inside ourselves."

Tracey looked at her boy amazed that he had taken all of that in. She said, "Wow Jake, I guess you were paying attention. Well, you are right but not knowing where he is has me crazy. I think I am more scared than anything."

Jake, almost 13, went over to his mom and gave her a hug. He was being a man for his mother without realizing it. She hugged him back finding some needed peace and comfort. It was the reverse of the restaurant hug 30 minutes earlier. They sat on the sofa next to each other, turned on the TV and began the wait for the missing man of the house.

*

*

*

Chapter 15

Handcuffs and a Heart Attack

It was approximately 8 p.m when Bob Slider's world caved in on him. As the handcuffs closed tightly around his wrists tears began to ooze from his eyes. He could not believe what was happening. All he wanted was a few pain pills. Instead he was being arrested and going to jail. It was not fair. It was not right. He didn't do anything. For crying out loud, the other guy drove into him.

Bob began to breathe rapidly and then a dull, aching pain gripped his upper back inside his right shoulder. Bob instinctively tried to reach up with his left hand to grab hold of the shoulder and rub it but the handcuffs prevented him from doing so. He began to sweat profusely and then hyperventilate. The fear and emotion of the moment were about to bring him down.

The young police officer noticed his new prisoner's distress and said to him, "C'mon man, try to relax. You'll probably be home in a couple of hours. I'm just following procedure. It will be all right."

Bob's brain heard the words but his heart ignored them. With his hands shackled behind him the big guy could not break his fall. He went down like a ton of bricks landing on his left side and smacking the side of his head into the pavement. The cop was stunned and said, "Oh no, I don't believe it." He called for the paramedics and knelt down next to his fallen prisoner. He checked to see if Bob was breathing. He was.

If you were arrested and were taking a prescribed controlled substance, that was just too bad. You would not be getting any of that 'medication' until you were released. Rules were rules and many a new inmate spent horrible nights in the county jail sweating profusely, vomiting, screaming, doubled up in pain, as they involuntarily withdrew either from alcohol or prescription pain 'meds'. Rehabilitation could not be forced on anyone. Fortunately for Bob, Boulevard General Hospital was only a few blocks away. Bob would get some kind of meds versus getting none.

The firehouse was less than a quarter of a mile in the other direction. The ambulance was on the scene in less than five minutes and the paramedics immediately took over. The handcuffs were removed and they immediately checked Bob's pulse and blood pressure. An oxygen mask was placed over Bob's nose and mouth and an IV of saline was started. Fifteen minutes later Bob Slider was in the emergency room at the hospital being stabilized.

The arresting police officer, following procedure, stationed himself outside the ER. As soon as he was permitted, he would be handcuffing Bob to the bed he was in. The drunk driver who had smacked into Bob's truck starting the whole chain of events was taken to jail by a back-up officer.

~~~~~~~~~~~~~~~~~~~~~~~~~~~~~

Tracey and Jake, exhausted from the emotions of the day, had unexpectedly fallen asleep on the sofa. Both were in sitting positions with their heads leaned back on the top edge of the sofa. Both were snoring loudly. Jake's snoring woke his mom. When she opened her eyes and looked over at the clock in the kitchen and realized it was after ten, she yelled out, "Oh my God, it's ten o'clock. He's not home yet." She shook Jake, "Wake up, Jake, wake up."

The boy opened his eyes and sat up quickly. "What—what's going on? Where is dad?"

"He's not home yet. He's not home."

"Where is he Mom? Where did he go?"

Tracey shook her head and pulled out her phone. She dialed Judi. "Hello---"

"Judi, I'm sorry to call you so late but I'm sort of freaking out. Bob is not home yet---"

"What? What do you mean—yet? Where did he go? How long has he been gone?"

"He wasn't here when we got home. The truck is gone too. I'm scared to death, Judi. I don't know what to do."

"Oh my God, and he has a suspended license. Okay Trace, put on some coffee. I'm coming over. We'll figure this out."

"Thanks, Judi. The door is unlocked."

Tracey put on a fresh pot of coffee and ten minutes later she and Judi were sipping it from their cups. Jake, sitting with them at the dining room table, was drinking Mountain Dew. They were all getting a late night dose of caffeine. They needed it. Judi said, "Well, how many places could he or would he go? He knows he isn't supposed to drive. He wouldn't go very far, right?"

"I don't know, Judi. He may have gone to see that guy, Zack. That is all that I keep thinking about. He went to see Zack Covello and now he's in trouble."

"Whoever Zack is you sure sound like you don't like him."

"Judi, he worked at Bildot with Bob. He started Bob on those pain pills years ago and I know Bob has called him to get some."

"I'm calling Tommy. I want him to call a bail bond office. They'll know if he got in trouble. They are on line with the county jail and getting fresh information all the time."

Judi called Tommy and he came over. He was not very upset about Bob's whereabouts. As a guy he just figured that he would be back and that the women were just overreacting. So he tried to be cool and calm their nerves a bit. "Trust me, he's fine. I'll bet you he will walk in here any minute."

"Tommy, while we are waiting for that minute to pass do you think you could call 'Big Al's' and check. If they have nothing on their computer then we are okay and can cross that off our worry list. Okay."

Okay Judi, I get the sarcasm. I'll call. I'll call."

Tommy did call and as he waited quietly for them to give a response to his question the two women and one 12-year old just stared at him waiting to hear a Yay or a Nay. It was a Nay. There was no Robert Slider on any police blotters. They all breathed big sighs of relief. Tommy never let on that he was beginning to have a real bad feeling about the whole situation. He surely was.

～～～～～～～～～～～～～～～～～～～～～～～～～～～～～

The ER doctor was quite sure Bob had suffered a severe anxiety attack that mimicked a heart attack. He ordered a 1 mg. shot of Ativan to temper Bob's anxiety. Bob was resting comfortably in the emergency room. His heart was beating perfectly, his blood pressure was normal and his respirations were fine. The doctor on-call told the police officer that Bob had suffered an apparent anxiety attack but that he would need some follow up testing just to be sure it was not a full blown heart attack. The officer was given permission to go back into his prisoner and 'secure' him.

As soon as Bob saw the policeman walking toward him his heart rate began to increase. When the cop nonchalantly squeezed the handcuff closed on his wrist and fastened the other side to the railing of the bed, Bob began to hyperventilate again and his heart rate soared to 160. The doctor heard the warning beep coming from the heart monitor and hurried over. He saw what was happening and said to the diligent policeman, "Is this man a wanted felon or something? I mean, is all this necessary? He's not going to try an escape. How about cutting the man some slack?"

"I'm just following procedure, doctor. This is what I am supposed to do."

"Look, I'll take full responsibility. As his attending physician I am telling you that the handcuffs are preventing his heart from regaining its natural rhythms. I gave him an anti-anxiety drug and it was working. Those cuffs have virtually cancelled that out. "

The policeman removed the cuffs from Bob's wrist and his heart rate immediately

began to decrease. The cop said, "Okay Doc. I see what you mean. Look, I have a bunch of paperwork to complete anyway. I'll be out in the waiting room."

The doctor smiled at him and proceeded to check Bob's pulse even though the heart monitor was flashing Bob's vital signs.

Bob was looking at them and they were talking about him and it was as if he was not even there. He kept quiet and just listened. His circumstances were not his to determine. He said to the policeman, "Officer, I really need to call my wife. She'll be freaking out wondering where I am. Can I call her and let her know what happened to her dumb husband."

The bit of self-deprecation softened the "newbie" cop a bit and he told Bob he could call his wife. Bob was not allowed to use his cell phone in the ER as it could interfere with telemetry within the hospital corridors so he was given a portable hand-held phone to use. Just as he was about to push the buttons to call Tracey someone said, "Bob, is that you?"

Bob lowered the phone and turned his head. It was Father Jim from Sacred heart Church. The priest said, "You do remember me, don't you? What happened to you?"

Bob was stunned to see Father Jim standing there and then he heard the doctor say, "Another late night call, Father?"

"Yes Scott, a sweet lady up in room 204, Ann Dowling. She was a parishioner. 94 years old and I managed to be with her at the end. Imagine that, 94 years old. Anyway, I use the ER as a shortcut when I leave the hospital and I noticed Mr. Slider in the bed here. He has a long way to go before he reaches 94 like Mrs. Dowling so I hope he is going to be all right."

Bob was thinking as quickly as he could. *Father called him Scott so they must be friends. What am I supposed to tell this priest? I don't even know the doctor's name except now he is Scott. What do I tell Tracey. Holy shit, I need a pill. How did I get into such a mess. At least the handcuffs are not on. The priest would freak out if he saw me in hand cuffs. Damn it, damn it.*

The doctor laughed a bit and said, "Yes Father, he should be fine. He may have a bumpy road ahead but I'm sure he'll be okay. Look, you talk to Bob and I will go check on some of my other ER patients. Good to see you Father."

"Yes, you too, Scott. Take care."

It was now the priest and the patient. The patient had a cop outside waiting to bring him to jail, he had a wife at home who had no idea where her husband was and now he had the parish priest standing by his hospital bed and all he could think about was roxycodone. Father Jim said to Bob, "So, what happened, Bob? That is sure a nasty looking scrape on the side of your face. Is that why you're here?"

Bob Slider could not help himself. He started to cry and shamefully covered his eyes with his big hand. Father Jim was bewildered. He had seen many folks break down in the hospital, especially after they had heard bad news. It could have been from a sudden death or an ominous diagnosis or possibly being told that their insurance was not in force. Many things triggered tears in a hospital setting. Father Jim waited a moment and then said, "Look Bob, Tracey is probably outside in the waiting room. I'll go outside and see if I can find her. I'll ask her what's going on, that's if you don't mind."

Bob instinctively blurted out, NO! Uh, no Father. She's not out there. She doesn't even know I'm here."

Father Jim's antennae shot up. He knew something was out of kilter with Bob Slider. He moved closer to the bed and looked at the big man lying there looking so pathetic. "Listen Bob, maybe there was a twofold purpose for me being here tonight. Mrs. Dowling was number one. I was blessed. She was 94 and loved her God her whole life and gave of herself to so many people. I was able to watch her go on her journey to see the Lord. She was so at peace when she breathed her last. It was a beautiful thing to see."

The priest paused, looked at Bob and said, "I do not sense very much peace going on with you. So, maybe you are the second reason I am here tonight. I must ask, why doesn't your wife know you are here? You guys have not split up have you?"

"No Father, nothing like that. It's nothing like that."

Just then the police officer came back to Bob's cubicle. He poked his head in and saw the priest. His reaction shocked Bob because the cop blurted out, "Father Jim, how you doing. Longtime no see."

"Billy, how are you, son. Good to see you. It's been a long time."

"Sure has Father. A couple of years at least. You look good, Father."

"The priest turned to Bob and said, "Hey Bob, this is an old altar boy of mine, Billy Tyler. Billy graduated Sacred Heart School, must be about ten years ago, right Billy?"

"Nine Father, nine years ago. Graduated college two years ago and here I am, a cop."

"So how do you and Bob know each other?"

The cop and the prisoner looked at each other not saying anything. The priest sensed the tension. He broke it by saying, "Okay fellas, what gives. I am a priest and you both know me so, come on, what is going on?"

Billy said to Bob, "He is my friend too, so do you want to tell him or should I?"

Bob teared up again and just made a motion with the back of his hand as if he were brushing some crumbs from a table. Billy took the cue and moved close to the priest and said, "I arrested him earlier tonight for driving with a suspended license. He is also on probation for DUI. He got so upset that his heart began racing and he collapsed. He was handcuffed and hit the side of his head on the asphalt. There you have it Father. I never met Mr. Slider before tonight."

Father Jim took a deep breath and said, "Oh, I see. Well now, that is an unexpected turn of events for me. Billy, can I talk to you outside for a minute?"

"Sure Father, sure. But I have to follow procedure and put the cuffs back on him.

"Okay Billy, do what you have to do. I'll wait outside in the waiting room. Try not to squeeze them too tight.""

Billy stepped over to Bob's bed, his handcuffs dangling from his hand. He turned and saw Father Jim walking away, the priest's subtle sarcasm ringing in his ears. Then he looked at Bob and saw the anxiety building in him as his face muscles seemed to contort. He said, "Tell you what, promise you won't try to escape and I'll put these away."

The young cop's attempt at levity worked better than any Ativan could have. Bob smiled a bit and said, "Thank you. I promise."

Father Jim brought Billy Tyler down the hall to a small prayer room that was near the entrance to the ER. They stepped inside and the priest closed the door. It was peaceful room, about 8 X 10 in size and it had a small desk with writing paper on it, a phone for people to use and a bible and some other inspirational materials. Father said, "This is nice and quiet. Okay Billy, I want to help this man and his family. What can I do?"

"Uh, look Father Jim, I don't know. Mr. Slider should not have been out driving. The irony is a drunk driver drove into him. He didn't do anything but, when we ran his license, he came up on the screen as having a record and being on probation. I had no choice but to arrest him."

"Billy, I want to call his wife. She needs to know what is going on. Secondly, I want you to do me a very big favor and hold off on taking him in. You can stall on that can't you?"

"Look Father, I would do anything for you but---but, gee, I don't know."

"Well, he has not been processed into the system yet, right?"

"Yes Father, that's true. The thing of it is---"

Father Jim interrupted and said, "Billy, I get it, okay. But I think I know what's going on with our friend in there and it is really not all his fault. He is a victim as much as he is perpetrator. But I have an idea and I need a bit of time. So, can you help me out?"

Billy Tyler, on the job for less than two years, had been indoctrinated into following procedure during his training at the academy. He was hoping that he was not going to be asked by his priest friend to take a serious chance with his job and his career. He was not sure what to do and was frightened. "Father Jim, I have to report in and let them know what is going on. What am I supposed to say?"

Father Jim saw the insecurity and angst in Billy's face and said, "Billy, I just want some time, maybe an hour or two. Look, he still has the IV stuck in his hand. It will be at least two hours before they remove the needle. So tell them the truth. "

Billy calmed down and said, "Okay Father, that makes sense. I think we'll still be here in two hours. Hey, how do you know it will be at least two hours?"

He shrugged, smiled coyly and said, "Well, I figure we need at least two hours, right?"

Billy chuckled. "Sure Father, I get it."

"Good, now I have to go talk to Bob."

"Okay Father, I'll go out in the waiting room and grab some coffee. Then I will report in and tell them the prisoner has not been discharged yet. We'll take it from there."

Billy Tyler walked out to the waiting room and Father Jim headed back to see Bob. But first he made a pit stop at the nurse's station. The ER nurse had her back to him and was looking inside a cabinet for some medications. Father said, "Hey Cathy, how are you doing?"

The woman turned her head and said as she turned it back, "Oh, Hi Father Jim. I didn't know you were here. What can I do for you?" The ER nurses all knew Father Jim who had made many an emergency visit to their job location. Father had, over the years, become friends with them. "Cathy, our friend in Bed 3, Mr. Slider, is he set for discharge?"

The woman turned to him and said, "Why Father, I think he has an escort waiting for him."

"Cathy, I know him and I was wondering if the possibility exists that it will be about two more hours before he is released?"

"No Father, that is not a possibility. Doctor Hilgren is on his way down to sign the release papers. He will be out of here in less than 20 minutes. I just have to remove the IV from his hand."

Father Jim smiled at the nurse who was looking at him knowing he had something up his sleeve. Father said, "Well, what is the chance that you might have something urgent to take care of with another patient and you cannot get to Mr. Slider for a while? Any chance of that?"

Cathy smiled coyly and said, "What do you mean by a while Father?"

"Well, you know, an hour or two. Would there be any harm if that IV stayed in a bit longer?"

She kept straight-faced and said, "Well, I do have to tend to some urgent paper-work in the triage room. So I guess It will be some time before I get back to him. But Father, it might be best to discuss this with Doctor Hilgren, don't you think?"

"Yes Cathy, I think so. One more thing, can you write down your fax number here. You may be getting a fax for me later. I'm not sure, but it is a possibility."

She jotted the number down and handed it to him. They both smiled at each other and went about their business. Father headed over to Bob's bed. When he got there he said, "How are doing Bob? Feeling better?"

"Well, I had an apparent heart attack and I am going to jail. I've had better days."

"Your wife must be frantic with worry. I would like to ask you if you mind if I call her. It might be better hearing all of this from me. What do you say?"

"I'm not sure about that. Hearing you telling her about me might really freak her out."

"Okay, good point. Your head seems pretty clear. Here, good luck."

He handed Bob the portable ER phone and watched him push the buttons. He stepped away from the bed as soon he heard Bob say, "Tracey, it's me."

Father Jim stood behind the curtain within earshot of Bob and listened carefully. He wanted some insight into the 'real' Bob Slider. He listened as Bob said, "Tracey, I'm okay. But I am in the hospital."

He could only imagine what Tracey was saying back so he tried to decipher it from Bob's comments. "Stop yelling Tracey, stop yelling. I'm okay. They think a heart attack."

Tracey screamed, "A heart attack! Oh my God, you had a heart attack?"

"Tracey please, calm down, I'm okay."

Father Jim had heard enough. He knew it was time to grab the phone. He stepped from behind the curtain and reached out his hand. Bob said, "Hey Tracey, Father Jim is here. He wants to talk to you."----------"Yes Tracey, Father Jim from Sacred Heart. Here he is."

"Hi Tracey, Father Jim here. Don't worry, Bob is okay. It seems he may have had a slight heart attack."

Tracey had Jake standing next to her on one side and Tommy and Judi standing on her other side. She said, "Father Jim, what is going on? How can he have a heart attack? He's only 38. What happened? What hospital is he in? How did he get to the hospital? Did you bring him there? Why are you there? Oh my God, is he dying?"

Father Jim became stern, "Tracey, please, take a deep breath and listen to me. He is NOT dying. He is okay. He is in some trouble however. He has been arrested. "

Tracey screamed out "Oh my God, no! Not again. Oh my God. Judi, he had a heart attack and he was arrested. Father Jim is at the hospital with him. We have to get over there. I have no vehicle. Can you take me?"

"Of course, Tracey. What hospital?"

"What hospital, Father?"

"Boulevard General."

"Okay, Father, I am leaving right now. Judi Pavano is driving me."

"Father said, "Okay Tracey that's good. Now, I have one important question for you before you leave. Please be honest with me. Does your husband have a drug issue?" Is he an addict?"

The priest was standing right next to Bob and Bob became angry. "You can ask me Father. I'm laying right here."

Father held up a finger to Bob more or less telling him to shut up. He did not look at him but instead listened to Tracey's answer to his question. Bob was not happy with how he was being treated and his desire for roxycodone was once again demanding his full attention.

Tracey said to Father Jim, "Yes Father, he does. Ever since he hurt his back they have taken over his life. In fact, Jake and I went to our first Nar-Anon meeting tonight."

"Okay, I see. Thank you. Now, you come on over to the hospital. We are in the emergency room. I'll see you when you get here."

The priest hung up the phone, stepped right next to the bed and said to Bob. "Give me your hand."

Bob slowly extended his unshackled right hand toward the priest. He had no idea what was happening and he felt intimidated by the seriousness of Father Jim. He said nothing and waited. The priest looked at him and said, "Bob, tonight can be a turning point for you. Ultimately it will be your choice. Now, I wish to pray with you for a moment."

He did not ask permission or if it was okay or anything like that, he just bowed his head and began, "Father in heaven, almighty and everlasting God, I am here with Bob Slider and we are both asking You to watch over him and guide him on his journey to recovery and to give him the strength and courage he needs to overcome the evil demon of addiction that has wrapped its tentacles around him. We both ask that you give his wife and son the patience and understanding so that they may all work together to revitalize their family structure and move forward doing all things that might be pleasing in Your eyes. We ask this in the name of Jesus Christ, Your Son, Who lives and reigns with the Holy Spirit, one God forever. Amen."

Father raised his head and lowered his hands. Never in Bob's life had he experienced a moment like that and he was almost in a daze because of it. Father Jim said to him, "Do you trust me Bob?"

"Sure Father, why not. If I can't trust you who can I trust?"

"That's good because I am going to try, with the help of the Good Lord above, to change this evening's projected finale. But first, I would like to anoint you if that is okay?"

"Uh—sure Father, I guess. I don't know what you mean but---that's fine. You know, I'm not a church going fella. Does that matter?"

"Don't worry about any of that. Now holdout the palms of your hands and bow your head. I am going to administer the sacrament of Anointing of the Sick to you. I know you have not been much of a churchgoer but I understand you were baptized as a child. This is the healing sacrament of the Catholic Church and will impart many graces upon you to help you on your journey to get well." Father Jim removed a small vial from his pocket. He said to Bob, "This is the oil of sacred chrism blessed by the bishop during Holy Week." He opened it and dipped his thumb in it. Then he extended his hand toward Bob and, with his thumb, made the sign of the cross on Bob's brow. He then did the same thing on the palms of Bob's hands. As he did this he said, "Through this holy anointing may the Lord in His love and mercy help you with the grace of the Holy Spirit. May the Lord who frees you from sin save you and raise you up."

Father Jim left quickly without saying anything more. Bob was deeply moved and also confused. He never felt this way before. It was as if his life had been taken from his control and bounced around between different venues and had miraculously landed in a good place.

He lifted his hands upward and looked at them closely, fixated on the oil that had been smeared into both palms. He just stared for a long while. Then he took his right forefinger and gently touched the oil in the palm of his left hand. He began to think the hands he was looking at were not even his, that they were special hands that belonged to a 'good' person. He was still frightened yet a sense of calm had grabbed hold of him and it was not from any kind of drug. He did not understand that, not yet anyway. He did like it.

Chapter 16

Father Jim; "Unbelievably Impossible"

Father Jim headed out to the waiting room and found Billy Tyler waiting patiently by the front entrance. "Billy, I'm sorry for taking so long."

"No problem, Father. No-one from headquarters has called me so I guess we're in good shape right now. But I have to check in just to touch base soon. I was just waiting on you. How much more time do you need?"
"I don't know for sure, Billy. Maybe 15 minutes. And I need to talk to Mr. Slider's wife. She should be here in another ten minutes or so. Now, do me a favor. If she comes in talk to her before she gets back to Bob. Her name is Tracey. Tell her I asked that she wait for me before she talks to him. We all have to be on the same page with my little plan."

"Okay Father, whatever you say."

Father Jim walked back to the privacy room where he had been with Billy earlier. He sat at the small table, blessed himself and said a short quiet prayer. Then he picked up the phone and dialed. A woman answered and she sounded half asleep. "Hello."

"Maureen, is that you?"

"Uh yeah---oh, Father Jimmy, It's you. Sorry, I was dozing on the sofa. Oh my, it is almost eleven o'clock. What's wrong Jimmy? Oh no, tell me you aren't about to ask for a room for someone?"

"Maureen, I need a room for someone."

She laughed a bit and said, "Oh Father Jim, what am I going to do with you?'

The priest laughed too and said, "Why, just get a bed ready for a new patient."

"Seriously Jimmy, I don't know. I think all the beds are taken. The earliest discharge would be tomorrow morning."

"Look Moe, this guy has been arrested and is in the hospital and I know we can help him. He has a wife and son and ----"

"Jimmy, please , it's me, Maureen, you know, little Moe. You do not have to sell me. I know you well enough to know that these people you call me about are on the edge and can be saved. But can't this one wait until after eleven tomorrow morning? That is only another 12 hours."

"Maureen, the cop who arrested him is waiting here at the hospital to take him to jail. I had to convince him to take the handcuffs off him while they were treating him in the ER. His wife and son are on the way, I just anointed the man, and I have to get this order approved so I can have the arrest cancelled."

"Oh my God, Father. Now you think you can have an arrest cancelled. I mean, you know bureaucracy. Once someone is put in the system, good luck getting them out."

"Well, I'm praying that he is not all the way into the system yet. The cop is an ex-altar boy of mine from Sacred Heart. He's young but he is trying to help me out."

"That poor young policeman. He doesn't have a prayer with you on the job."

They both laughed loudly and Maureen said, "Father, I'll call you back in about ten minutes."

"Please Moe, can you make it five. I'm under the gun here."

"Father Jim Daniels, you are impossible. Okay, let me hang up so I can get busy."

Father went back to the waiting room and walked over to Billy who was getting quite antsy. "Oh good, you're back. So, tell me Father, what's going on?"

"I am waiting for a call back from a dear friend of mine, Maureen Comerford. She is the administrator of the Kolbe Wellness Center in St. Petersburg. I am trying to get our friend admitted tonight."

"Father, he is already under arrest. I cannot do that. Plus, Kolbe Rehab is not on the list. It is a private facility and in another county. They have no agreement with the county."

Father Jim put his hand on Billy's shoulder and looked him dead in the eye and said, "Billy, Billy, Billy, God is in charge of this entire evening and the last I saw, Bob Slider was still in a hospital bed and not in a jail cell. So, bear with me son, please. This could turn out to be a memorable evening."

The young cop just shook his head and smiled, "Father, you are unbelievable. Okay, I'm sitting tight like you ask. But I don't know how long I can avoid calling in."

The priest laughed and said, "I was just called 'impossible' and now you just called me 'unbelievable'. So Billy Tyler, which am I? Impossibly unbelievable or unbelievably impossible?"

Billy shook his head and said, "Ah, come on Father. You're neither one. But you are definitely a good Samaritan, no doubt about that."

The priest and the cop turned as they heard someone calling out, "Father Jim, Father Jim, where is he. Is he all right? We got here as quick as we could."

"Yes Tracey, you can relax, he's all right. Hi Judi, hi Tommy. And Jake, how are you son? Hope you're okay."

Just then Father's phone started chirping. He looked at the screen and saw Maureen's name. He answered and said, "Maureen, hold one second, please."

Then he turned to Tracey and the others and said, "Please, all of you, wait until I finish with this call before you go back to see him. I must talk to you first. This is Billy Tyler. He accompanied Bob here. You all introduce yourself to each other and I will be back in a few minutes."

They all nodded in the affirmative and Father Jim turned his back to them and walked across the room talking to Maureen. The five of them watched the priest and no-one said anything to anyone including Officer Billy Tyler, who was becoming quite captivated by the way Father Jim was handling the sticky situation.

Finally, Tommy Pavano introduced himself to Billy and then he introduced the others to him and they all nervously shook hands. The situation was quite surreal. The young policeman was shaking hands with the people who were the husband, father and friends of the man he had arrested. The four of them were nervously smiling at him. He smiled back, raised his eyebrows and shrugged his shoulders ever so slightly. Not one of them said a word.

Father Jim had been a classmate and close friend of Maureen's older brother, Joe, and when Joe enlisted in the Marine Corps, he had asked his best friend, Jimmy Daniels, to keep an eye out for his little sister, Maureen. Jimmy agreed and life went on.

Life is filled with the sudden and the unforeseen and dramatic change can happenquickly. Joe Comerford was killed in action in Afghanistan in 2003. At the time Maureen was three years into college. She had been hanging with a fast crowd and was using different drugs, her drugs of choice being un-prescribed oxycontin and Xanax often times mixed with alcohol, an extremely deadly mix. As for Jimmy, he was in the seminary and was only a year and a half away from ordination.

Maureen's mom and dad were faithful, church-going Catholics who had no clue about the depth of their daughter's addiction. They knew her grades had slipped and that she had missed many classes but the drug use had turned her into a great liar. She could also schmooze them into believing anything, especially her dad. After all, she was the youngest child and a daughter, the proverbial "daddy's little girl". Their naivete was probably good for them. Plus, they had their powerful faith and they had Jimmy Daniels.

When a distraught Maureen overdosed on Xanax and alcohol on the night of Joe's Funeral, she collapsed on the bedroom floor. It was almost midnight when her mom found her and she called Jimmy who was home from the seminary for the funeral. He hurried over to find the young woman drooling and comatose. She was close to cardiac arrest. He called 911 and, if it had not been for Jimmy Daniels, Maureen would have died.

He kept his promise to his best friend and took Maureen under his wing. He got her

into rehab visiting every day that he could. He learned as much as he could about the disease of addiction. Every time he visited Maureen the first thing he would do was hold her hands and say a prayer. He would visit, talk and upon leaving, pray with her again. The transformation was remarkable and Father Jim insisted that it was the hand of God that placed all of the necessary graces in place for Maureen who chose to grab onto them and let them help her get clean.

Maureen Comerford kicked her addiction, finished school and went on for her Master's Degree. Within three years of her graduation she was in charge of the substance abuse division at the county jail. Now, ten years later, she was the Director of Kolbe Rehabilitation Center, a facility that could handle up to 80 addicts at a time and had among the finest staff and equipment anywhere. Maureen Comerford was a woman who had "walked the walk", climbed to the mountaintop and raised and held high the drug-free flag of victory. The Kolbe Center thrived under her insightful direction.

As Father and Maureen were about to finish their conversation Maureen said, "Okay, Jimmy, everything is done, you have your room waiting and all you have to do is ask for Nancy when you get there. One last thing, what kind of insurance does your guy have?"

Bob Slider did not have insurance that qualified him for Kolbe. Father Jim did not care about trivialities. "I have no idea, Moe. What's the difference? We'll work that out when we get there."

"Jimmy, come on, I have to have something to input into the system . Go and check for me ---please."

"Okay, hold on."

Father Jim walked back toward the quintet waiting on him and said, "Tracey, what kind of insurance does Bob have?"

"Temporary Medicaid."

"Okay good, that will work. Do you have his Medicaid number with you or does he have it?"

"I guess he has it."

"Okay, I'll be right back."

As Father headed back to Bob she impatiently said to him. "Father Jim, I want to see my husband. This is ridiculous me waiting like this."

"Tracey, please, I need to talk to you first. We all want to help the man back there, right? So please, give me a few more minutes."

Tracey breathed deeply and said, "All right Father. Go ahead."

Father Jim headed back to the patient section of the ER. Officer Tyler followed him.

"How you doing Bob?"

"Okay Father. I'm better."

"That's good, you look better. Tracey and Jake are waiting outside but I just needed your insurance ID from you. You have it with you, right?"

"Uh yeah Father, sure. Can you hand me my pants. My wallet is in the back pocket. The ID is in there."

Billy Tyler said, "I'll get them."

Bob's clothes had been removed by the ER nurses when he was brought in by the paramedics. They had been placed in a little cubby in the corner of the examining cubicle. Billy picked them up and felt around and lifted the wallet from the back pocket. He handed it to Bob who started to nervously fumble through it. Any cop would have become suspicious at the instant agitation. Billy said to his prisoner, 'Here, give me that."

Bob reluctantly handed it to the policeman who opened it and said, "What are we looking for?"

Father Jim said, "His Medicaid ID."

"Here, give it to me. I know just where it is," Bob said.

Billy Tyler was suspicious. He held the open wallet up in front of Bob but did not hand it to him. "Go ahead, Mr. Slider, pull it out. You still have that IV in your hand, no sense aggravating it."

Bob had placed the altered prescription in his wallet next to his Medicaid card. He found the card and, seeing the altered script next to it, became nervous. Then, in his quest to appear nonchalant, he watched in horror as his hands began to shake as he tried to separate the card and script. He could not make the shaking stop. As the card was lifted from the wallet the script came along with it and fluttered downward landing on the floor next to the bed. Billy Tyler said, "I got it."

Bob Slider was now sweating and red flags were flying in front of the officer. The cop said, "What's wrong with you man. What are you so nervous about? Are you---oh, wait a minute."

Billy looked at Bob and then at the piece of paper in his hand. He opened it and knew immediately why his prisoner was shaking . He said, "Oh man, are you kidding me. Is this why you drove over here? Are you nuts?"

A puzzled Father Jim, said, "What's going on, Billy?"

The cop looked at Bob and said disgustingly, "You altered or forged this script, didn't you? Let me tell you something, you did a lousy job. I could tell immediately."

Billy was plain old pissed off. He had been doing everything in his power to help Father Jim help Bob Slider. He was not following proper protocol and was, in effect, jeopardizing his young career in law-enforcement. He looked at Bob and said, "Don't say a word. You're playing all of us and I, for one, do not like being made a fool out of."

Father was now getting nervous. "Billy, what happened? What's going on?"

"Okay Father, this script is why our friend was over this way this evening."

He handed the script to the priest and Father looked at it and said, "I don't understand, Billy. It is a prescription, right?"

He looked at Bob who was ready to bust out crying—again. Billy said, "Should I tell him Mr. Slider, or do you want to? I mean the man is doing his damnedest to help you out and save your ass so maybe you should tell him."

"Billy, I don't rightly care who tells who what. Someone just tell me something, please."

"Sorry Father, but your friend here is carrying a prescription for a controlled substance and it has obviously been tampered with. He was over in this area because, I can guarantee you, he was taking this to the Kauflin Pharmacy to try and fill it. Kauflin charges a bit more and in return they accommodate folks, know what I mean?"

"Yeah, I do. I know about Kauflin. Is that true Bob? Is Billy right about that?"

Bob, tears once again streaming down his face, nodded. Father looked at him and was thinking, *So near yet so far. Dear Lord, I need a bit of help. Soften Billy's angry heart so he listens to me. I mean, listens to you as*

I talk to him. Oh Jesus, you know what I mean. He grabbed Billy by his arm and gently guided him away from the bed. "He looked at him and said, "I need one more little favor."

"You know Father, I'm angry. He tried to scam all of us and we are simply trying to help him. And you know, that script was so poorly altered anyone would have noticed it. He is so lucky that you came by tonight. He has no idea."

"Billy, he is a victim of prescribed medications. He is a drug addict and doctors set the table for him to become one. We both know about these things. He was fortunate tonight. That script would have immediately put him in prison. I think God is in the driver's seat tonight. Understand."

"Father, this whole thing is in my face. What would you have me do?"

"Well, if you somehow lost or misplaced that script and couldn't find it, wouldn't that be a twist of fate. Then we might still be able to change the path he is on and save a good man from himself. You have to admit, he certainly is not nasty or cocky like so many of the folks you deal with. He is more like a big baby crying and everything. He is so scared. This could be the time to help save him from himself."

Billy Tyler breathed deeply and feigned a sneeze. As he went to cover his nose and mouth the piece of white paper he was holding somehow fell from his hand. Father Jim saw it flutter downward and as he said "God bless you", he placed his size 12 shoe over the illegal prescription. Billy patted Father Jim on the arm and walked away. He did not notice Father Jim quietly blessing him. The young cop just wanted his shift to be over. He paid no attention to the priest picking the script up and tearing it into tiny pieces.

Father quickly called Maureen and, when she answered, he said, "Okay Moe, he has Temporary Medicaid. Here's the number."

"Oh my God, Jimmy. We don't take Medicaid and we are not on a county list for county aid. Your guy, in effect, has no insurance."

"Wait a minute Moe, I know from experience there are certain situations where an exemption can be made, right?"

"Father Jimmy, I love you, but ---oh, all right. I'll do something. But we might need some cash up front."

"Cash—no problem. I know people. All I need is for you to fax the admission approval over here. Here is the fax number. I got it from the charge nurse. Then I can give a copy of that to the police and I think that will satisfy this 'almost arrest'. Hey Moe, I love you too."

"You owe me a steak dinner that, as usual, I will wind up paying for. Okay."

"Talk later Moe. In fact, I will probably see you over at Kolbe tomorrow."

"Bye Jimmy. See you tomorrow."

Father Jim went back to the family and the pensive, aggravated police officer. He said, "Hey Tracey , do you mind if you and I go down the hall for a minute or two. I have to talk to you."

"What about me, he is my dad."

"I agree Jake, but that is up to your Mom."

"Yes, of course, and Judi and Tommy too. They are extended family and have been along for this ride from the get-go. They should all come."

They all went down to the privacy room and it was unoccupied. "This is perfect. No one is in here. Let's go in," Father said.

Facing the priest with the arresting officer distancing himself to the side of the room near the wall, Father Jim explained to them what had happened up to that point. Tracey, wanting desperately to go back to her husband, finally said, "Father, please, what is the bottom line. Is he going to jail? How much trouble is he in? Actually, I don't even care. I just want to see my husband. I'm going back there."

Tracey opened the door and began hurrying down the corridor toward the ER waiting room. Father hurried after her and stepped in front of her. "Get out of my way," she said.

"Please, Tracey listen to me. I need two more minutes. Just two minutes. I have made arrangements with the Kolbe Rehabilitation Center to accept Bob as an inpatient effective

immediately. I have not told him about any of this. Officer Tyler has been working with me to expedite this and we owe him an enormous thank you. Now, we all have to be on the same page with all of this and--"

"Father Jim, I like you. I know you have a caring heart and that you mean well but I want to see my husband and I want to see him right now."

"Okay Tracey, fine. I just wanted to give him his options before you all went in to see him. I was going to tell you as soon as I told him."

"Guess what, Father Jim. That man and I have been married 14 years. We are partners in life. We may not go to church much but that doesn't matter. Whatever you have to tell him you can tell US together. Understand. Now, let's go talk to my husband."

Young Officer Tyler was feeling overwhelmed. This was his arrest to begin with and his priest friend had taken the entire situation completely over. He hurried after them. As Father and Tracey were nearing Bob's bed he said loudly, "Excuse me Father, I need a word with you—right now, in private—please."

Tracey said, "I'm sure you fellows don't mind me listening in on this. It is about my husband, right?"

"'Sure Tracey," Father said. "Right you are."

Tracey thought and seized the moment. She said, "Know what, I will go see my husband for a minute, alone, while you two talk. Then you can fill both of us in, okay?"

The priest and the cop looked at each other and then just nodded to Tracey. She quickly headed back to her husband.

Father Jim had been pushing his agenda and had taken his young friend Billy a bit for granted. They stepped outside the privacy room for a minute and the priest caught Billy off guard. He said , "Billy, I apologize. I have not taken your job and your feelings into account with all of this. I have been so consumed with getting this guy out of his predicament that I was rude to you. I am very sorry. It wasn't right."

"Uh—well Father, I understand. You were trying to help someone out. I get it. Look, I want to help people too. But I arrested him and they know I am here with a prisoner. What am I supposed to do? Now you just went and told everyone you had him admitted to Kolbe Rehab. What do you expect of me anyway?"

Father Jim raised his eyebrows and opened his eyes wide. Then he displayed an impish smile, almost like a child who had been caught with his hand in the proverbial cookie jar. Billy said, "Oh no, Father, I don't like that look in your eye. What are you thinking now?"

"Billy, it seems to me Mr. Slider's behavior warrants him being Baker Acted. What say you?"

"Father Jim, he is fine. He isn't crazy and he isn't acting crazy. He's here because he was stupid. Last I heard it was not a crime to be stupid."

The priest was determined. He had lined up the ducks and now he wanted them all to march one after the other to the beat of his drum. "Billy, if he is Baker Acted he does not have to go to jail. He can legally go to Kolbe Rehab, right?"

"But Father, a person has to be a danger to themselves or someone else for them to be Baker Acted."

The priest looked at Billy Tyler and said, "Okay Billy, what's your point? He's driving with a DUI conviction and carrying an altered script for a controlled substance and was in a minor traffic altercation. It seems to me he is a definite danger to himself and others."

"Come on Father Jim, you know it is not the same and—" The cop paused and looked at the priest and began to smile. He shook his head and held up his hands. '"Father, I surrender. You win." Then came the youthful sarcasm. "But you had better discuss this with the doctor in charge. He has to sign off for me to do this. Oh yeah, then maybe you should discuss it with the guy's wife. Oh, I forgot, maybe you need to discuss it with the arresting officer who has to sign off also. Oh, that's me, isn't it. Oh, I also forgot, how about the prisoner and patient. Maybe he might want to hear how we are all about to say he is plain NUTS."

"Father Jim began to laugh. He said, "Billy, that's quite funny. You're the cop and you surrender. I love it. I needed a slap upside the head and you just gave me one. Thank you. You are right. I have been a bit overbearing in my quest to help this man. But it changes nothing. Either this guy goes to Kolbe or to jail. What do you say. Should we tell him?"

"Okay Father, like I said, this cop surrenders. Let's do it."

CHAPTER 17

Rehab Trumps Jail

Father and Billy walked the short distance back to Bob's cubicle. As they stepped around the closed curtain they saw Tracey sitting on the edge of the bed holding her husband's hand. Bob's neck was nestled in the crook of Tracey's right arm and his puffy eyes were closed. Wetness surrounded them. The big, burly, blue-collar guy looked like a child who had finally found peace in his mother's arms. The couple's tender appearance together presented Father Jim with an unexpected insight into the love that flowed between them and it also affirmed for him that he was doing the right thing. "So, how is the patient feeling?"

As Tracey moved her arm out from behind him Bob opened his eyes, wiped them and sat up straight. He was a bit embarrassed and said, "I'm okay, Father."

"Good, Bob, good. We have to talk seriously and quickly. And I intend to be to the point and blunt. Is that okay with the two of you?"

Tracey was tired and getting exasperated. "Father," she said. "just tell us what you have in mind. Please."

"Okay, I don't know the whole story so I will be as brief as I can be. Bob, you have an addiction to pills. When or how it started I do not care. That is the reason you are here and that is the reason you

189

were arrested. That is also the reason you have a record and violated probation. That more or less sums it all up, right?"

The wife, the priest and the cop stared at him waiting for an answer. None of them blinked, not even once. Bob shook his head up and down and said, "I don't know what happened. How did I get this way? I really didn't do anything wrong."

Father Jim said, "Stop it Bob. This is no time for self pity. This is your time to face reality. Are you an addict? Yes or no?"

"Yes, yes ,yes. I am. You all know I am. I can't stop thinking about those damn freaking pills. Thinking about them is like having squirrels running around inside my head. There, are you all satisfied? I admit it. I'm an addict. Now, can somebody help me? Tracey, I'm sorry. I don't know what to do."

Tracey was standing still and her tears flowed freely. She did not even wipe her eyes. Billy Tyler was thinking how pitiful his prisoner seemed to be. Father Jim said, "Okay, everyone take a breath. Bob, I have one question and I want a 'yes' or 'no' answer. Do you want to get clean and get your life back?"

"Yes, yes, I do."

"Good, now I have managed to get you admitted into the Kolbe Wellness Center over in Tampa. It is one of the foremost rehab centers in the entire southeast. You will go there tonight and might be there for up to 60 days. You understand? Your new life starts right now, tonight. If you screw up you go to jail, simple as that. What do you think, Tracey?"

The partner of the man in the bed wiped her tears and said, "I can't believe it. That's wonderful. I have heard of that place. But it is very expensive, isn't it. We don't have insurance like we used to."

"We'll talk about that another time. First things first. There is a slight glitch in the entire discharge and admission procedure that has to be addressed."

"What's that, Father?"

The priest slapped his forehead with the palm of his hand. He said, "Oh my God, I just thought of something. Hey Billy, is Paul Henninger your captain?"

"Uh, yes Father. Why?"

"I shall return in five minutes. Man oh man, God is good."

The priest hurried out and down the hall to the privacy room. He wanted to make a call without ears listening and eyes glaring at him. Everyone, sopped with the enthusiasm that had just poured down upon them, watched him leave. Tracey said to Billy, "Officer, can I ask my son and my friends to come back here?"

"I don't see why not, and, do me a favor and call me Billy, okay. In fact, you wait here and I will go get them."

Tracey feebly smiled. She knew he was not her enemy. "Okay Billy, thanks."

A minute later Jake was hugging his dad and, even though it had only been a few hours, it was almost as if a family reunion was taking place. Tracey told them about Bob being admitted to Kolbe and Judi was dumbfounded. She knew about the place. About ten minutes later Father Jim came back in and said, "Oh great, all of you are here. You all know what the plan is, right? We are going to Kolbe tonight."

Judi said, "I have been there, Father. Someone in my family was a patient there. Very nice facility."

"Yes Judi, it certainly is. Hey Billy, come here a minute."

"Yes Father, what is it?"

"Call Captain Henninger. He's expecting your call. We don't have to Baker Act anyone."

Billy looked at the priest and was speechless. He just walked away to make the call.

Things processed smoothly and quickly from that point forward. Father Jim's expected fax was at the nurse's station. Capt. Henninger had told Billy that, as the commanding office, he could override the arrest because it was a medical necessity. He also commended Billy on his patience and maturity in dealing with a complex problem. Doctor Scott Hilgren, before leaving and discharging Bob, signed a form validating the necessity of Bob's being taken to Kolbe.

Jake said his goodbye to his dad and was amazingly stoic as he did. They hugged each other tightly and Jake said, "Don't worry dad, I'll watch out for mom."

Bob rubbed his boy's head and said, "I know you will, son. I love you."

"Love you too, dad."

Then it was Tracey's turn. She and her husband just held each other quietly for about a minute. Then Tracey kissed him and said, "I will talk to you tomorrow. You take care of yourself and be strong. I know in my heart this is the best thing that could happen to you, and to us."

Bob was going through a myriad of emotions. He wanted to go home. He wanted to be in bed with Tracey listening to the short, staccato snorts she made as she snored away the night. He desperately wanted some oxycontin or some xanax. He did not like being with this priest who had seemingly came out of nowhere and taken over his life but there was a part of him that liked it. He smiled at his wife feebly and said, "Okay, I can do this. We can talk tomorrow."

Tommy got permission from Billy Tyler to take Tracey to where Bob's truck had been parked to see if it was still there. Miraculously, the vehicle had not been impounded and Tracey and Jake climbed in and drove it home. Father Jim's night was not over yet. He was the one transporting Bob to the rehab hospital over in Tampa. As Father pulled away from the emergency room exit he said to his passenger, "Well Bob, we sure kept the Good Lord busy tonight. He must be exhausted."

Bob Slider had been saved from going to jail. His blood work had shown that he did not have a heart attack. He had no money and, without the necessary insurance coverage, was being taken to a top notch rehabilitation center and being given the opportunity to get his life back on track. He simply said, "If you say so Father, if you say so."

The priest hit the brakes, turned around and pulled back into the hospital parking lot. It was late, he was tired, he was hungry and he wanted to take a shower. Now he was also offended. He stopped short in a parking lane and turned off the engine. He extended his arms to the steering wheel, leaned his head back and sighed.

Bob was unnerved. He did not understand what had come over the affable, smiling priest. He sat there, saying nothing, anxiously awaiting for what was next. Finally, while still looking straight ahead, Father said, "What kind of condescending crap was that, Bob?"

Bob's insides curled. He was not sure what had come over the priest. Could it have been his quick response to the priest's comments? No, no way, but---"I don't know what you mean Father."

"Bob, let's get something straight. First of all you know damn well what I mean. You basically mocked my comments about God being kept busy by us tonight. Yet here you are, being given an opportunity to start over and it never would have happened if Ann Dowling, a sweet, gentle 94-year-old woman had not needed a priest at her bedside as she passed from this life. Her being here is the reason we crossed paths tonight. Otherwise, you would be in county jail by now. You would have had your probation revoked and, like it or not, off to Chipola Correctional up in the panhandle. You are an addict Bob, no doubt about it. And trust me, rehab trumps prison."

Bob did not know how to respond. So he began to agree. "You're right Father. I'm sorry. I appreciate everything you've done tonight."

The priest was not in the mood. "Stop it, Bob. Do not, I repeat, do not try to schmooze me. You are happy that you are not going to jail. That is true. But you don't have any plans to get clean. So, all the tears back in the hospital were temporary. Once you knew you were not going to jail they dried right up. Admit it man, right now you want some pills, end of story. Right or wrong?"

"Well, okay, so what. My back is killing me. I need some. That doesn't make me a bad person, does it?"

Father Jim turned and looked at Bob Slider. He shook his head back and forth and said, "Okay, let's just get going. I'm going to turn on my rosary tape and say the rosary. You can join me if you wish. Otherwise, just be quiet. "

The only noise heard for the next half hour was the monotone repetition of 'Hail Marys', 'Our Fathers' and Catholic hymns played between each decade. Bob fell asleep and Father Jim was not sure if he was faking sleep so he did not have to talk or if he really was sleeping. The priest did not care. He was happy to oblige and not have to talk either, whether Bob was faking or not.

Kolbe Rehab's official name was Maximilian Kolbe Wellness Center but everyone called it Kolbe Rehab. It had been named after St. Maximilian Kolbe, a Polish priest who was a victim of the Holocaust. Father Kolbe had traded his life at Auschwitz for that of a Jewish man who had a wife and children. His reward from the Nazi's was starvation. After two weeks in a dungeon, Father Kolbe was still alive. So they lost patience and gave him a shot of carbolic acid to finish him off. He held out his left arm so their job would be simple.

Declared a saint by Pope John Paul II in 1982 Maximilian Kolbe was declared the patron saint of drug addicts and, at the dedication by the local bishop, the center had been placed under Father Kolbe's spiritual protection.

The center outside Tampa, near the Dale Mabry Highway, was set almost a quarter of a mile off the road and if someone was going there for the first time, it was not easy to find, especially at night. Father Jim had been here many times and knew exactly where it was. He drove down the road toward the main building, pulled under the concrete overhang at the entrance and turned off the engine. It was ten past midnight. Besides the dim night time lights in the lobby the place was eerily quiet. Father turned to Bob and said , Okay Bob, we have arrived."

Bob, opening his eyes, let out a big breath and said, "Oh, okay."

"C'mon, follow me."

The priest did not walk to the front doors but instead walked down the side of the building following a path lit up by blue solar lights spaced about two feet apart and only a foot off the ground. About 20 feet down the pathway was a door. Father Jim stopped and, squinting in the dim light, keyed in some numbers on the touch pad next to the door. A message flashed, "Please ring bell". He pushed the bell next to the door jamb. A few seconds went by and a voice, electronically raspy, came from a speaker above them, "Yes, may we help you."

"Hi, this is Father Jim Daniels. Nancy is expecting us."

"Hold on please."

Both men stood there, waiting and not saying anything. A few seconds passed and the raspy voice came from the speaker again, "Father, can you key in your password please?"

Father said, "I already did. I was instructed to ring the bell."

"I'm sorry Father. After 9 p.m. the door has to be unlocked by us. Try to key in again and this time I will makes sure it opens. "Okay, thanks. Here goes."

Father Jim looked at the keypad mounted on the wall and once again pressed out the letters, L-I-T-T-L-E-M-O-E. As soon as he finished a buzzer sounded and the door opened inward. "Okay Bob, were in. Let's go."

They began to walk down a long corridor which led to another large door. It was nighttime in a rehab center and everything was in lockdown mode. They could see a man and a woman peering through the single pane of tempered glass in the upper center of the door. Father said, "I think that is Nancy."

They both stopped at the door and a big, dark-skinned man put his face to the glass and looked at them. Then he turned and looked at the woman. Another buzzer went off and that door opened in. The lady smiled and said, "Hello Father, how are you?"

"I'm fine Nancy, thanks. This is Bob Slider. You have been expecting him."

"Yes we have. Hello, Mr. Slider. Good to see you. This nice man next to me is Micah Post. He is in charge of security this evening. Well now, Mr. Slider, I understand you have had a long day. If you'll follow me we'll get you admitted."

Father said, "Do you need me for anything else, Nancy?"

"No Father. Just give me the paper work and we'll take it from there."

"Okay Nancy, here you go. Everything should be there."

"Thank you, Father. You have a safe trip home."

Bob, realizing this was it and he was going behind locked doors started to really get upset. "Uh, wait a second. That's it. I'm here. Do I get anything to calm me down? Can I call my wife? I don't think I like this."

Nancy and the priest looked at each other. Micah tensed up and prepared himself for the unexpected. Father said, "Hey Nancy, do you mind if I talk to Bob alone for a moment?"

"Of course not, Father. We'll wait right over there."

Nancy and Micah stepped away from them and Father Jim said to Bob, "Look, I'm sorry for getting on you like that before. I guess I'm just tired. You should understand that these people are going to help you. You'll be okay. I have seen the wonders that happen here. Trust me, please."

"Can I call Tracey?"

"Bob, that is not up to me. They have a system here. You have to ask them. Now, I know you have not been a church guy or anything like that. It doesn't matter. You are a good man. Just try to understand that God does love you and will help you. So, all I ask is that you be open to Him. That's all. When all is said and done, we make our own choices and have to accept responsibility for them. That applies to each and every one of us. God will help you get through all of this but you have to allow Him to help you. He does not force Himself on anyone. So, if you have the inkling to talk to Him, consider giving it a shot. You certainly have nothing to lose, right?"

"I never thought about it like that, Father. You're right, I have nothing to lose."

Nancy came over to them and said, "Father. You go ahead. Everything is fine."

The priest knew what she meant and said, "Okay Nancy, I understand. Bob, I'll be praying for you and I'll see you soon. You'll be fine. Just open that heart of yours."

"I want to call my wife right now."

Nancy held up her hand and Father just turned and began to walk toward the exit. Nancy said to Bob, "Mr. Slider, you cannot call your wife tonight. Maybe tomorrow. We'll see."

"What do you mean , maybe tomorrow? I need to talk to her now."

"Nancy said, "Mr. Slider, do you mind if I call you Bob?"

"Uh, no."

"Okay, that's great. Now, let us get you settled in for the night. It is late and maybe we can have the nurse see you and get you some meds to relax you a bit. What do you say?"

Nancy had said the right thing. Bob answered, "Okay, I could use something to calm me down."

Bob Slider was processed into Kolbe Rehab and by 1:30 a.m was in a room. He was given a 10mg Librium capsule to take and by 2:00 a.m, exhausted from a day he would never forget, was sound asleep.

*

CHAPTER 18

Start of a 'New Day'

R elieved that Bob was safe and with the emotions of the previous day behind them, Tracey and Jake were both sleeping like babies. Tracey never heard her cell phone chirping at 6:30 a.m. She never heard it at 7 or 7:15 either.

Bob had found a wall phone that patients could use in the main conference room. He was desperate to talk to Tracey. He was positive that she could help him and he was sure that she could somehow, some way, come and get out him out of this place. He felt certain that he did not belong there. Inside his disarranged mind he knew he was misunderstood. After all, he was only trying to get some pain relief medication for his back. He was not a criminal. He certainly was not a drug addict. For crying out loud, the doctors had prescribed the medicine he was taking. They gave it to him. It was legal. He also was absolutely convinced that if his back stopped hurting he would never take another one of those stupid pills. The fact was, inside his own topsy-turvy world, Bob Slider knew 'jack-squat' about himself.

It was now 7:18 a.m. and someone said to Bob, "Hey man, you see that sign? You can't be touchin' no phones until after nine o'clock. You gonna get in trouble."

Bob was startled by the skinny, long-haired man standing off to his side. He turned and looked at him and then turned to look at the sign to the right of the phone. Bob had seen it but had just ignored it. This time he looked and paid attention. The sign read, *PHONE HOURS: 9 a.m. to 8 p.m.*

Bob mumbled, "Screw that, I need to talk to Tracey." He began to dial again and another voice came from directly behind him. "Excuse me, you're Mr. Slider, right?"

Bob turned and a man about 6'5" and who weighed in at about 275 pounds was standing so close to him that their bodies were virtually touching. The man's huge square head was bald as a cue ball and he looked down at Bob through black, horned-rimmed glasses. Freckles were splattered across his scalp in all different shapes and sizes. Bob tried to move back but there was no place to go. The man smiled and said, "My name is Jonathan. I am one of the rehab specialists here and I have been lucky enough to have you assigned to my group. So tell me Bob, oh, I'm sorry, you do not mind if I call you Bob, do you? After all, we WILL be seeing a lot of each other." Bob, intimidated by the stranger and insecure in his new surroundings, said, "Uh no, that's fine."

"Okay then Bob, let me ask you. Can you read? Do you need remedial reading help?"

"Bob looked at Jonathan and said, "Can I read? Of course I can read. Why would you ask something like that?"

"Because Bob, there is a sign right in front of your face and apparently you do not seem to understand what it means. I just assumed you could not read."

The sarcasm from Jonathan was raining down on Bob and he felt an anger well up within himself. "Yeah, I can read fine, okay. And I saw the sign. I just need to talk to my wife."

Jonathan turned to the other man and said to him, "Hey Skip, don't you have something to do?"

"I don't think so."

"Yes you do, Skip. Now, go take your shower and get ready for breakfast."

Skip shrugged and slowly walked away. Jonathan turned back to Bob and said, "Okay Bob, I understand that you are new here so I am going to cut you some slack. Now, pay attention."

Bob looked at Jonathan and wanted to just shove him as hard as he could and tell him to back off. But, he didn't. He did tighten his lips and Jonathan could see the anger in his new patient's face. "Okay Bob, I understand that you are pissed off at me right now. But here's the thing. I do not care. I do not even care if you come to hate me. I'm here to help you. You are here because you are a drug addict. This is not a vacation spa. You are in a rehabilitation hospital because you are sick. But in here we have rules and they are expected to be followed, by everyone. Now, you cannot call your wife until after you see Doctor Cunningham. He will begin making rounds after 9 a.m. Okay, any questions for me?"

"Bob answered, "I'm not sure. Wait a minute. What did you mean when you said I was assigned to your group?"

"Good question, Bob. There are a number of full-time counselors on staff here. I am one of them. We each have groups of patients assigned to us. There are three counselors to a group. I have the day shift, from 7 a.m. until 3 p.m. Charlie works the night shift. You met him briefly last night. Jennifer has the evening shift from 3 until 11 p.m. After you shower and have breakfast I will give you an itinerary and a breakdown of the program here. Our group had 18 people and now, with you, it is 19. We meet four times a day, we all have a set recreational schedules and we eat together.

You'll see as we go along."

"I need clean clothes. What should I wear?"

"You can put on a hospital gown or wear what you had on last night. When your family or friends visit they can bring you some fresh clothing. So, go shower and eat something. Then we'll talk some more."

"Okay, um---just one more thing Jonathan. Can I get some medication for my back pain?"

Jonathan smiled slightly and said, "Dr. Cunningham will discuss your situation with you. He is the only one who can prescribe anything. Don't worry, he'll give you something. In the meantime eat some fruit. Go have a banana or an apple. There is always fruit available. It is good for you and it helps with the cravings."

Jonathan walked away and Bob stood there feeling lost in a place where he knew he did not belong. He wanted some oxycodone or at least a couple of Xanax. He saw bananas and apples and peaches in a bowl near the nurse's station and went over and grabbed a banana. He peeled it back and took a bite. He headed back to his room for his first shower in rehab. He also began to think about leaving as quickly as he possibly could.

~~~~~~~~~~~~~~~~~~~~~~~~~~~~~~

It was after 9 a.m. when Tracey opened her eyes. She stood up, stretched a bit , yawned twice and walked over to Jake's room. Jake was supposed to be in school by 8:30 and he was

still sound asleep. Tracey said, "Jake, Jake, you're late for school."

"Oh Mom, do I have to go. I'm so tired. I don't want to get up. What time is it anyway?"

"It's after nine Jake." Tracey paused, looked down at her boy and said, "Oh, don't worry about it Jake. Just stay in bed. You're already late. Plus, yesterday was a long day. I have to see if I can contact your father. I hope he's all right."

Tracey turned on the computer and googled Kolbe Wellness Center. It was located out near the University of South Florida off Fletcher Ave. "Dang", she said. "That's a long ride every day."

She looked at the phone number on the screen and dialed. She waited and finally the voice menu went into its routine. *You have reached the Maximillian Kolbe Wellness Center. Please enter your access code. If you do not have an access code press zero and the operator will assist you.*

Tracey pushed '0' and waited. Music began to play and then, after an eternity of maybe two or three minutes, a live person picked up. "Good morning, Kolbe Wellness, may I help you?"

"Yes, good morning. My name is Tracey Slider. My husband was admitted last night, sometime after midnight. His name is Bob, I mean Robert, Robert Slider. Can you connect me to him?"

"Do you have an access code <u>Mrs</u>. Slider?"

"No, he just was admitted last night. I was not even there."

I'm sorry Mrs. Slider. You will have to wait until you hear from your husband. We cannot release any information to anyone unless they have the proper access code."

"What do you mean, you cannot reveal personal information? He is my husband, he was admitted there last night. This is ridiculous."

The operator tried to be calm and give Tracey an idea of what the protocol was. "Mrs. Slider, you need an access code to call in. If your husband is a patient here he will call you with the access code sometime today. Do you understand?"

"What! What do you mean IF he is there? I KNOW he's there. I need to speak to

someone in charge. Give me your supervisor."

"Mrs. Slider, please. Pay attention to me. I'm asking you to just listen to me carefully. Can you do that, please?"

"Tracey breathed in deeply and said, "Okay, okay, I'm listening."

"Thank you. Now, Mrs. Slider, Hippa Laws forbid us from releasing patient information over the telephone. Do you understand? So, like I said, If your husband is a patient here I GUARANTEE he will call you sometime soon with an access number. Do you understand?"

"Rules, rules, rules, all I want to do is talk to my husband. This is so crazy."

Mrs. Slider, we do not even know if you are really his wife. I'm sure you are but the initial contact has to be from him. Now, if he is here, he will be in touch. Try to relax and think about what I have told you. Don't worry, he will be in touch if he is here. Now, you have a nice day."

The lady hung up and Tracey stared at the phone. Jake came out from his room and said, "Mom, why you yelling? What's going on? Did you talk to dad?"

"Talk to dad, yeah sure. They won't even admit to me that he is there. We have to wait until he calls us. I can't believe it. I'm his wife and---I'm going over to Judi's. I'll be back in a few minutes."

Tracey, still in a nightgown and bathrobe, hurried over to Judi's house but Judi had already left for work. She rushed back home and, as she hurried past Jake, she said to herself, "I know, I'll call Father Jim. "

Jake, staring at the TV, turned his staring to his Mom. He said nothing as he watched her rifle trough some papers on the table, pause and run out the door. The boy was thinking she was going crazy. Then she hurried back in carrying a church bulletin in her hand which she had left in the truck. She dialed the Sacred Heart Church office number. As soon as she heard the phone being answered she said, "Yes, hi, this is Tracey Slider calling. I need to talk to Father Jim. Is he there?"

A pleasant, professional voice said, "I'm sorry, Mrs. Slider. Father is saying the 9 a.m. children's Mass. He won't come back to the office until, well, probably 10:30. Can you call back then?"

"Oh my God. Okay, okay, but please tell him I called and I must talk to him. He knows what it is about."

"Certainly, Mrs. Slider, I'll tell him when I see him."

Bob finished his shower and dressed in his clothes from the day before. He had not shaved and still felt a bit unkempt. He walked out to the large room that was bordered by patient's rooms that ringed the perimeter of the building. It was obviously a multi-purpose area because there was a 46" flat screen TV, several sofas and lounge chairs, and some tables and folding chairs on the one end of the room. In the center of the floor was a pool table and a Ping-Pong table.

On the other side of the room folding chairs were set in place, about ten across and four rows deep. There was a lectern facing the chairs and this was obviously where meetings and discussions were held. In the middle of the room a metal curtain track was fastened to the ceiling and extended wall-to-wall. Heavy, mechanically activated, partition curtains were snuggled up against the wall on each side of the room. When meetings were in session the curtains were drawn closed so the folks not scheduled could lounge around watching TV, play pool or cards or just talk. The curtains were sound-proofed and, when closed, almost gave the folks attending the meeting the necessary quiet and privacy required.

It was now about 8 a.m. and the place was suddenly filled with people talking, sitting, laughing and arguing. There was an unexplained nervousness in the air and it was as if the entire place was filled with the 'jitters'. The people appeared to be getting in line for something and Bob did not know what he was supposed to do. A guy bumped into him by mistake and said, "Oh, sorry man, my bad."

Bob said, "No problem."

The guy said, "Hey, you're new. When did you get here?"

"Last night."

"Well, my name is Calvin. C'mon, we have to get our morning meds."

"I don't know if I get any. I haven't seen the doctor yet."

"Get in line. They'll give you something. If you're in here they know you need it. C'mon, follow me."

Calvin squirreled his way into the line and Bob knew he was cutting and felt foolish.

Someone yelled over , "Hey Calvin, you ass-hole, get in line like everyone else."

"Up yours, Vinnie."

Bob backed away from Calvin and began to slink toward the end of the med line. Vinnie said, "Yo Calvin, you're a real putz. After breakfast maybe we should take it outside."

Bob watched as Jonathan moved down the line and went over to Calvin. All he did was stop next to him and Calvin sheepishly went to the end of the line. Then Jonathan walked over to Vinnie. He looked at him for a few moments and everyone could see that Vinnie was scared even though he held his ground and stared right back at the big counselor. Jonathan said, "Vinnie, what am I going to do with you? You just can't bite that lip of yours, can you? Maybe you should take me outside? What do you think Vinnie, want to go outside with me?" Vinnie succumbed quickly and said, "Uh, no Jonathan."

"Good choice. Now look, it is early in the morning and I want to have a fairly peaceful day around here. So, apologize to Calvin for calling him names and let's all get on with our peaceful day. What do you say, Vinnie?"

"Okay Jonathan, you're right man. Hey Calvin, sorry man, didn't mean nothing."

Calvin waved to Vinnie, Jonathan gave Vinnie an agreeable smile, and the line began to move forward. Bob was amazed how simply Jonathan had neutralized an impending confrontation. Jonathan walked over to Bob and said, "Be careful who you hook up with here. Remember, everyone is just like you, an addict. Your main focus has to be on yourself and your recovery. Do not let anyone detract you from that, understand? I look at you and my instincts tell me that you are a potential success story. Just try to ignore anything negative you might hear from the people you will be meeting."

Bob was processing the remark, 'everyone is just like you' and said, "Okay, Jonathan. Thanks. One other thing, Calvin said I should get on line for meds. But I didn't see Dr. Cunningham yet. Do I get something now?"

"Wait here, I'll find out."

Jonathan went up to the nurse and the nurse looked at the list. He walked back to Bob and said, "There is something there for you. I don't know what. So stay right here. After you get your meds you will have breakfast. After breakfast you and I will sit and go over the itinerary we have in place. Then you will see Dr. Cunningham and then you will go to your first group. Okay, Bob, enjoy your breakfast. Hey Calvin, show Bob where the dining room is, okay?"

Calvin answered, "Okay boss, got ya."

Bob followed the line and when his turn came the young nurse standing next to the med cart said, "You're the new one, Mr. Slider, correct?"

Bob shook his head and smiled. He was struck by how small the nurse was. She was at the most, five feet tall, maybe less than that, and very thin. She had blond hair cut in a short shaggy style and had a very pretty face with big, brown eyes, a tiny nose and a dimple on each side of her mouth. She said, "Okay Mr. Slider, we have this for you. It is some Librium. That may change after you see Dr. Cunningham."

She handed Bob the little paper cup with the black and torquoise pill in it. As he took it from her she said, "My name is Diane, I'll be praying for you."

Bob, surprised that she had said that, answered, "Thanks Diane, appreciate it."

Calvin, who was near the end of the line, yelled over, "Hey Bob, wait for me man. I'll show you where to go. We can eat together."

Bob just shrugged and stood there. Diane called Bob close to her and, turning her head to him said, "This is your first day so let me explain something to you. Calvin is harmless enough but you may not want to take what he says too seriously. He kind of makes things up. Understand?"

Bob smiled and Calvin came up to him. "C'mon Bob, today is pancakes and sausages."

Bob followed Calvin through two swinging doors at the end of the meeting room and around to the right. Following Calvin into the dining room he quickly took stock of his new 'eating place'. Everyone's eating place is important to them and Bob's first impression was favorable.

The place was clean, it was painted with soft yellows and greens, had recovery slogans tactfully and purposely hanging on the walls and soft music was playing. The room was almost 30' X 30' and had folding tables located separately in a random, yet orderly, fashion. All were covered with pale yellow, plastic table cloths with green place mats placed in front of each chair. In the center of each table a clear plastic vase was placed each holding a bouquet of flowers. Although artificial it was hard to tell them from the real thing.

Bob mimicked the others and picked up his tray first and then the silver ware and then his plate. By the time he was finished being served his tray was full. He had a bowl of fresh fruit, two biscuits, three sausage patties and four large pancakes. At the end of the line he was given some orange juice and a large mug of coffee. He could not believe how good it all looked.

Calvin said to him, "Good food here. Nothing like Windjammer."

"What's Windjammer?"

"Oh man, you are a newbie, aren't you. Windjammer is the county rehab over near McDill . Their food sucks. Hey, come on, sit over here with me. I can introduce you to some people"

Bob followed Calvin thinking about the fact that Calvin knew what kind of food was served in other rehab facilities. He never considered that people might do rehab multiple times. Calvin sat down near a man and two women. He said, "Bob, sit down here. This is Gracie, Dennis and Janice. Hey you guys, meet Bob. He came in last night. He's a first timer."

Bob looked at Calvin not liking the phrase 'first timer' at all. It made him feel as if he was in prison surrounded by repeat offenders. "Hey Bob," Janice said. Gracie smiled and Dennis just nodded. Bob smiled at them and placed his tray down next to Calvin. Gracie said, "You can sit on this side Bob or do you think I have lice or something?"

Bob was taken back by Gracie's curt remarks but Dennis said to her, " Gracie, don't start with the guy. He just got here. So shut up. Hey Bob, don't pay no attention to her. She can be a pain in the ass. Just ignore her."

"Screw you Dennis. Stay out of my business."

Just like that Jonathan was standing there. "Is there a problem here guys?" he asked.

"No problem Jonathan, we're good," Dennis said.

Gracie and Janice smiled and said nothing while Calvin held his head down as he took a bite out of a blueberry muffin. Jonathan said, "This is Bob's first morning here and he is a bit nervous so, while you guys are having your nice breakfast, why don't you explain to him how we do things around here. I would appreciate that. I'm sure Bob would too, right Bob?"

Bob nodded meekly wishing he could go just go home. He was not like these other people. No way. He said to Jonathan, "Yeah, that would be fine. Hey Jonathan, when can I get that code so I can call home?"

"I'll set that up right now. Come see me right after you finish breakfast."

Jonathan left and the four patients quietly ate. The two women seemed a bit hostile, especially Gracie, and they made Bob nervous. Dennis was not saying anything and was acting quite nonchalant and comfortable in his surroundings. Calvin was yammering away about who knows what and as he did, Dennis kept looking over at Bob rolling his eyes and slowly shaking his head.

Dennis suddenly got up, carried his tray around the table, placed it next to Bob and sat down next to him. He leaned his head a bit toward Bob as if he was letting him in on something special and said, "Look Bob, I'm glad to meet you. I can tell you are not like these other bozos. I'll bet you have a wife and kids, right?"

"Bob perked up and looked at Dennis. "Well yes, I do. How did you know?

"Because I can tell you are not a real addict. That's how. In fact, I'll bet you were hurt and they started you on pain meds and then you could not get any, right?"

"Exactly Dennis, exactly. Now I'm being punished for shit that wasn't my fault. It is all a bunch of crap."

"How did you wind up here?"

Dennis was drawing a naïve Bob Slider into his little web. But Jonathan was watching and, just like before, suddenly he was standing there. "Hey Bob, if you are done with breakfast I would like to talk to you."

"Bob was almost done and he said, "I'm done, sure thing."

As Bob got up to leave with Jonathan, the big counselor looked at Dennis. Actually, he looked right through Dennis because Dennis was a con artist and Jonathan knew it and Dennis knew that he knew it. Jonathan said, "Dennis, we can talk later, know what I mean?"

Dennis answered, "No need Jonathan. I get the message."

After breakfast Bob watched as most of the patients more or less congregated together in threes or fours. It seemed that everyone belonged to a small clique and quickly gravitated to it. Near the front of the room opposite the TV side a man sat at a table and Diane sat next to him. There was a box filled with files on the table and Diane was sorting through them. Suddenly she called out, "Keith, come on over."

One of the men in one of the small groups walked across the room and sat down. Bob asked Vinnie, who was standing next to him, what was going on. Vinnie told him that the man at the table was Dr.Cunningham. Bob was shocked that by the time Vinnie had told him what was going on, Keith had gotten up and left and Diane had called out another name. And so it went for the next several minutes until a buzzer went off.

The hanging curtains began to slowly travel across the room while a number of patients slowly walked over to the TV side and the others headed to the chairs near the lectern. It was 'group' time. Jonathan said to Bob, "You come with me. You will go to your first group meeting after lunch."

Jonathan directed Bob to a small room adjacent to the nurse's station. It had a small table and two chairs. Jonathan sat at the table and placed a folder down. He pulled out a sheet of paper and handed it to Bob. "Okay Bob, here is your schedule. This is the way your day will go until Dr. Cunningham decides differently. Let's go over this."

Bob quickly found out that his day was seriously organized. A patient must be up by 7:30 a.m., shower and be in line for meds by 8. Then it was breakfast, see the doctor, group, break-time, lunch, meds, group, free-time, dinner, group, meds, and then to bed. 10 p.m., lights out. Sunday was visitation day. After two weeks visitations could be increased up to two days a week. That depended on the patient and their individual progress. After going over the daily schedule Jonathan said, "Any questions?"

"I really have to call my wife."

"Like I said, Bob, Dr. Cunningham will fill you in on that. In fact, I think it is your turn to see him. Go ahead, he is a good man. One more thing, if you have a problem of any kind, come to me. I can help you and I want to help you."

Bob looked at this big, bald man and was not sure what to make of him. Was he sincere or just following his job description? Did he really care? He would have to wait to find out.

〃〃〃〃〃〃〃〃〃〃〃〃〃〃〃〃〃〃〃〃〃〃〃〃

Tracey was sitting at her kitchen table drinking coffee and staring at her phone. There was nothing worse than not being able to do anything or talk to anyone or to be completely uninformed about a situation you were deeply imbedded in.

The phone she was holding was a device that could inform, convey, record, take photos, make videos, give directions and connect people anywhere at any time. At that moment it was no more than a useless piece of junk. Then it sprang to life and began to sing. The screen lit up and the words, Sacred Heart Church, appeared on it. The woman's heart sighed relief as she pushed the connect button and said, Hi, Father Jim, is that you?"

"Yes, Tracey, it is. What's wrong? Did something happen?"

"I tried to call Bob and they won't even tell me if he is there. I'm his wife and they won't even talk to me. Please, I just need to know that everything is all right?"

"Oh Tracey, trust me, he is fine. Let me explain how it works. The hospital will not tell someone over the phone anything about a patient. After all, it might be a law firm representing someone in a divorce proceeding or it could be credit collectors calling to get inside information on someone or even someone's place of employment so the facility has to be careful in their screening process. You can understand that, right?"

"Yes, I suppose. So how long do you think it might be before I get to talk to him?"

"I can't answer that. But trust me, Bob will be calling you. They will give him an access code to give you and he will call you and give it to you. After that, when you call him, you will input the code and they will connect you. So, he has to make the first call. You will just have to be patient. Anyway, he is fine. I dropped him there myself, remember."

"Yes Father, point taken. I apologize for being so insecure with all of this. I'm just worried about him."

"I understand, Tracey. Look, what is your schedule like today?"

"I go into work at six this evening. Otherwise, wide open unless something happens with Bob."

"The reason I asked was because I was hoping you could get back to some Nar-Anon meetings right away. You are traveling in unchartered waters with this rehab business and you might get some valuable insight into what it is like to have a loved one as a patient in a place like that."

That makes sense Father. They may have some afternoon meetings. I'm going to check."

"Well Tracey, I can tell you this. I know that Calvary Methodist does have meetings on Tuesday and Thursday afternoons at 2:30 p.m. In fact, Jake could go too. School is out at 2:15, right? You could bring him along."

"He did not go to school. We were both so exhausted after last night we overslept. I let him stay home."

Tracey momentarily looked at her phone. She knew he must have had this information ready for her. She sort of smiled and sort of winced simultaneously. The priest was coordinating her moves in his quest to help her. She was not sure if she liked it or if it was a bit too intrusive. Tracey said, "Father, I don't know. What if Bob calls me while I am at the meeting?

"Tracey, you have a cell phone, right?"

"Oh my God, my cell phone. I'm sorry."

Father Jim chuckled and said, "That's okay, Tracey. You have been through the ringer with all of this. Anyway, if he does call it will read 'private caller' so you cannot see the hospital number. Answer it and excuse yourself from the meeting. It's not a problem."

"Okay Father Jim, okay. I really have to thank you for all you are doing for Bob."

"Tracey, I have to say something to you and you might think this is a bit weird. But I believe that last night a miracle took place for your husband. He was on his way to jail, end of story. My being there for Ann Dowling at that moment in time was heaven sent. So I didn't really do anything. God could have called her home an hour earlier or an hour later. But timing was everything and all of our paths crossed at that moment in time. God had a plan and I was part of it as was Anne, rest her soul. It is truly beautiful the way it all worked out."

Tracey said, "Oh Father, I guess---"

Father cut her off, "Look, this is a faith thing. Because of it I have absolutely no doubt that is why things played out like they did. You don't have to believe it and that is okay. But just keep on praying Tracey. Trust me, it is the best medicine out there."

Okay Father, I will. Thank you."

"You're welcome. And if I hear anything else I will call you right away. By the way, will I see you at Mass on Sunday?"

"Uh, yes Father. Jake and I will be there."

Bob walked over to the table, stopped and stood in front of Dr. Cunningham and Diane. Diane smiled at him and said, "Well, hi again Bob, this is Dr. Cunningham. This is Bob Slider, Doctor, he came in late last night. I mentioned him to you earlier."

The doctor was flipping through a stack of papers. He looked up at Bob for a moment and said, "Have a seat, Bob. Nice to meet you."

Bob just smiled a bit, sat down and the doctor went back to flipping through the papers he was holding. Bob quickly felt tense and timid. After a few quick moments that seemed to last forever the doctor said, without looking up, "Well, you must be another one of Father Jimmy's people. I can't believe what I am reading here."

Doctor Cunningham lifted his head a bit and, with his eyeglasses leaning on the end of his nose, peered over them looking into Bob's eyes. He stared for a few seconds and, once again, it was as if time was standing still for Bob. Dr. Cunningham, without blinking, said, "Do you have any idea how fortunate you are Mr. Slider? Let's see now. You were convicted of a DUI, have a suspended license and you are out driving while on probation. Right there is jail time. SO, you have a traffic altercation, are arrested and have a possible heart attack. Am I getting this all in order?"

Bob just nodded his head and tightened his lips. This was embarrassing. He was being treated like a child.

Doctor Cunningham continued, "Now, for some reason the arrest vanishes and your heart attack is quickly diagnosed as not a heart attack. You might ask yourself, how can they know that so quickly? Beee-cause, your blood work was analyzed so quickly. And then, to top it all off, you have Temporary Medicaid as your primary insurance and you wind up in the Maximillian Kolbe Wellness Center a private facility that does not accept Medicaid. Can you explain how all of that happened?"

Bob shrugged and guardedly answered, "I guess I was pretty lucky."

Diane's eyes opened wide because she knew what was coming. Dr. Cunningham said. "Lucky! You think you were lucky? Are you a religious man Bob? Do you believe in God or a Higher-Power or anything like that?"

Bob was becoming rattled. This doctor was getting quite animated and intense. Bob said, "Well, I guess so. Sure. In fact, Father Jim-----"

The doctor stopped him and said, "Father Jimmy, I knew it. God Himself directed Father Jimmy Daniels to you. You have been blessed my friend, truly blessed. Now, let's see what you do with the opportunity that has been heaven sent to you. And, make no mistake, it has been heaven sent.

Bob was sitting there, hands folded on the table, looking across at this doctor who was rambling on about at how 'blessed' Bob was. First it was Father Jim and now it was Dr. Cunningham.

Bob was starting to feel as if God was being rammed down his throat.

The doctor saw the expression on Bob's face and said, "So, you think you were lucky, do you? Well my friend, let me tell you something. Lucky is winning the lottery and many of those 'lucky' folks wind up more miserable than they were before they won."

Doctor Cunningham stopped talking and leaned back in his chair. Tilting his head backward, as if he was looking at the ceiling, he ran his hands over the top of his head. He puffed up his cheeks and let out a big sigh. Then he lowered his head and looked across the table at Bob. "Bob, I'm sorry. I did not mean to get so zealous about your case. It is just that I have been around the block and have seen many things and what happened to you is a not the norm. Plus, I am good friends with Father Jim. He has delivered a number of patients to the doors of this facility and, well, never mind. I can't discuss them. So tell me, how did Father Jim wind up involved with you?" "He just happened to be in the hospital last night and walked by my bed as he was leaving. He recognized me from his church."

"He just happened to be there? Small world, right? And you go to Sacred Heart?"

"Uh, no, not really. I went to Mass there on Thanksgiving and my neighbor introduced me."

Dr. Cunningham smiled and said, "So, you met him one time and he walks by your bed in the emergency room weeks later and remembers you. And here you are. That's beautiful. I love stuff like that. Don't you?"

Bob looked at this doctor but did not want to admit he was not sure of what he believed. He was starting to believe that maybe there was something to this God and faith thing. But it was a distant feeling, like a stirring going on down deep inside him. He said, "Yeah, I guess maybe I do. But I have never thought about that kind of stuff."

Dr. Cunningham knew he had hit a nerve somewhere and that his new patient had something unique to think about. He said, "Anyway, I am what most people call a 'shrink'. From the way I have been rambling, you must think I need one myself." He laughed a bit and continued, "Anyway, my diploma says, Psychiatrist. And, in case you did not know, I am a medical doctor first. All psychiatrists are. Psychiatry is a specialty, like some people are cardiologists or internists or allergists, understand?"

"Yes, I have an orthopedist for my back, Dr. Nelson."

"Victoria Nelson?"

"Yeah, you know her?"

"As a matter of fact I know her very well. She is a fine lady and a fine doctor."

"I can tell you one thing. She sure does not like giving out pain killers."

"Well, she does pro-bono work over at Pinellas Pines Rehab. She and I have also worked together on occasion. She knows about pain pills and she has a point. Look where you are."

Bob breathed in deeply and said nothing. His eyes quickly scanned his surroundings and for the first time the reality of his situation impacted him and a chill ran down his spine.

Dr. Cunningham said, "Okay, I am prescribing 10mg Librium 3x a day for you for five days. We will see how that goes. I will be back Thursday and you and I will have a one-on-one for about a half an hour or so. In the meantime, Jonathan will monitor your progress and I will determine how you are doing based on his reports. Understand?"

Bob shook his head up and down and said, "When can I call my wife. She needs to hear from me. And what are the visiting hours so I can tell her when she can come?"

The doctor said, "Hold on Bob, not so fast. Jonathan will give you an access number later today. Then you can call your wife. You give her that number so she can call you. She cannot get through without that number. As far as visitation, well that might be a week or so. Our objective is to help you get straight. It will probably be at least a week."

"That stinks, I need clothes and personal things. She has to bring them."

"As long as she has the access code she can bring you things and leave them at the front desk. No razors. We have our own safety razors here. You have to use them. Okay Bob, I am falling way behind schedule. Jonathan will give you your access number later and I will see you Thursday morning."

Doctor Cunningham signaled to Jonathan who came right over. "Jonathan," he said,

"Can you take care of getting Bob his access number and some personal items please?"

"Sure thing, Doctor. Come on Bob, follow me and I'll get you a few things."

Diane, who had been quietly sitting and observing, looked at Bob as he stood up to leave. She smiled at him, folded her hands in prayer and said, "Remember."

He knew what she meant and had an unusual desire to do so. He did not know how.

*

*

CHAPTER 19

Time to Get Real

Tracey had not even put the phone down when Jake asked, "What's going on Mom? Is Dad okay?"

"Yes Jake, Father Jim said we will hear from him some time this afternoon. So don't worry, everything is okay."

That was good enough for Jake and he went back to staring at the TV. Tracey decided that going to a Nar-Anon meeting was a good idea but she was not sure if she should bring Jake along. She just needed some time by herself interacting with people who understood her situation and with whom she could talk freely without Jake listening. The thought was very appealing. After thinking about it she decided that she would go by herself. She would just tell Jake to wait for her to get home.

It was 12:30 p.m. and she looked around the house, realized how neglected it had been over the past several days and began to clean. She turned her head as a truck rumbled to a stop in front of the house. It was Greg Margolese. "Hey Mom, Mr. Margolese is here."

"Yes Jake, I see him. Nuts, I don't need this now."

"Should I tell him you're sick or something?"

"No Jake, it's okay. I don't want you lying for me. That's not right. Don't worry, it's no big deal. I can talk to him."

She put down the trash bag she had in her hand and walked to the front door. She opened it just as Greg was about to knock. "Oh, hi Tracey. How are you?"

Tracey, unaware of how worn out she looked, answered, "Fine, Greg. How are you?"

Jake was standing right in back of his mom and Greg said, "Oh, hi Jake. No school today?"

Tracey, unaware that Jake had shadowed her, turned to her boy and said, "Jake, is there something you need?"

"Uh, no Mom."

"Well that's good. Then go inside while I talk to Mr. Margolese, okay."

Jake turned and headed to his room and Greg could tell something was wrong. He waited until Jake left the room and said, "Tracey , I'm sorry for popping in like this but I was in the neighborhood and I thought I would stop by. I wanted to talk to you and Bob about something. If this is a bad time I can come back."

Tracey never dealt with Greg. That was Bob's thing and he was the one who always interacted with him. That was how she liked it. Maybe it was Greg's ever-present, staid demeanor but she did not particularly like the guy and she was happy being the secondary tenant. But this day was a bit different than days gone by. Bob was almost put in jail the night before and was now in a rehab hospital, she had no money and Christmas was less than two weeks away. These thoughts smashed together at one time creating a perfect emotional storm. She looked at Greg and burst into tears.

She could not help it and felt like a fool. "Oh my God, I'm sorry," and she ran into the kitchen to get some tissues as she tried to compose herself.

Greg stood there, lost in a world he rarely traveled in. He was looking at uncertainty, confusion and vulnerability. In Greg's ordered life these were foreign objects. He did not know what to do. He looked into the house watching Tracey in the dining room area pulling paper towels from the roll to use as tissues.

Greg, always sporting a business like demeanor and rarely digressing from that, felt his compassionate side sneaking out. He slowly walked into the house and walked over to the weeping woman. He stood there waiting for an inner guidance that was evading him. He wanted to just leave. But he didn't. He started to talk and said, "Tracey, please, is there anything I can do? I don't see Bob, where is he? Is he all right? Jake isn't in school. Is he sick? Is there anything I can help you with?"

Greg's rapid, nervous questions calmed her. She wiped her eyes and took a deep breath. "I'm so sorry, Greg. It has just been—well, look, Bob's in the hospital and---"

"The hospital? Why is he in the hospital? What happened? Is he going to be okay?"

Greg Margolese's genuine concern was a side of him that Tracey had never seen or even thought that the man had. But he was actually a caring kind of guy who just tried his best to keep business as business. "Okay Greg, we know you a longtime and I know Bob considers you more than a landlord. He considers you a friend. So I will tell you exactly what is going on."

Greg looked at Tracey and said, "Thanks Tracey, I appreciate that. I consider you folks my friends too."

They both sat at the table and Tracey offered Greg some coffee which he accepted. Tracey felt surprisingly at ease with the rigid landlord and she felt a bit guilty that she had never really given him a chance to just be himself around her. She said, "When Bob hurt his back they put him on pain pills. These pills were narcotics and they were very addictive. He started taking more than he was prescribed and ran out. I never told you about any of this because, well Greg, you are the landlord and everything and I was afraid and—"

He stopped her and said, "Afraid, afraid of what. Afraid of me?"

"Oh God, I don't know. Maybe I was. I know he wasn't. Look, he went out last night with the truck and got arrested."

"Arrested! Bob was arrested? For what? What did he do?"

"Greg, a few months ago He was arrested for DUI. He is on probation and his license is suspended. Anyway, he goes out last night trying to get pills and gets in an accident and just like that he's in handcuffs."

"I can't believe this, Tracey. I had no idea all of that was going on. The reason I thought

Bob wasn't staying in touch was because of his back being hurt. By the way, that is why I stopped

here today. But we can talk about that in a minute. Please---finish telling me what happened?"

"Well, he got so upset he collapsed right in the street. They thought he had a heart attack---"

"A heart attack! Bob had a heart attack?"

"Well no, but they thought it was but, actually, it was from anxiety. They took him to the hospital."

"So Bob was arrested, might have had a heart attack and wound up in the hospital. I can't believe it. But he is okay, right?"

"Yes, I think so. I am waiting to hear from him."

"Wow Tracey, you sure have been through it. How is Jake doing with all of this?"

Once again he had surprised her by asking about her son. "He's an amazing kid. He really understands and I even brought him to a Nar-Anon meeting. They have a group for kids like Jake called Narateen."

"I don't know what that is. What is Nar-Anon. Is it like AA?""

"Exactly, and just like AA has AL-Anon for families of alcoholics, NA is Narcotics Anonymous and has Nar-Anon for families of addicts."

"So Bob is an addict and it all started when he hurt his back doing work for me. I can't believe it. I feel so badly about all of this. I guess I am to blame for a lot of it."

Tracey, who was already learning about addiction, got a bit indignant. "Greg, you are not to blame. We all make choices. Bob chose to use too many pills and then chose to go out without a license while on probation. You did not make him do that and neither did I. He made a choice and there were consequences. Do you understand?"

"I guess so."

"One more thing you should know. I found out that he had tried some of these pills before he hurt his back. Some guy at work had given him some and, well, don't ever think it is your fault. It isn't."

"I have read about this pill epidemic in the newspaper but I have never seen it affecting people I know. I read where many people have died from accidentally overdosing. It's hard to believe."

"Well Greg, the priest from Scared Heart happened to be in the hospital last night on a sick call and just happened to see Bob when he was leaving. Next thing you know he takes my husband under his wing. He happens to know the arresting officer, and he also knows the person who is in charge of Kolbe Rehab. Just like that my husband, with no insurance to cover it, winds up in a top-notch rehab center instead of jail. Father Jim told me it is a miracle that everything happened the way it did."

Greg sat there just looking at Tracey as his brain tried to process all of the information it had just received. It was not an easy thing for a man who always had his "ducks in a row" and planned out every day several days in advance.

Greg Margolese rarely, if ever, allowed himself to be sidetracked by anything but this was one of those rare times. "This is all so unbelievable Tracey. You guys sure have had a rough year. First you lose your job and then Bildot closes; and then Bob hurts his back and now he's in rehab. Unbelievable. No wonder you're upset. You have every right."

"Well Greg, I'm learning how to pray. I know God is there but we have never really paid attention to Him. But he sure helped us out last night."

"I believe that too, Tracey. We all need to pay more attention, especially me. I have been blessed and I tend to take a lot for granted. God has been good to me and my family, that's for sure."

Once again he had shown another side of himself. Greg Margolese was also man of faith. Tracey and Greg had known each other for 12 years but this was the very first time they actually had gotten to know each other. She looked at him and smiled and he timidly smiled back at her. Then he said, "I came by for a reason. I told you both that I would zero out the rent through December because of his back injury. It has been three months and I wanted to ask you a favor."

"Sure Greg, if we can do something for you we would be glad to."

"Okay, this house you are in is one of my bigger income earners. It also carries a hefty mortgage. I cannot afford to make the payments on it any longer especially with the housing industry in the tank and so many homes 'under-water' as they say. I really need to have the rent that this house generates ."

"Oh my God, Greg, we can't---"

He held up his hand and said, "Whoa, slow down Tracey. I need to run this idea by you."

"My heart just sank, Greg. I mean, the thought of losing our home and everything. I could not handle anymore today."

"Tracey I have a two-bedroom, one-bath house over on 72nd Terrace. I just put a new water heater in there and it has central heat and air. It has a great yard and is in very nice shape. It does not have a garage but it has a carport. It also has a big shed in the back that Bob could use to store his tools and equipment. I am asking you to consider moving over there. It is only a few blocks from here so it would not affect Jake's school zoning or anything like that. If you guys are willing to do that I will only charge you $200.00 a month rent for the first year. The second year might see a slight increase."

Tracey stared at Greg. She was absolutely flabbergasted. "I don't understand. How can you—I mean, did you say $200.00 a month?"

"Yes Tracey, I did. Look, I own that house outright. I also feel responsible for the situation Bob is in with his back and all. I can cover my expenses on that house with $200.00 a month. The downside is you have to move out of this house by January 1st."

"That's only a few weeks away. But that would be a life saver for us. I can pay that easily with my job at the supermarket. I just don't know how we can move out by January 1st. I mean, oh my God, that sounds impossible."

"Don't worry, I'll help with that. So, what do you say?"

"I have to talk to Bob and---no, I don't have to talk to him. I won't even tell him. He needs to do this rehab thing. When he comes home I'll just pull up to a different house. It will be a new year, a new life, and a new house to live in. Yes Greg---it sounds perfect. Wait a minute. I think I should bring Jake in on this. It's his life too. I'll be right back."

He watched as she went back to get her son. A few moments later she came back and Jake was once again standing close behind her. Tracey said, "He fell asleep. I had to wake him." She turned to her son, gave him a hug and said, "Sit down Jake, I want your opinion about something."

Jake, surprised at being included in a conversation with the landlord, perked up. "Okay, what's going on?"

She explained Greg's proposal as simply as she could. Jake shrugged and said, "You know Mom, you and Dad have been really worried about the money thing for a long time now. I think this is a great idea. Maybe you guys will start laughing and joking around more if you don't have to worry about money every second. I'm still going to have my own room. Yeah, I say you should do it."

Tracey looked at her son and tears welled up in her eyes. Greg Margolese, impressed with the maturity Jake was showing, said, "Hey Jake, since you are home from school, want to make twenty bucks?"

"Yeah, sure, Mr. Margolese. What do you want me to do?"

"Well, I am cleaning out a house over on 58th Place. My trailer is in the driveway. I just need a bunch of the junk in the house thrown into the trailer. Later on in the day I will bring it to the dump. What do you think?"

"Yeah, sure. Twenty bucks. I could use twenty bucks. Let's go. It's okay Mom, right?"

"Oh, of course Jake. Of course."

Greg clapped his hands together and said, "Great. I'll drop you off at the house, Jake. I have some heavy duty gloves you can use. I'll pick you up in about two hours. Tracey, you let me know what your schedule will be and I will try to coordinate everything, okay."

"Okay Greg, I have to talk to Bob. I have not spoken to him yet so I do not know what visiting hours are. Can I call you tomorrow?"

"Sure thing Tracey. No problem. Okay then, I have to get going. If you should need anything, anything at all, call me. And thank you. "

Tracey Slider hugged her son and held on to him for about 15 seconds. "I love you Jake. I am so proud of you."

Greg and Jake walked out to the truck and she watched them climb in. The big red F-350 rumbled to life and disappeared down the street. She went over to the table, sat down, lifted her almost empty cup of coffee and truly enjoyed the lasts few cold sips. She shook her head thinking, *Did I ever misjudge that man. $200.00 a month. No one would believe me if I told them my rent was $200.00 a month. And what is he thanking ME for? And Jake—what a kid I have.*

Tracey suddenly felt secure in the fact that God was definitely watching out for them. She whispered, "Thank you Lord, thank you so much."

~~~~~~~~~~~~~~~~~~~~~~~~~~~~~~~~~~~

Bob had attended his first group meeting at 11 a.m. The moderator of the group was one of the patients who had been there at least two weeks. Jonathan was the counselor on duty so he sat to the side observing and making sure that a proper decorum was maintained.

The man who called the meeting to order was Dennis. Dennis opened the meeting with the Serenity Prayer. Then he welcomed the newcomers. One was Bob and the other was a woman in her mid-twenties who had only arrived within the last hour or so. Dennis asked Bob if he would tell the group something about himself. Bob, nervously stood up and said, "I have never done anything like this before. I don't know what to say."

Dennis replied, "Just tell us your name and a little about yourself. That's enough for now."

Bob said, "Okay, my name is Bob Slider and I used to work---"

Jonathan interrupted saying, "I'm sorry, Bob. Dennis should have advised you of the protocol. He looked over at Dennis. "Isn't that right, Dennis?"

"Yes Jonathan, you're right. I'm sorry."

Jonathan knew that Dennis was a serial manipulator and purposely did not explain the protocol hoping Bob would reveal something about himself that he did not have to. Dennis said, "For you new people, this is an NA meeting. You do not have to tell us your last name. You do not even have to speak if you do not want to. Go at your own pace and just say what you want to. Is that enough, Jonathan?"

Bob watched as Jonathan glared at Dennis. He could tell that Dennis was not one of Jonathan's 'favorite' people. Jonathan snapped at Dennis, "Dennis, you wanted to run meetings and here you are. Have you changed your mind? Would you rather not run the meeting? That is no problem. You know what, never mind. Hey Calvin, why don't you introduce yourself and show Bob and our new friend over here how it is done."

Instead a woman stood up and said, "Hi ya'all, my name is Luanne and I am an addict."

Everyone answered, "Hi, Luanne."

Luanne continued, "Mah drug of choice is oxycontin and I like some of those dang

Xanax too. I have smoked a lot of weed and did some coke when I was a teenager. I have been to rehab two other times and I am truly praying to God that He helps me conquer this demon once and for all."

Luanne sat down and Dennis said, "Thank you, Luanne. Does anyone else want to speak."

Suddenly there were three hands being raised. Dennis pointed to another woman who was older and had tried her best to look presentable even though she was in a rehab facility with limited cosmetic resources. "Hi everyone, my name is Theresa and I am an addict.

All replied, "Hi Theresa."

"Well, my drug of choice has been Valium but I have tried all that other crap too like Ativan and Xanax and Librium. Yeah, I like those benzos for sure. I even tried Triazolam because I couldn't sleep. Oh yeah, all of it was prescribed. You just have to know how to play the doctors and I'm good at it. Anyway, I am 53 years old and I think that if I want to make it to 54 I had better get my crap together and get off this stuff once and for all. Maybe then my kids will talk to me again."

Theresa sat down and there was a pause from everyone as they absorbed Theresa's words. Dennis said, "Thank you Theresa. Who else had their hand up?"

Jonathan said, "Hold on Dennis. Hey Bob, why don't you get your feet wet. Give it another shot."

Bob stood up and nervously said, "Um, hello, my name is Bob and, ugh, well, I got here---"

Jonathan stopped him. "Bob, come on. You heard how the other folks introduced themselves. Everyone, including you, is here because of one primary reason. So, how about saying it. I know it isn't easy but you have to take this step."

Bob, standing in front of strangers, felt like his very soul was naked and exposed. He had fought this moment tooth and nail, even with Father Jim the previous night. But now it was time. They were all waiting and they all knew what he was going through. Luanne said , "Come on now honey, you can do it. It's all right."

Bob looked over at Luanne and nodded. He took a breath and began to speak, "Hi, my name is Bob and I---I—um, oh my God, I am a freaking drug addict." With that he broke down and wept openly.

Silence grabbed hold of the group and then Luanne got up and went over to Bob and hugged him. She said, "That's okay honey. It's okay for a grown man to cry once in a while. It shows ya'all got some heart. You just manned up. I'm proud of you."

Jonathan watched carefully as the scene played itself out. Unnoticed but watching from her office was Maureen Comerford, the director and Father Jim's close friend. She wiped a tear from her eye. It was a happy tear.

The meeting ended at a little after 12 and it was time for lunch. Jonathan called Bob over and walked him across the room. "I just want to tell you that I know it was hard for you in there. But you did good Bob. You confronted your addiction. That is the first step. Be proud of what you did. It was not a weakness, it was a sign of character. I'm proud of you."

Bob was stunned. Jonathan was 'proud' of him. He could not believe he liked that fact. It reinforced him. "Thanks, Jonathan."

"You're welcome. Now go have some lunch and afterwards I will give you your access code so you can call your wife."

Bob smiled and Jonathan extended his hand. He and Bob shook hands and Bob, feeling better about himself, headed into the dining room. Jonathan walked down the hall to Maureen's office. He knocked on the closed glass door and she waved him in. "That was a nice moment in there with Bob Slider. What do you think of him?"

"I think he will be okay, Maureen. He is definitely not one of those hard core addicts. I think he just got caught in the unknown world of pain medication and was overwhelmed. My experience tells me he could be a one-shot rehab patient and recapture his life. We'll see, you never know."

"We sure don't, do we. Anyway, he was very close to going to prison and he does not

belong in prison. God had his back last night through my friend, Father Jimmy. That priest is something."

Jonathan was well aware of Maureen's friendship with Father Jim and he just smiled. He said, "Can I get an access code for Bob. I told him I would give it to him after lunch."

"Actually, Jonathan, I would like to talk to him after lunch. Could you just send him to me. I'll give him his access code."

"Okay, Maureen, that's fine. Well, I had better get over to the dining room and make sure everything is okay. See you later."

〃〃〃〃〃〃〃〃〃〃〃〃〃〃〃〃〃〃〃〃〃〃〃〃〃〃〃〃〃〃

Back in Pinellas Pines Tracey was flitting about the house doing this and that without giving anything she was doing much thought. Nervous energy had her washing up the dishes and wiping out the microwave and even washing the bathtub. Then she took the kitchen curtains down and put them in the washer. She put in some detergent and walked away without starting the machine. She poured herself some coffee, put the cup down and a few minutes later could not find it.

The whole time she was thinking about moving to the other house, about Bob not having called yet and about Christmas being right around the corner. She was not sure about not telling Bob about moving. She was starting to think that maybe she should. Jake had been incredibly 'grown-up' about the move but it was the only house he had ever lived in. She thought that she would get some feedback about everything at the NA meeting. Surprisingly, she was amped up and in no way despondent. The confusion she was now feeling was that of a "good confusion" because, once sorted, it would lead them to preservation. "Damn it ," she said, "Where did I put that coffee."

Tracey did calm herself down, got ready and left for the meeting. She arrived at Calvary Methodist at 2:15 and went down the stairs to the meeting room. There were only a half dozen people there but, to her relief, Grace was one of them. She walked over to Tracey and hugged her saying, "I didn't expect you Tracey. So glad you came."

"Thanks, Grace. Father Jim from Sacred Heart told me there was a meeting today. I'm glad he did. I need some advice."

"Well good, that's what we're all here for, to help each other. Go ahead and sit down and we'll get started. I'm not running the meeting today, Frank is."

Tracey sat down and Grace sat next to her. Another woman sat next to Grace and they hugged each other. Then Grace introduced Tracey to her. "Tracey, this is Donna. She has been coming for a while."

Tracey smiled, reached across Grace and shook Donna's hand. "Nice to meet you Donna."

"You too Tracey."

Then Frank opened the meeting with the Serenity Prayer and then talked about Step T"wo of the Twelve Steps; *we came to believe that a Power greater than ourselves could restore us to sanity.* Tracey had not heard Step 2 yet and the words impacted her deeply. She was surely coming to believe that God was the power working in their lives. She was glad that she had come to the meeting.

After about 15 minutes, Tracey got her chance to stand and speak. "Hi, my name is Tracey and my husband is in rehab---" She paused when the singing of her cell phone came from inside her purse. She hurriedly took the phone out and saw on the screen, 'private number'. Finally, it had to be Bob. "Excuse me," she said. I'm so sorry but I have been waiting for this call."

She answered the phone and, hurrying to the back of the meeting room said, "Bob, is that you?"

"Yeah Trace, it's me. I couldn't call until now."

"Yes, I know about the access number. Father Jim told me. Are you all right, Bob?"

"I guess so. It is a pretty nice place and all. Tracey, I need some clothes. It's not like a regular hospital where you can wear a gown and lay in bed. Everyone is wearing regular clothes."

"Well, when are visiting hours? I'll bring your clothes with me."

"That's another thing. I'm not sure. Maybe Sunday."

"Sunday? That's a longtime. It's only Tuesday. Can you wait that long?

"Yeah right, I should wear the same stinking clothes all week. No---I cannot wait until Sunday."

Tracey felt anger well up inside her but bit her lip. She knew he had to be either scared or insecure. "You just told me visiting hours are not until Sunday."

"Yeah, I know, but you can come out here and drop them off for me?"

"Okay Bob, if I 'm allowed I'll try to get out there tomorrow morning."

"Good, now I have that access number. You need it to call me and also need it so you are able to drop my stuff off here. Got a pencil and paper?"

"Yes, go ahead. What is it?"

"S1944PPF"

Tracey said, 'Okay, S1944PPF, is that right?"

"Yup. Now when you call you have to key that in and then the phone will ring in my room. If I don't answer that means I'm at a meeting or something. Leave a message and I can call you back, understand? Do not tell anyone the access code."

"Who would I tell?"

"Well, apparently someone could answer and ask you to repeat the code because it didn't take correctly or something like that. That won't be true. Just say you want to talk to Bob. If they won't connect you call the operator."

"Sounds like a spy organization or something."

"Well Tracey, I am finding out that if someone has my code they could maybe use it to give access to someone who could bring drugs to them or something. I don't know how. But then I would get blamed. I'm new at this but, bottom line, do not give the number to anyone you do not know or trust."

"Well Bob, I miss you. But I have to admit, I am glad you are there. Things were sure getting out of hand."

"Yeah Tracey, I know, I know."

"What are they giving you for medication?"

"I get some Librium 3X a day. I get re-evaluated Thursday."

"Bob, when is it a good time to call you?

"Well, dinner is at 5:30 and 6:30 to 7 is free time and then we have a group meeting.

So I guess 6:30 to 7."

"Okay Bob, I am at a meeting and I have to go. I'll call you later."

"What kind of meeting are you at?"

"It is a Nar-Anon meeting Bob, for family members of addicts. Ask them about it at your NA meeting. You know sweetheart, Jake and I both love you and we want to do all we can to help you back to where you were."

Bob said, "Are you telling me that my son is going to meetings where they talk about his father? That is such crap Tracey. Thanks a lot."

Tracey was shocked. "Bob, what is the matter with you? We are just trying to do our best in our own way to help you and—"The sudden sound of silence caught her attention. Tracey lowered her phone from her ear and stared at the screen. The signal was gone. Bob had hung up on her.

Maureen Comerford looked across her desk at Bob Slider. The anger in him was obvious. She said nothing and continued looking at him. Then she sighed, leaned forward and folded her hands on her desk. "You know Bob," she said, "You and I just finished having a nice conversation. You said all the right things about getting 'straight' and feeling sorry for your wife and son and how hard you are going to work at getting your life in order. And what did I say in response?"

Bob, feeling like a child being questioned by the teacher, said, "You said, 'good for you Bob. Good for you'. I hope you mean it."

"That's right and then I gave you your access code and had you call your wife from here. The truth is, I wanted to observe. It helps me understand my patients better when I see them interact with the people they are most familiar with. Do you understand?"

Bob looked at Maureen, took in a deep breath, lowered his head and exhaled. Maureen, once again, said nothing and waited. Bob lifted his head and looked at her. She said, "So, the first chance you have to really be yourself you lash out at the person who is closer to you than anyone else on this planet and hang up on her. Did that make you feel good about yourself?"

He sat there shaking his head back and forth as tears ran down his face. In less than 24 hours Bob Slider had cried more than when he broke his wrist as a six year old. Maureen said, "I am glad you are crying Bob. You should be crying. It means you do care. But here it is in a nutshell. It is time for you to 'get real'. Do you know what I mean by that?"

"Yes, yes, yes. I know. I know."

Maureen knew that when a person kept saying 'I know, I know' it usually meant 'shutup, shut-up'. "Okay Bob, you call that wife of yours back right now and talk to her like she deserves to be talked to by her husband. I will even step outside for your privacy. Like I said, it is time to 'get real'. You can start with the number one person in your life, your wife, Tracey."

*

*

*

*

CHAPTER 20

Embracing Truth

Maureen got up and stepped out of her office giving Bob the chance to 'get real' with his wife. She watched through the glass as Bob called her and spoke to her. She waited patiently for him to finish his conversation thinking about the long, unknown journey they had embarked upon. She knew that never again would the road they traveled be free from potholes and detours. Watching carefully, she read his lips as they formed the words 'I'm sorry babe' and 'I love you'. That was her clue to come back in and she did, saying to Bob, "Bob, please let me talk to Tracey for a minute before you disconnect. You can stay right here and listen. I just want to say hello and introduce myself."

"Did you hear, Tracey? Yes, that's right. Okay, here she is."

Maureen took the phone from Bob and said, "Hi, Mrs. Slider. My name is Maureen Comerford and I am the director here at Kolbe."

Tracey became a bit nervous and simply said, "Oh yes, Ms. Comerford, Father Jim mentioned your name last night."

"Please, call me Maureen. And may I call you Tracey?"

"Oh sure, of course, Maureen."

"Good. Now, I would just like you to understand that our objective here is twofold.

Naturally we want our patients to be drug free when they leave here. In fact, usually within 72 hours, the drugs are out of their system and there is no physical need for them. Unfortunately, the brain still thinks the body needs them. That is the real problem. It takes a long time for a person to reprogram their brain to not want these drugs. The addict is the only person capable of doing that and it can be a lifelong battle for them. So, we have programs and support groups to fight back. Am I overwhelming you yet, Tracey?"

"Well Maureen, I never knew that. It sounds like addiction can be very hard to overcome if the brain needs to be retrained."

"Exactly, Tracey. You seem to understand and it is important that you do. Secondly, when patients leave here we try to have them in the best possible frame of mind, believing in themselves and ready to confront the demons that await them."

"That makes a lot of sense. What can I do to help?"

"Come for your first visit Sunday afternoon. This way ---"

Bob cut her off. "Excuse me, Maureen, what about my clothes? I need clothes."

"I know Bob, I know. Be patient. I was just getting to that. Tracey, if you can bring some of Bob's clothes out and leave them at the reception desk in the lobby, that would be great."

"Okay. I'll try to do that tomorrow. This way I can find out where the place is and everything. Oh, one other thing. Can I bring our son, Jake, to visit? He's almost 13."

"Tracey, I will leave that up to you. You know what your child can handle better than I do. Some of the patients here can be a bit, let's just say, intense. So I leave it you. He is more than welcome to come and see his father. Pray on it."

"Thanks Maureen. I'll do that."

"Okay Tracey, it was good talking to you and I look forward to meeting you. Do you want to say good-bye to Bob?"

Maureen handed the phone over to Bob. He felt trapped. His wife and this strange woman had taken over his life. He did not even have clothes to wear. He wanted roxycodone. He took the phone and said, "Yeah Tracey, I'm here. I don't want Jake coming out here."

Maureen tapped her finger on her desk to get his attention. He looked over at her and she held up her forefinger and moved it back and forth. Then she held her fingers to the sides of her mouth and pulled her lips up into a smile signaling Bob that he needed to 'smile' too. He rolled his eyes and said, "Okay Tracey, I'll see you Sunday afternoon. Love you."

He disconnected the call and handed Maureen the phone. She said, "You are experiencing some serious withdrawal, aren't you? You want something, don't you?"

"Yes, I need something. I hate this feeling. It's like something is ripping me apart from the inside out."

"Yes, I know. It's not fun. But it will get better. This is a rehab center so you have to go through it, like it or not. You are not due for any more meds for about four hours. Try eating a banana and then drink some water. That helps. As far as Jake goes, he knows what is going on with you. You could turn this into a learning experience for him by showing him how tough his Dad really is. I would like you to think about that. "

Bob took a breath and left Maureen's office. His withdrawals were amped up and starting to rage. He was thinking, *I can't believe that woman. She tells me she knows how I feel. Yeah, right. She don't know squat. She couldn't last ten minutes going through what I'm going through.* Jonathan saw him and knew the stress had exacerbated his symptoms. He walked over to Bob and said, "Follow me."

Bob followed the big counselor out the door and down to a room on the other end of the building. It was a work-out room with free-weights, two tread-mills, an elliptical and several exercise bikes. Jonathan said to Bob, "If you're going through withdrawal, sweat it away."

Bob was surprised and said, "You kidding me?"

"Bob," Jonathan said, "I do not kid around about withdrawal. Since your heart is fine the exercise will help with the detox and so will drinking a lot of water. Did you ever use a treadmill?"

"Uh, no, I haven't."

Jonathan showed Bob how to use the treadmill and said, "For your first time we will set this on a low setting. Once you are used to it you can crank up the speed."

Bob clipped the disconnect cord to his shirt and started the machine. Fifteen minutes later sweat was pouring from Bob's body as the rubber roadway traveled under his feet. Jonathan told him to slowly bring the speed down and stop. He did and when he stepped from the machine Jonathan handed him a bottle of water, tossed him a towel and asked, "Well, how do you feel?"

"Dang Jonathan, that was much more strenuous than I ever thought it would be."

"You're sweating profusely and we had the speed set pretty low. But that will help you with the detox. Stay well hydrated and drink lots of water. Keep flushing your body out."

Bob just looked off into space and stared. He said, "I think it did help."

"Good, I'm glad. When you have free time take advantage of this room. It can only help you. Okay buddy, you better clean up. It is almost time for group."

Tracey was back with her Nar-Anon group sitting there trying to process her conversations with Bob and Maureen Comerford. She appeared to be in somewhat of a daze and Frank, the moderator, asked her if everything was all right. She never even heard him ask her. He said louder, "Excuse me, Tracey. Are you all right?"

Grace reached over to her and said "Tracey, is everything okay?"

Tracey snapped to and said, "Oh, I'm sorry. I was waiting to hear from my husband and he finally called. That's all."

Frank asked, "Is he all right. I mean you don't have to say anything if you don't want to. But we are all here to help each other and it is all confidential. "

Tracey looked up at the man she had just met fifteen minutes earlier and said, "Okay, he was taken to rehab last night. This is the first time I talked to him. The phone conversation was, well , it wasn't what I expected."

Donna said, "You thought he would be sort of like meek or something and he was nasty, right? I mean Tracey, he is an addict and addicts think of themselves as victims and then they treat the ones who really love them like cow dung. It is crazy but that is the way it is. Am I wrong? Did he talk to you like crap or what?"

"Yes, he did. He acted ticked off at me because he did not have clean clothes to wear. He left the hospital last night and was driven straight to rehab. I mean, I didn't even know how to get a hold of him and it's my fault. So yes, he treated me like crap."

"Well Tracey," said Frank, "That's why we need each other here. We love these people and we have to know and understand that it is the addiction speaking and not the person. Sometimes that is very hard to do, very hard."

"I spoke to the director out there and she said I should wait until Sunday to visit him. But I guess I will bring some of his clothes out tomorrow and drop them off."

"Donna said, "Do you mind if I ask where this 'place' is?"
""No, it's the Kolbe Wellness Center in Tampa."

Frank said, "Whoo—that is one fine place Tracey. He is a lucky guy to be in there."

Tracey said, "I never heard of it until last night and I heard it was a good place. I'm glad you told me that."

～～～

Bob went back to his room and took a shower. It felt very good and he stood under the intense spray allowing the pounding water to beat on the top of his head and cascade down all around him. After a while he stepped from the shower and began to dry himself. His dirty clothes were lying in a heap on the bathroom floor and he realized he had to put them back on. "Damn," he said. "That stuff must smell. I can't wear that. This is bull."

He stepped from the shower with the bath towel wrapped around him and poked his head out of the door. He saw Jonathan across the way and called out to him. Jonathan walked over and said, "Yes Bob, do you need anything?"

"Jonathan, my clothes smell. I can't wear them."

"Where are they?"

"They are still on the bathroom floor."

Jonathan walked past Bob, went into the bathroom and picked up the clothes. He held them to his face and sniffed them. He said to Bob, "These aren't so bad. Here, spread this stuff out over the chair. I'll be right back."

Jonathan left and was back within a minute holding an aerosol can in his hand. He walked over to Bob's clothes and sprayed them all over. "There you go, scented Lysol. Now you'll be germ free and smell like a lilac bush."

"Come on Jonathan, that's not funny. Aren't there any old clothes around here that are clean and that I might borrow until my wife brings my stuff out here?"

"Group starts in five minutes Bob and you need to be there. If you do not want to wear the clothes wear a hospital gown. They are freshly laundered and do not smell. It is your choice. "

Bob, disgusted, said, "Okay, whatever. Where are the gowns?"

"There should be a few on the shelf in your closet. Look there."

A few minutes later Bob appeared wearing the freshly sprayed, lilac scented clothes he had on since the day before. Jonathan peered over at him from the other side of the room and felt a moment of self-satisfaction. Bob had swallowed some pride. It was a good moment for him although he did not know it.

Everyone migrated to the meeting side of the room, the curtains were drawn closed and the afternoon group was ready to begin. Bob sat down with the rest of the patients and watched as Dennis walked up to the lectern. Bob was a bit surprised when Dennis began by saying, " Good afternoon everyone. I'm not going to be moderating this afternoon. We have a special moderator and, oh, here she is."

Dennis walked away from the lectern as Maureen Comerford stepped to it. It was the first time that Bob had been able to view the entire physical woman. She was wearing a crisply tailored taupe suit and it flowed gracefully over her perfectly contoured body. He was struck how shapely she was and how she seemingly glided across the floor exuding confidence. Her hair was auburn with pronounced, natural streaks of burnt–sienna flowing throughout.

Maureen's face was perfectly formed and her striking blue-eyes quickly grabbed one's attention. Bob Slider realized that she was just plain beautiful. Maureen stood at the lectern, looked out at the patients looking up at her, smiled and said, "Good afternoon everyone. My name is Maureen and I am an addict."

Everyone answered, everyone except Bob Slider who was temporarily speechless. "Hi ,Maureen."

Maureen smiled and said. "It has been more than two weeks since I have stood up here like this and I guess some of the new folks are a bit surprised to see me here. The fact of the matter is I am a recovering addict. For me, every day is a fight. Every day I say the 'Serenity Prayer' at least 50 times. I have worked and fought and I have beaten my addiction down. However, I know that it never goes away. I know that it is always lurking, waiting to pounce, waiting to catch me in a moment of weakness. So, I have chosen not to let it ever beat me again."

"Since I am the director of Kolbe this is your opportunity to ask me a few questions. You know, like how does a user like me get to be a director of a fancy rehab hospital?"

Janice quickly raised her hand, "So how did you do it, Maureen? Because, to tell you the truth, I think you're making this all up to, you know, like motivate us or something. That's what I think."

Maureen smiled and said, "Actually Janice, that makes sense to me. Okay, does anyone else think the same thing? Do you think that this is a motivational technique to help you all get clean?"

Skip, Calvin, and about six others raised their hands. Maureen said, "Okay, here it is. Number one, all of us here, including me, make choices. Number two, we have to accept responsibility for those choices. None of us became an addict because we were made to. Some of us were prescribed meds that were addictive and we abused them. Choices. Some of us wanted to be 'cool'. Choices again. When I was in high school and in my first years at college I made choices. These choices almost killed me. Then I made different choices and here I am."

Calvin said, "Like what was different for you? You standing there telling us about choices is dumb. Sometimes you got no choice but to make the same choices like when you need food to eat and stuff. Nothing is ever different for me. So what am I supposed to do about it. I got no money, I got a record, no one wants to give me a job. What choice does someone like me got?"

Maureen got a bit angry and also was exasperated. She knew Calvin was one of those folks who would more than likely 'repeat'. The man would not accept responsibility for any of his actions. Things that happened to him were never his 'fault'. She looked at Calvin and said, "Calvin, you have a family that cares about you. I know, because I have met them. That is all I am going to say to you now. If you decide to share with your NA family here, that's your choice. But do not ever tell me you have no choices to make. I have 'walked the walk' Calvin. I know the world you come from. So, you might consider reading over the Twelve Steps. That is your choice. We all make choices Calvin, each and every one of us, and we own those choices, like it or not."

Maureen looked at the addicts staring up at her and for the moment felt totally inadequate and actually felt a shiver run through her. Who did she think she was telling them what to think or feel or do. She was an addict like them. She sat where they were sitting. She took a breath and continued speaking. "My brother, Joe, was in the Army and was killed in action in Afghanistan. I loved Joe. We were very close. The night of his funeral I overdosed on booze and benzos. Xanax I think. Maybe some other stuff too. I don't have a clue. Anyway, I almost died. But Joe's best friend, Jimmy, saved my life. He stayed with me and prayed with me and helped me recover."

"I finished college, went on for my Master's Degree in Social Work, received all my certifications and here I am. But I had Jimmy. You all have family or friends or clergy or someone in your corner too. And, there is always NA. You never have to be alone. Do not allow pride to get in your way of succeeding. If you falter, don't be embarrassed. Turn it over to your Higher Power. Turn to your family or friend. Go to an NA meeting. There is always someone, somewhere you can turn to."

"Anyway, I want you to know I understand what you are going through. Please do not try to con me because I have, as the cliché goes, 'been there, done that'. My staff and I will do all we can to help you in your recovery. However, you are in charge of your own lives. You have a choice to make. This is the opportunity for all of you to embrace the truth no matter how painful it might be. Have faith, stay strong and you can succeed. And by the way, I love you all."

Maureen stepped from the lectern and did not make eye contact with anyone. She purposely and slowly walked back to her office. Most of the eyes in the small audience followed her. Many of those eyes were filled with tears.

_____

Tracey arrived home close to 4 p.m. She no sooner stepped from the truck when Judi pulled up. Judi yelled over to her, "Hello girl-friend. Don't go anywhere. Stay right there, I have some news for you."

Tracey stood still watching her best friend as she ran over to her. "Tracey, you won't believe what happened. Oh, how's Bob?"

"Bob's fine, Tracey, what won't I believe happened."

"Helen quit. She walked out in a huff. She got into a fight with Mr. White and started screaming and cursing at him. It was unbelievable."

"Oh my God, Helen? Mild mannered Helen? She flipped out?"

"She was so mad about her paycheck being messed up. They shorted her almost $150.00 and with Christmas so close she became upset. She went to Mr. White and he told her he was not sure if it could be fixed until the next pay cycle was complete. Helen just lost it. It was awful."

"But he didn't say for sure she wouldn't get the money, right?"
"Right Tracey, but Helen has been under a lot of pressure at home. She has that guy living with her and he's a free-loading drunk. But she won't throw him out and he takes her for every dime she has. I don't understand it."

"Oh Judi, I just came from a Nar-Anon meeting. So Helen is another one who has a problem making choices. It is like an epidemic of 'bad choices' going around."

"Yeah, you're right. We have to wait and see what happens but the way Helen was carrying on in front of everyone I do not think she will be able to get that job back. She went too far. In fact , she picked up a bunch of paper sacks and threw them at Mr. White. They just fluttered all over but it was a terrible scene. They could press charges against her if they want to."

"Poor Helen. That's awful. And right before Christmas."

"So, how was your day. You went to a Nar-Anon meeting. Good for you."

"Judi, can you come in for some coffee. I have a lot to tell you, a lot."

"Sure Trace, let me just go home for a second and get out of this uniform. I'll be back in ten minutes."

Judi came back to Tracey's and they sat and had coffee and Tracey shared the entire day with her friend. Judi could not believe what Greg Margolese had offered them and, although she was not very happy about the Sliders moving out, she was happy about the opportunity afforded them. She also was quite happy that Father Jim had become such a positive influence in their lives.

As they chatted the phone rang. Tracey looked at the screen and saw that it was Shop-

Well Supermarket's number. "It's the store," she said.

Judi watched as Tracey answered. "Oh, hi Mr. White. What's going on? Do you need me to come in earlier than six?"

Tracey looked over at Judi and opened her eyes wide and began pointing to the phone. Judi was dying to know what her manager was saying. Then Tracey said, "Well, yes, absolutely. I would love it. You won't be sorry, Mr. White. Yes---thank you. Bye bye."

Judi was staring and as soon as the phone clicked off she said, "What, tell me, what's going on?"

"He just offered me a full time cashier's position. I can't believe it. Oh my God, that means benefits and 36 hours and oh my God Judi, that's like over $1800.00 a month and with the new rent of $200.00 we can" ---Tracey began to cry. So did Judi. The both stood and hugged each other. Then Judi said, "Let's join hands and thank God for this and also ask Him to watch over Helen."

Tracey said, "Oh Judi, if Helen hadn't lost her temper like that I wouldn't be thanking God for anything. Someone had to lose their job so I could get one."

"Tracey, didn't you just tell me about an epidemic of bad choices going around. God may have something better in store for Helen and I believe this is what He wanted you to have during this Christmas season. She grabbed Tracey's hands, bowed her head and said, "Father in heaven, thank you for giving Tracey and her family this fresh opportunity and we ask that You watch over Helen. Keep her safe and let her know that You are there for her, we ask this in Jesus' name. Amen."

Just then Greg's truck rumbled up. Jake jumped out and ran into the house. He was all excited. "Hey mom, hey Judi. What's going on? What's to eat Mom, I'm starving."

"I guess Mr. Margolese worked your butt off."

"No Mom, actually, he is pretty cool. I always thought he was like stuck up or something. But he's not. In fact, he paid me thirty bucks instead of twenty and all I had to do was drag a bunch of junk out from the house and fill his trailer with it. It was kind of easy."

"You're right Jake, I guess he is pretty cool. Now, I have some news for you. I was just offered a full-time job at Shop-Well. That will be a big raise in pay and with moving to the other house with less rent we'll be okay money-wise. How does that sound?"

"Mom, that is so awesome. And then Dad will come home and be all better and everything will be okay again. I guess there really is something to this praying thing."

Tracey and Judi looked at each other and smiled. It had been a good afternoon.

*

CHAPTER 21

Choices

Mr. White had asked Tracey if she could come in at five o'clock instead of six. He wanted her to fill out the additional paperwork that was required for a full-time employee as there were healthcare and 401K options that now had to be considered. There was even a voluntary stock option plan that was available for full-timers. Things sure had taken a positive turn in the Slider family.

Tracey finished her paperwork and had about 20 minutes to spare before her final shift as a part-timer began. She decided to walk outside the store to get some air and stretch her legs. The store entrances and exits were located on each side of the store. As she walked from the west exit down towards the east exit a man ran past her bumping into her slightly. Startled, she turned to see three of the young stock clerks who worked at Shop-Well running after him. "There he is, let's get his sorry ass," one of the clerks yelled.

Tracey watched as the three young men from the store chased after the man. She noticed that he was quite a bit older and shabbily dressed in worn and dirty clothes. He wore a dark red baseball cap that crowned his long, dirty hair which complimented his scruffy beard. Any hope he had of escaping the three younger and faster men was futile. In fact, the man actually had a pronounced limp and could hardly run at all.

Tracey kept watching and gasped in horror as the three young guys caught up to him. One of them tackled him right in the store parking lot executing a beautiful, open field tackle that would have made any football coach smile. The man fell in a heap smashing his dirty head into the asphalt. The three men did not wait to see if the guy was all right. They just stood him up and began dragging him back to the store. Blood was running down the side of his face.

Tracey was stunned at the violence the man was being subjected to. She watched as Mr. White came out from the store at the same time two police cars pulled up with their red and blue lights flashing. Tracey was sure this guy must have committed a serious offense. She watched as the policemen got out of their cars and slowly and matter of factly walked toward the men. The one cop said, "Oh man, it's our friend Harold. What's it this time Harold, popcorn?"

A small crowd quickly formed and Tracey could not help but cringe at some of the things she was hearing that described the bleeding, humiliated man. Words such as *waste, useless, pathetic, bum, and scum bag* were a few. Some people had an obvious sense of compassion on their faces while others seemed to harbor a disdain for the bleeding, dirty, 'criminal'. Tracey found herself so upset she became sick to her stomach. The other cop held out his hand to the man and said, Okay Harold, hand it over."

Harold, holding his one hand over his head wound, reached under his shirt and pulled out a sandwich. The cop shook his head and said, "Well, Harold, looks like you're turning into a gourmet. This is roast beef, not bologna. What, now you're too good for bologna? "

Tracey, holding her hand on across her belly, walked over to Mr. White and said, "Mr. White, is all of this because he stole a sandwich?"

"Yes Tracey, it is. And it is not his first time."

"It's not even a five dollar sandwich. Can't I just pay for it?"

"Look, Tracey, what are we supposed to do? This is not Harold's first time doing this. He probably wants to get caught. Then they take him to jail and he stays a while, gets cleaned up and fed. They release him and then he does this again. Sometimes he is taken into a rehab facility and he stays a month, gets cleaned up and sober and then hits the streets again. He apparently has a serious drug problem and this is his life."

"That's so crazy Mr. White. Why would anyone want to live like that? Oh God, look at him. His head is bleeding all over the place. They should call an ambulance. They didn't have to tackle him like that."

Just then an ambulance did pull into the parking lot. Mr. White said to Tracey, "I hate seeing this. If I thought it would help him I would pay for the damn sandwich myself. I did one time and before I knew it eight of his friends were in here looking for free food. What are we supposed to do?" I don't know. Do you?"

"Uh, I guess I don't know what to do. Does he live around here?"

"He lives on the streets. He's one of our homeless people. Someone told me he used to have a good job and a family and everything. He supposedly came here from Wisconsin. I have no idea what happened in his life, no idea. I sure do not understand it. I guess we just have to pray for him."

Tracey said nothing and watched as the man sat on the rear end of the ambulance while the paramedics tended to his head wound. Fifteen minutes later the ambulance drove away with the man inside. One of the police officers went along. She turned and watched as Mr. White and the other policeman went into the store and completed some paper work at the courtesy counter. It suddenly impacted her that the night before her own husband had been arrested, hit his head on the asphalt and was taken to the hospital. An overwhelming sense of dread filled her. She said quietly to herself, "Oh my God, oh my God. Please dear Jesus, don't let that happen to my husband, please."

Tracey finished her shift at ten o'clock and headed home. She was still unnerved by the homeless man who only wanted something to eat and had been manhandled so unceremoniously. She wished she would have known about him when he came into the store because she was sure she would have immediately bought him a sandwich and drink before he tried to rob the place. But, in her heart of hearts, she knew she had seen him in the store once or twice before and always hoped that he would not come to her register.

The next morning Tracey packed up some of Bob's clothes in a carry bag. She placed some personal hygiene products, some homemade chocolate chip cookies and a "get well" card with a husband/wife personal note written in it. She was confident that when he read the note he would know immediately that it would be a "very good thing' for him to get well and get home ASAP.

She drove Jake to school and told him about the previous evening's trouble at the store. She was stunned that Jake teared up and said to her, "Mom, I need to go with you to see Dad. I think I'm scared about what's going on with him."

She reached over and grabbed her son's hand. "Don't worry Jake. Your dad will be fine. He has us, right? We are a family. And you and I together will never let anything like that happen."

"Promise, Mom?"

Tracey's fledgling faith sprouted a few new buds and she said, "Jake, we are giving this over to God. He will help us get through anything. Now, pray along with me."

Jake squeezed his mom's hand as she prayed, "Hail Mary, full of grace, the Lord is with you, blessed---oh Jake, I'm sorry. I can't remember how it goes. Okay, ---Oh Lord, please watch over us, especially my husband and Jake's dad, thank you and Amen. Sorry Lord, I'm not very good at praying . But I will get better at it."

Jake appeared to appreciate that personal moment with his mom and he smiled and said, "I think God liked that. It came from your heart, know what I mean?"

She just looked at her son and then said, "Come here and give me a hug."

They hugged and she kissed him goodbye. Tracey waved to him as he walked toward the school entrance and then she reached over to the back seat and grabbed the carry bag. She placed it on the passenger seat next to her and began her first drive out to the Kolbe Wellness Center. The only time she moved her hand away from the bag was when she had to shift gears.

The drive took almost an hour but Tracey found the place easy enough. But she was quite disappointed that her access to the facility was so limited. She drove up to the front entrance and the guard at the station asked for her access code and her driver's license. They were validated and then the bag was searched. Bob's shaving razor was not acceptable. The cookies were also not acceptable. They might be laced with something and there was no way to tell. She was advised that the patients had plenty of food and snacks always available to them and that the safety razors for shaving were given out by the hospital. In less than five minutes she was turned around and leaving.

As she drove down the winding road toward the Dale Mabry Highway she stopped and got out of the truck. She stood there looking at the building that held her husband behind its walls. It was not fenced and it had no razor wire or guard towers or anything like that surrounding it. It actually looked quite tranquil. Then she noticed that across the road from where she was standing was a bronze statue of a man. Slowly, she walked over to it.

Tracey stood still in the mid-morning sun and stared at the figure. It was of a frail man dressed in a striped prison uniform with the number, 16670, emblazoned across the left breast. The statue's right arm pointed toward the building and the face on the statue appeared to be peaceful and serene.

To the side and set back about a foot or so from the statue was a plaque. Tracey looked at it and began to read: *This facility is dedicated to St. Maximilian Kolbe, a simple, Catholic priest who, as a prisoner of the Nazis at the Auschwitz Concentration Camp, traded his own life to save the life of another. On August 14, 1941, after almost two weeks of starvation, the Nazis injected Father Kolbe with carbolic acid. He was 47 years old. He was declared a saint by Pope John Paul II on October 10, 1982. Father Kolbe has been declared the Patron Saint of drug addicts and their families. St. Maximilian Kolbe, pray for us.*

Tracey finished reading the plaque and turned to look back at the statue. As she stared at the bronze face, snippets of the man the statue honored filled her head. The little thought pieces quickly ran together and she saw a frail man, kind and gentle, standing in front of a towering prison guard, looking him right in the eye. Tracey could sense that he was filled with peace and unafraid. Then she saw him being dragged away and thrown into a dungeon and finally being injected with poison days later, willingly holding out his arm for his executioner. All of that happened inside her head in a matter of a few seconds. As she walked back across the road to her truck she said quietly, "St. Maximilian, I'm not sure how this works but please pray for Bob and me and Jake too. And all of the other people who are patients here."

As she climbed into her truck a shiver ran down her spine. She paused and took in a deep breath. In a moment's time Tracey's nagging doubts had disappeared.

Tracey began her drive home feeling a bit lightheaded and squeamish in her stomach. She knew she needed something to eat. A "Mr. Donut" sign caught her eye and she pulled into their parking lot. She had no sooner stepped from the truck and taken two steps toward the store entrance when an unkempt, dirty looking fellow came meekly over to her and said, "Excuse me ma'am, any chance you could spare some change for some coffee?"

She had no time to respond when a man came out from the store yelling, "Hey you—I told you to get the hell away from my store. Now beat it or I'm calling the cops."

The dirty guy turned and quickly walked away. The man walked toward Tracey and said, "I'm sorry ma'am. But these drugged soaked, homeless people drive me nuts. I hope he didn't bother you any."

Tracey felt herself getting angry. She said to the man, "Well, he looked hungry and I was going to get him some breakfast. They have to eat too, don't they?"

The man stared at her. "You're passing judgment on me, aren't you? You think I don't care. Let me tell you something lady, that guy and his buddies come here every day at four o'clock and I give them maybe four or five dozen donuts from the morning shift. Every single day, lady. So don't be so high and mighty with me. How many homeless people did you feed today, huh?"

The man's words hit Tracey like a sledgehammer and she teared up. The guy said, "Look, I'm sorry. I'm sorry. Please don't cry on me. I know you were going to feed that guy. I apologize. I just get frustrated sometimes. So many of these men and women have no place to go. I do my best but—hey look, my name is Gus. Come inside and let me buy you a coffee and a donut. And please, don't cry."

⁓ ⁓

Tracey arrived home close to noon. Her experience at "Mr. Donut" had been very enlightening. The previous day she had looked on as a homeless man was chased down, captured, and then taken to the hospital in handcuffs for treatment to a head injury he suffered in his apprehension. And it was all he because he was hungry and tried to steal a sandwich.

At Mr. Donut another hungry, homeless man had been run off because he wanted something to eat. Tracey's initial reaction was that these people were being treated like stray dogs and that people did not care and just wanted them to 'get lost'. She had quickly learned that it was not the case. Many people did care. Mr. White wanted to help. Gus fed homeless people every day of the week. But there were so many homeless people sometimes the numbers were simply overwhelming.

Tracey went to the fridge and took out some iced tea. Gus had given her a half-dozen donuts to bring home and she took a chocolate covered crème out of the bag. She took a big bite and stopped in mid-chew opening her eyes very wide. "Oh my God, oh my God."

She had just realized that Bob was scheduled to see his probation officer on Thursday which was tomorrow. She knew that if he found out where Bob was he would know that he had violated his probation. That would mean immediate jail time. She started mumbling, "Oh my God, what should I do? What should I do?"

She stood up and began to nervously pace around the house. She finally stopped moving, took a deep breath and said out loud, "Okay Tracey, calm down. Thursday is not today. It is tomorrow. What to do? What to do? Maybe I should, I know, say a prayer."

Alone in her living room, Tracey Slider folded her hands and recited out loud the only prayer she knew, "God grant me the serenity to accept the things I cannot change, the courage to change the things that I can and the wisdom to know the difference." She added, "Okay God, I need some help here. Amen."

She felt a bit calmer but she still had no idea as to what she should do. She sat back down at the table and took another sip of coffee. She looked at the phone lying next to her hand and, just like that, picked it up and punched in the numbers for the probation department. She patiently listened as the voice-mail prompts went on and on. Finally, the message said, 'for Mr. Hendley, press 6'. She pressed 6. The phone rang a few times and a woman answered and said, "Mr. Hendley's office, this is Ms. Gibson, may I help you?" Tracey answered, "Yes, this is Tracey Slider. I wanted to speak to Mr. Hendley. Is he in?"

"I'm sorry Mrs. Slider but Mr. Hendley is away on vacation. He won't return until the middle of January. I'm taking over his caseload while he is away. Is there something I can help you with?"

Tracey was not sure what to say. She had spoken to Mr. Hendley a few times and was comfortable with him. This was an adventure into the unkown. She said, "Well Ms. Gibson, my husband, Robert Slider, has his appointment tomorrow morning. He has been sick and I wanted to--"

Ms. Gibson interrupted, "Excuse me Mrs. Slider, could you hold on for a second."

Tracey heard papers rustling and was rapidly becoming frightened. She thought, *Please Lord. Let this work out. Please. Please.* Ms. Gibson's voice came back and Tracey snapped to attention. "Mrs. Slider, Mr. Hendley left me a list of certain clients that are going to be getting , well, let's just say, a kind of Christmas gift. Your husband is one of them. He is always respectful and courteous, is always on time for his appointments, and is doing his best to fulfill his probation requirements. Because of that he does not have to report in until January 17th. He gets the month off. How does that sound?"

Tracey was astounded. Just like that her problem was over and done with. She had harbored wild thoughts of her and Jake freaking out as Bob, kicking and screaming and crying, was dragged away to prison on Christmas Day and poof!---just like that, everything was okay. She said, "That's wonderful, Ms. Gibson. Thank you."

"You're welcome, Mrs. Slider. You and your family have a nice holiday."

"Yes, you too Ms. Gibson. Merry Christmas."

Tracey flipped the phone closed, sat still and listened to the quiet in the house. After a few minutes she raised her eyes upward and smiled a Thank You.

Tracey had one more quandary to deal with. She was supposed to visit Bob for the first time on Sunday but she was also scheduled to work from noon until 8 p.m. that day. It was imperative that she see her husband but she did not want to be taking off from work when she just had been promoted. Plus, Mr. White had no knowledge of any of the problems she was dealing with. She might have asked Judi for an alternative schedule but Judi had already left to visit with her mom and was not due back until Saturday. Tracey decided to take the same approach with Mr. White as she had done with the probation office. Except this time she would not call, she would go talk to him face to face.

Tracey got into her truck and drove over to Shop-Well. Before she went into the store she once again paused to say a personal prayer. This time she just talked to God and asked for His help, apologized to Him for being such a pain and then thanked Him for being so good to her. She was starting to really enjoy talking to God and when she stepped from the truck she felt a certain sense of peace inside her. As Tracey headed toward the store she was standing taller and walking faster.

She walked into the store and over to the courtesy counter. Sally McGovern was selling lottery tickets to a very large man who was sitting in an electric, courtesy cart. The man had a stack of tickets that were being run through the machine and Tracey knew it would be sometime before Sally was finished with him. Sally saw Tracey standing there and, without stopping from inserting tickets, said, "Tracey, I have something for you . I'll be done here soon. Sit tight."

"Sure, Sally."

She headed over to the cushioned bench that was against the wall and sat down. The big man was spending some 'big bucks' on all different kinds of Lottery tickets. She watched as his total price hit $250.00. The man neatly stacked his tickets, put then in a plastic carry case and slowly drove himself out of the store. Tracey walked back to the counter and said to Sally, "Did he really spend $250.00?"

"He sure did. It's not that unusual. Anyway, I have something for you." She reached

under the counter and took out an envelope. "Here you are, Mr. White left this for you. I think he changed your schedule. He asked me to give it to you if you came in."

"Thanks, Sally."

Tracey went back to the cushioned bench and opened the envelope. Her hours for

Sunday had been changed. She did not have to come to work until 4 p.m. There was a note included. It read, 'Tracey, my apologies for the change to your schedule but one of the cashiers needed the evening hours for a family event. I hope you don't mind. If there is a problem, let me know'. It was initialed , EW .

Tracey was shocked. Once again her prayers had been answered. Visiting hours at Kolbe began at 11 a.m. She could go there Sunday morning, leave by 2:30 and still be back in plenty of time for work. And no-one at work would know anything about it. Tracey stood up, did a slight fist pump, left the store and headed home.

⌐⌐⌐⌐⌐⌐⌐⌐⌐⌐⌐⌐⌐⌐⌐⌐⌐⌐⌐⌐⌐⌐⌐⌐⌐⌐

It was Thursday afternoon and the patients at Kolbe rehab were just spending an hour of scheduled free-time prior to dinner. Some watched TV, others shot pool, some played cards and about half of the folks milled around outside in the courtyard. Smoking was permitted in the courtyard and about half of the patients were smokers. The cigarette break was a welcome moment of relaxation for them. Quitting smoking could come later. Kicking one addiction at a time was hard enough.

Bob had come out and sat down at a picnic table by himself. Just like that Dennis came over and sat down across from Bob. He pulled a pack of Pall Mall from his pocket and offered the pack to Bob. Bob just shook his head 'no' and Dennis fired up his smoke. Dennis was a short, stocky guy who seemed to be in charge of things and filled with confidence. He had a full head of sandy colored hair that he combed straight back and he had a tattoo that said "MOM" on his right bicep. He had been "cozying" up to Bob since Bob had arrived and Bob, being alone and insecure, liked it.

"So Bob, how you doing? Two days in, right? Listen man, don't worry, you'll be fine. I've been here three weeks. This is my second time.

I actually like it here. Great food, the staff is awesome and that Maureen Comerford is a sweetheart. Do you know her pretty well?"

"Uh, no, I just met her yesterday for the first time."

Dennis was doing his thing and softening Bob up. He was becoming his 'best friend' and Bob did not even know it. "Yeah Bob, me and Maureen go back a ways. I knew her when she was a user. She was something. It is amazing what she has managed to do with her life."

"You knew her way back? Really?"

"Yup, sure did. Hey Bob, listen, I was wondering if you could do me a small favor?"

Bob got nervous. He answered, "Well, I guess, if I can. I don't know what I can do for anyone while I'm in here. What is it?"

"Well, Maureen does not come in until tomorrow afternoon. She would take care of it then, us being good friends and all, but I really can't wait until tomorrow. I have to call my wife. It is really important."

Bob was puzzled to say the least. "Don't you have an access code to call out with? We all do, right?"

Dennis stared at Bob and said, "So---you calling me a liar? You think I embarrassed myself coming over to you like this just for the hell of it? I don't even know you man and I come to you asking a possible new friend for a little help and right away you treat me like a jerk. Man, I had you all wrong."

Bob was totally dumbfounded at Dennis' reaction to his simple question. He was momentarily speechless and stared at Dennis. The guy lowered his head, took a drag from his cigarette and just shook his head back and forth. Bob suddenly felt guilty and said, "Wait a minute man, what's wrong? I only asked you a simple question. Maybe I can help you but I don't know what you want. "

Dennis lifted his head and without turning to bob said, "I told you I have to call my wife."

"Bob said, "I don't understand, Dennis. What can I do to help you call your wife?"

"Oh man, I'm sorry for jumping at you like that. Look, I lost my access card. It is the second time and I feel like an idiot. Last time, Maureen gave me a new one right away. But she's not here and I can't ask Jonathan because he'd never believe me. He don't understand people like Maureen does. I just need to call home. That's it Bob. That's the favor. Just help a dumb guy call his wife. That's it."

Bob was not sure what to do. He had been told not to give his code to anyone. But Dennis was a guy just like him who only wanted to call his wife. Anyone could lose his code. Dennis helped Bob decide. He said to Bob, "Look, you dial the phone for me. I never have to even touch your card. Then you put the card back in your pocket and we're done. What do you say, Bob? How about helping a guy out. All you have to do is dial the phone. That's it."

Bob shrugged and said, "Okay, I guess it's all right."

"Oh man, that's great. I'll owe you big time for this. Come on, let's go."

Dennis stomped out his smoke and headed for the rec-room. Bob dutifully followed.

Dennis pulled the door open and held it for Bob. As Bob was about to pass Dennis a voice called out

"Hey Bob, could you come over here? I need to see you for one second."

Bob turned and saw it was Jonathan. He said, "Yeah, sure Jonathan. Be right there. Hey Dennis, give me a second. Jonathan wants to see me for a minute. I'll be right there."

Bob walked over to the big counselor who had just happened to stay an extra hour to fill in for Jennifer who was going to be late this day. "Yeah Jonathan, what's up?"

"Look Bob, you are new here and I just wanted to remind you that it is choices you made that brought you here. You may be asked to make choices while you are here also. If that happens, make them wisely."

"What   do   you   mean?"
"I'm just going to say this to you. If you are entertaining any thoughts about using your access code for someone else, you may want to rethink that decision. That's all. We all make choices Bob and we have to accept responsibility for those choices. I understand it is not easy to say 'NO' to someone but there are times when it is the right thing to do. Okay, that's all I wanted to say. You are a big boy. Just remember, you own your decisions."

Jonathan turned and walked away. Bob could not believe it. Jonathan knew exactly what was going on. Now he had to tell Dennis 'NO'. That was the only way out of his predicament. He turned and walked back to Dennis who had stepped back outside and lit another smoke. Dennis looked at Bob and knew something was up. He also played it off. "I suppose Jonathan gave you a quick pep talk about something or another. Well, he does that a lot when you're new around here. Come on. I have to make that call."

Dennis put out the cigarette and opened the door, holding it for Bob. Bob stood in place and did not move. Dennis said, "Come on man, let's go. It will be dinner soon."

Bob looked at Dennis and said, "Hey man, I can't do it. It's against the rules. You have to use your own access card."

Dennis said indignantly, "What? You bailing on me? No favor for poor, pathetic Dennis. Is that what Jonathan told you? Well, screw you, Bob. Just wait till you need something."

Dennis knew immediately what had happened because it was not the first time the staff at Kolbe had foiled one of his subtle cons. The man was a manipulator and they watched him closely. As Dennis stormed away from Bob he walked right into Jonathan who had come around from the other side of the courtyard and entered through a different door. Bob watched as Jonathan put his hand on Dennis' back and guided him out of the rec-room. Bob headed over to the exercise room, got on a treadmill, turned up the speed and quickly tried running away from himself.

*

*

*

CHAPTER 22

Merry Christmas (to some)

Bob and Tracey Slider had always been hard-working, bill paying, tax payers. Upstanding, middle class Americans, they flew their flag on national holidays and decorated their house not only on Christmas but also on Halloween. They never could have imagined living through the year that had passed.

They had been thrust into a strange world, a world they had only heard about. That world was for the people with unknown faces who comprised the statistics that were talked about on the news channels. That world was for the unemployed, those on food stamps and Medicaid, those who asked the local church help pay their electric bill. That world was for those who were unable to work because of an injury or illness. It was a world with drug addicts. It was also the world where beyond the horizon was a place called "Homeless". As the year came to a close the Sliders had become part of that world but had managed to veer away from the Horizon looming before them.

Tracey had been quite concerned about providing Christmas for Jake. Every penny she earned was accounted for and there were no 'extra' dollars anywhere. An unexpected Saturday phone call changed everything. She answered the phone and heard, "Hi Tracey, this is Pete, from St. Vincent de Paul. How are you?"

"Oh, hi Pete. I'm fine thanks. How are you and Dee?"

"Oh, we're good, thanks. Listen Tracey, I wanted to ask you something. If you feel funny about it just tell me no."

Tracey, wondering what in the world he was going to ask, said, "Sure Pete, no problem. Ask away."

"Well, tomorrow is our annual Christmas Giveaway. Every year we do this and we provide toys for over 400 kids in the area who otherwise would have nothing under their tree. We also supply Christmas dinner to close to 250 families, just like on Thanksgiving."

"That sounds like a wonderful thing, Pete. But I have dinner covered."

"That's good but I'm not really calling about the dinner. Tracey, we always have a hard time finding gifts for teenagers. But something unexpected happened and I thought of you. Actually, Father Jim thought of you, too. Anyway, does Jake have an iPad?"

"An iPad? I wish."

Pete laughed and said, "Well now, Santa visited us a bit earlier than expected and gave us six iPads to give to the older kids. You want one for Jake?"

Tracey answered loudly, "Oh my God, Pete. Are you kidding me? Yes, yes, I want one for Jake. Oh my God, I can't believe it. Yes, yes--- Thank you, thank you."

"Okay Tracey, I am so glad I called you about this. Now, tomorrow is our Giveaway from 1 p.m. until 4 p.m. Come over anytime during those hours and I'll have it waiting for you."

Tracey was not sure what to say. She expected to be back from Kolbe by 3:30 p.m. but was worried about being delayed. She wanted that iPad for Jake but she was not sure whether or not she should mention what was going on with Bob. She said, "Pete, what if I cannot make it by 4 p.m.?"

"Tracey, is there a problem with Sunday?"

"Uh, maybe, I'm not sure."

"I spoke to Father Jim. How is Bob doing?"

"You know about him then. Well, Jake and I are going to see him for the first time tomorrow. I was worried I would not be back in time."

"Look, I am an usher at the 8 a.m. Mass. Why don't you meet me after Mass and I'll

see that you get the iPad then. Okay?"

Tracey's tears were instantly triggered and she sniffled and said, Okay, Pete, thank you and God bless you."

"See you tomorrow morning."

Judi got home from work and called Tracey asking her if she and Jake would go to 8 a.m. Mass with her and Tommy in the morning. After Mass they would all go to breakfast at the Park Slope Diner. Tracey couldn't believe it. This Saturday had already turned into one fine day.

Sunday morning they all went to Mass together and Pete was in the narthex greeting folks as they came in. When he saw Tracey with Jake, he went over and greeted them and asked Tracey if he could speak to her privately for a moment. They went into the ushers' room and Pete gave her the iPad which fit perfectly into her oversized purse. She hugged Pete and said ,"God bless you and thank you."

"Tracey, don't thank me. You have to thank all the folks who donate this stuff. Without them there would be nothing for anyone. Oh yeah, one last thing. What size clothes does Jake wear and what size shoes?"

"His shoe is a size 9 and his clothes, oh, he's growing so fast, a size 16 to 18. Why?"

"Tracey, you never know what to expect at this time of the year. Christmas is a time for miracles and, working with St. Vincent, I have seen many unexplained things happen. Like the iPads. They are expensive and someone donated six of them. There are some really good and generous people out there. So, who knows. I wanted those sizes just in case."

After Mass, Father Jim made a point of saying 'HI' to Tracey and Jake and told them he hoped to see them Christmas morning. There were too many people wanting to say 'HI' to him for him to have time to be able to do any more than say 'HI'. The group headed to Park Slope, had a fine breakfast and by 10:30 Tracey and Jake were on their way to the Maximilian Kolbe Wellness center. Christmas was the following Friday.

It was a beautiful Sunday morning with the temperature at about 70 degrees and the Florida sky cloudless and virtually royal blue from horizon to horizon. They pulled up to the entrance and Tracey stopped and said to Jake, "I have to show you something."

Jake stepped from the truck and followed his mom to the St. Maximilian Kolbe site. They stopped and Tracey said, "This got to me Jake. Look at the statue and then read the plaque. I was quite taken with it and I wanted to just show it to you."

They stood for several minutes and Tracey said, "He must have been a very brave man, don't you think?"

Jake just shook his head up and down. "I guess so. I never heard of him, Mom.'

"Me neither, Jake. But now we have. I looked him up on the computer and bookmarked the site. He was an amazing man. If you want to find out something about him and the Holocaust it is right at your fingertips when you get home. Okay, time to see dad."

When Tracey and Jake had last seen Bob he was in the hospital and looked absolutely horrendous. He was pale and appeared to be forlorn and desolate. Tracey was actually afraid of what she was about to see and Jake was simply afraid of the place. They had their access code validated and were directed to the elevator.

A few minutes later they stepped off on the third floor and walked down an empty hallway to a set of swinging doors that opened from the center out. Tracey pushed the buzzer and a voice came from the wall speaker asking for the patient's name. "Robert Slider," Tracey said.

The doors swung open and there was Bob coming around the corner of the nurses station. "Hey you guys, come here. Give me a hug. Hey Jake, how's my boy?"

They were both shocked. It was like the 'old' Bob Slider and the 'old' Dad was there. It had only been six days and a transformation had taken place. They all hugged each other and Bob said, "Come on in, let me show you around this place. It isn't the Ritz but it ain't bad. Hey Jake, are you hungry? Grab some fruit or donuts. They have them all over the place."

Tracey smiled and said to Bob, "You've been here less than a week and I think you have gained weight."

"Maybe so Trace. They keep you eating to keep your mind off other things, know what I mean."

Bob showed them his room, the exercise room and the dining room. They were impressed with the dining room. It did not look like a cafeteria but rather, it had a 'down home' feel to it. Then they took the elevator down and went out to the courtyard. After they had sat, Tracey said, "This place must agree with you. You seem so upbeat. You seem like your old self. What about your meds?"

"Tracey, Jake, listen to me. I am done with drugs. I swear, I am finished, finito. I have seen and heard too much in six days. I do not want to be in that world. I can take ibuprofen if I have pain. I also think I am going back to school when I get out of here."

"I can't believe it, Bob. You look and sound like you're supposed to, like you were before. I mean, thank God you are being like this instead of—well, you know what I mean."

"Look, I met this guy in here, his name was Dennis. He was running the NA meetings and it was like he was everyone's friend. Then he tried to scam me out of my access code. I almost fell for it but Jonathan—he's a counselor here--- I love that guy--- he set me straight and told me I had a choice to make. So I chose not to give the code to Dennis."

"Good for you hon, I knew you were tough."

"Yeah Dad, way to go."

"Well, it's not so easy but I am trying. Anyway, like I was saying, then Dennis was gone. I asked where he was and they told me he 'left'. You see, we are not prisoners here. Dennis has been here before because his work made him come here. Since this is a private facility no one is court-ordered here. They go to county rehab centers. Anyway, Dennis wanted to use me to get drugs. I said 'No' and then I saw Jonathan speaking to Dennis. Next thing I know, Dennis is not here. He wanted drugs more than getting straight and he was only here because his work made him come. He didn't really care."

"So what do you think happened to him, Dad?"

"Who knows Jake. Hopefully he will be okay. Who knows."

Tracey said, "So tell me about you going back to school. That sounds like a great idea. You can't do heavy lifting anymore. I'm all for it."

"Well, I was talking about it with the job counselor here. There are lots of options with financial aid available and other programs. The truth is I am thinking about going into radiology. You know, learn how to do X-Rays and Cat Scans and MRIs and stuff like that. St. Petersburg College has a program and, well, when I come home I am going over there to see what's available."

Tracey and Jake were both staring at this man, completely delighted by his attitude and demeanor. Tracey said, "Well, I have some news for you. I was offered full-time by Mr. White and I start today at four o'clock."

"Wow Trace, that's great. I'm proud of you. You have really worked hard since I hurt my back and all. That will sure help a lot. And once I get back working we'll be okay again."

"I have some other news too. I asked Jake about this and he said it was a good idea. Actually, it is a great idea and it was Greg's idea not mine."

"Greg? Greg Margolese? You were talking to him. I can't believe it. And you were getting along?"

"Yes, we were. You know, I never really gave him a chance. I always thought he had an attitude or something. He is actually a good man."

"Damn right he is. I told you that. Anyway, what is the 'great' idea he had?"

"You know the house he has over on 72nd Terrace?"

"Yeah, it's that rinky-dink cottage he has. What about it?"

"If we are willing to move in to that house he'll only charge us $200.00 a month for the first year. We haven't paid rent where we are since September and he has carried us since. It seems like a smart move for us. Actually, we have no choice, do we?"

Bob became quiet and his expression seemed to change from upbeat to glum. Tracey and Jake both noticed the change and it was Jake who broke the growing tension. "Dad,' he said, "It's okay with me. It's only $200.00. Nobody pays rent that cheap, right? Sounds like you made a smart move making friends with Mr. Margolese."

Jake had inadvertently hit the nail on the head. His 'Dad' had made the decision and Bob smiled and said, "Well, I guess it does make a lot of sense. When does he want us to move?"

The rest of the time together went very well. At 2:45 Tracey and Jake said their good-byes and headed home. It had been one of Tracey Slider's best weekends ever.

Jake was on Christmas break and Greg offered the boy some work while he was on vacation. Jake jumped at the chance and by Christmas Eve had earned $150.00. Pete's wife, Dee, had called Tracey and told her that Holy Family Parish had some left over clothing donations from their Christmas party and she had a pair of brand new, size 9 Nikes. Tracey was so excited. New Nikes and an iPad, Jake would flip out.

Tuesday night Bob called Tracy and he was quite upset. News had come in that Dennis, the man who had left Kolbe after Dennis refused to 'help' him, was found dead in his car on Monday. He had overdosed on roxycodone, passed out and his heart stopped. Neither Dennis nor his family would be having a Merry Christmas this year. "Are you all right Bob?" Tracey asked.

"Yeah, I'm okay. Maureen came in and talked to me about it. She told me that if anyone should ever suggest to me that it was my fault he died I should ignore them. Dennis made his choices and the consequences led to his death."

Tracey sighed and said, "Okay Bob, I love you. So does Jake. We'll be out Christmas day."

"I love you too, Tracey. Oh yeah, one more thing. I said a prayer for you today. How about that for a Christmas miracle?"

Tracey put down the phone and cried the happiest cry you could imagine. Indeed, it was a very blessed and merry Christmas.

EPILOGUE

We might ask what are Bob Slider's chances of remaining "clean" and staying off addictive drugs? We might think that Bob's home life with his wife and son and their respect for him as a husband and father would overwhelm his having any thoughts of "using" again. Common sense might lead us to think that Bob will never again take the chance of getting arrested and being put in jail. Unfortunately, when you are an addict and have given your brain the signal that taking a little pill will give you "pleasure", the brain does not forget it.

When a person begins using narcotics they, in effect, rewire their brain to disguise something harmful as "good". This takes place in the "limbic" system of the brain and is extremely hard to eliminate. These "false good" feelings are what cause habitual drug abuse.

What happened to Bob Slider after leaving rehab? Did he stay clean like he said he would? Did he go back to school and get a radiology certification? Did he mange to keep his family together? Some folks like Bob do conquer their addiction. But it is an ongoing everyday battle. Some folks fail over and over. Some lose everything and wind up on the streets. Others overdose and die alone. It is tragic. As for Bob Slider, when all is said and done his future is up to him and his ***Higher Power***.

The links below provide insight into the homeless and drug epidemic that fuels the numbers in our homeless population.

http://www.endhomelessness.org/library/entry/SOH2016

www.national**homeless**.org/factsheets/addiction.pdf

Please pray for all those who have no Home to go to--anywhere

www.ingramcontent.com/pod-product-compliance
Lightning Source LLC
Chambersburg PA
CBHW061606120626
46550CB00004B/1633